For Mark McNestry
with love and gratitude
and
In loving memory of Angus Suttie
(1946–1993)

Even the death of friends will inspire us as much as their
lives ... Their memories will be encrusted over with sublime
and pleasing thoughts, as monuments of other men are over-
grown with moss; for our friends have no place in the
graveyard.

Henry David Thoreau

Contents

viii *Contents*

Preface and Acknowledgements

————◦◦◦◦————

When I began working on this book, far too long ago now, my friends were sceptical. The question of values, they tended to mutter, was the prerogative of the Moral Right, a code for the attempted reestablishment of what goes by the label of 'traditional' ways of life: a reaffirmation of 'family values', hostility towards the advances made by women during the past generation, fear and loathing of homosexuality, and a deep anxiety caused by the growing diversity both of public life and our private arrangements.

Today, as I at last complete the book, values have shot to the top of the political agenda on both left and right. As traditional ways of life fragment under the revolutionary changes of our times, as social identities are reshaped and remade, as well-established political alignments collapse and new alliances are painfully constructed, as the public sphere is redefined, and the boundaries between public and private shift, as epidemic disease returns to haunt the imagination of the postmodern world, and as the flame of love flickers in the cold draught of various forms of hate, debates over values encapsulate our uncertainties about how we should live.

My concern in this book is with value debates as they inform the debates about sexuality, and with debates about sexuality as they help us to understand the significance of questions of value. For sexuality is at the heart of contemporary anguish about values: to that extent my sceptical friends were right. Where they were wrong was in thinking that the value-laden discourse of the morally conservative did not deserve a considered response from liberals and radicals, because such ideas were self-evidently ill-intentioned. I believe, on the contrary, that the failure of pro-gressive thought to counter effectively the values of the right has left a vacuum which stymies effective defence of what I believe in, the values of sexual diversity and freedom of choice.

As this suggests, I do not attempt in this book an 'objective' exploration of either the question of value in general, or of sexual values in particular. Value debates are about taking sides, about placing yourself in a tradition or traditions of arguments extending through time which necessarily conflict at many points with other traditions, other values. We can rightly require that the debates are conducted dialogically and democratically – that seems to me an absolute prerequisite of argument in a pluralist world. But I do not expect, or even hope, that the positions I have adopted will evoke universal agreement.

On the contrary, I hope my arguments will arouse debate and controversy, even among my friends, for that is the only way we can advance towards the radical humanism that this book attempts to advocate, a humanism which values individual free-dom and celebrates the rich diversity of human goals, and there-fore must expect disagreement as the price we pay for autonomy and choice.

How to live with diversity is the main theme of the book. The reader will not, therefore, find prescriptions here about how to live; it is precisely that form of the value debate which I am hoping to combat. I do attempt, however, to offer a framework for thinking about the issues that need to be confronted in asking that question, how shall I live? My argument, in brief, is that many forms of life can be 'moral' or ethically valid, especially with regard to the erotic. It is not so much what you do, but how you do it that should matter: less a morality of acts, more an ethics of relationships. Concepts such as care, responsibility, respect and love have become the currency of recent debates around personal behaviour. I argue that these are important virtues, but they cannot, and should not, be identified with any particular form of domestic arrangement or sexual activity. They embody values that inform a variety of lifestyles and 'experiments in living'. Their meaning needs to be struggled for, not assumed.

For whatever the fantasies of particular traditions, the legitimacy of any set of values cannot in the end depend on the claim that Truth, Revelation, Science or History are on their side. Values are human inventions, products of complex histories and the intermingling of many individual and collective aspirations and anxieties. Values depend on us, what we want or desire. At the moment there appears to be a high degree of uncertainty about values, leading among many to a search for new absolutes. I, however, see uncertainty as a challenge: to find ways of living, and loving, together, in a world without intrinsic meaning or foundational givens, which are securely rooted in our common humanity and our care and responsibility for others. This book is a contribution to that aim.

The book has taken considerably longer to complete than I originally intended, and in that time I have incurred many material, intellectual and emotional debts. I have to thank the University of Manchester for electing me to a Simon Senior Fellowship during 1989–90, which gave me the space to begin work on the book. I am grateful to the University of Michigan where I was welcomed as a visiting fellow at its Institute for the Humanities in 1991, a visit that provided a stimulus for writing first drafts of some of these chapters. The Humanities Research Group at the University of Windsor, Ontario, similarly provided intellectual encouragement and the spur to writing during my visit in early 1993.

During most of the time I worked on the book I was gainfully employed in the Faculty of Economics and Social Science at the University of the West of England, Bristol. I am very grateful to the Dean, Peter Glasner, for his constant support, and to his colleagues for their stimulating company, and occasional distraction. I must particularly thank Jem Thomas, Simon Thompson and Ian Welsh for their comments and intellectual encouragement, and Helen Robbins and Lesley Gander for their practical backing. I finished the book soon after I moved to South Bank University, and I am grateful for the welcome my new colleagues gave me, and their forbearance as I met my deadlines.

This book is partly about friendship, and my friends have been all I could have asked for. I want particularly to thank Lisa Adkins, Bob Cant, Emmanuel Cooper, Barry Davis, Liz Fidlon, Sue Golding, Jill Grinstead, Janet Holland, Ken Plummer, Kevin Porter, Alex Potts, Martha Vicinus and Simon Watney for their sustenance, material and intellectual, at various times. David Clark and Chetan Bhatt read parts or all of the book in draft, and I am grateful for their illuminating comments and support. I am also grateful to Chetan Bhatt for the many conversations I have had with him over the years which have never failed to stimulate me, and which have informed some of the arguments here (though he is not to blame for any recalcitrant conclusions I may have reached!).

Some of the arguments set out in the book have been rehearsed in my classes, in numerous seminar and conference papers, and in several articles, though in substantially different, earlier forms: *The Sphere of the Intimate*, Manchester Sociology Occasional Papers 29, University of Manchester 1991; 'Invented Moralities', *History Workshop Journal* 32, Autumn 1991; 'Values in an Age of Uncertainty', in Stanton 1992; 'Living with Uncertainty' and 'Necessary Fictions' in Jacqueline Murray (ed.) *Constructing Sexualities*, Windsor, Humanities Research Group, University of Windsor, Ontario; and 'Rethinking Private Life' in Clark 1994. I am grateful to all who invited me to give papers, to students and seminar and conference participants who engaged with my views, and to the various editors concerned for their comments and support at the time. I have seized the licence of the author to modify or revise my earlier views where appropriate.

For permission to publish from copyright material, I am grateful to the following: to Bloodaxe Books for the quotation from Jackie Kay's poem 'Close Shave', in *The Adoption Papers*, Bloodaxe Books 1991; to Faber and Faber Ltd, and Farrar, Straus & Giroux Inc. for the quotation from Thom Gunn's poem 'In Time of Plague', in *The Man with Night Sweats*.

Finally, I owe an overwhelming debt to three people. Micky Burbidge has been a constant and sturdy friend through thick and thin for many years. I can simply thank him.

I met my partner Mark McNestry as I began work on this book. He has lived with its various vicissitudes, been patient with my anxieties, sustained me through doubt, and given me all the love and support I could have wished for. The dedication is a small token of my deepest thanks.

My friend Angus Suttie died before I could complete the book. His bravery in the face of mortal illness, and the courage with which he faced his premature death, gave me unforgettable insights into the importance of living life well. Those final months with Angus also taught me something new about friendship, love and intimacy, and the value of the human bond. I have tried to convey some of what I learnt through this book.

INTRODUCTION

Values, whose Values?

---◆---

... a tour of perplexities, not a guide for the perplexed.
Judith Shklar, *Ordinary Vices*

All the symbols of the carnival idiom are filled with this sense
of pathos and change, with the sense of the gay relativity of
prevailing truths and authorities.
M. Bakhtin, *Rabelais and his World*

A CHANGING SEXUAL LANDSCAPE

There's an oil painting in the Museum of Modern Art, New
York, by the Chilean-born artist, Matta (Sebastian Antonio Matta
Echaurren). As you first look at it, the overwhelming impression
is of darkness and formlessness, a dark night of the soul. Gradu-
ally you notice that the black wash is less uniform than it first
appears. It has been partially rubbed away to reveal gradations
in the blackness, and this in turn highlights the apparently ran-
domly distributed, indefinable and mysterious shapes which seem
to float or explode in the shade, entwined in spirals and webs of
white lines.

Matta's painting is entitled *The Vertigo of Eros*, and the canvas is
ineffably but unmistakably sexual. As you continue to stare at it,
what you see is less the initial cosmic darkness and more the
imagery of fire, roots and sexual organs floating dreamlike and

evocatively in the void, until the imagery becomes the totality of what you see: an almost mystical world of sexual flux. Matta is quoted as saying that the title of his work derived from a reading of Freud: the life force, Eros, is constantly challenged by the death drive, Thanatos, which produces in most people a state of vertigo that must be constantly combated in order to achieve a sense of equilibrium and stability (Franc 1992, p. 128). Sexuality, it seems, is a field of infinite possibilities, shadowed by dissolution and death.

We can read too much into a single painting, or the life of a single artist, but there is something emblematic about Matta's painting, and career, which speaks to my concerns, and to the purposes of this book. Matta originally studied architecture in the Paris office of the arch-priest of modernism, Le Corbusier, famous, even infamous today, as the progenitor of machines for living stretching heavenwards into the pure air. The artist later, however, gravitated towards the Surrealists, whose group he joined finally in 1937. *The Vertigo of Eros* was painted after his absorption of surrealism, in 1944. A journey beginning in the idealistic yet disciplinary purity of modernist hubris, gave rise to a striking and disturbing but also highly charged landscape of chaos and disorder, and sexual excitement. Order and entropy, threat and opportunity, fear and attraction: these seem to me to sum up the confused trajectory of sexuality amidst what Nietzsche called the 'tropical tempo' of modernity.

The idea of 'sexual flux' is a characteristically postmodern trope, but it is integral to the whole modern discourse of sexuality, what I have called elsewhere the 'sexual tradition' (Weeks 1985). We can see this if we cast our minds towards the major codifications of sexuality during the twentieth century, the sexological texts which have helped shape the ways in which we think the erotic (see Bullough 1994). The rise of a science of desire, from the late nineteenth century, was in large part a response to a perception of the duality of the sexual: simultaneously, but contradictorily, a boundless sea of highly differentiated and excessive desires, and a massive continent of sexual and gender patterning and symmetry. Sexologists attempted to recognize the first by cataloguing and categorizing the varieties of sexual experience, while at the same time affirming the second, the majestic norms of heterosexual life which marginalized, devalued and often execrated the deviant, the perverse. Part of the enduring, if ambivalent, attraction of the greatest of these pioneers, Freud, is that he both recognized the contingency and flux of sexuality ('polymorphous perversity'), and of gender and object choice ('bisexuality'), and immediately sought to harness them to the complex cultural necessities of 'normality' (Coward 1983). But in this he was only a more subtle and profound representative of a major intellectual endeavour, which in turn responded to, and shaped, an opening up of sexual possibilities and a crisis of sexual certainty which continues to this day.

The impact of sexology is not my concern here (see Bullough 1994); rather I want to underline what the codifications embodied in sexology tell us about sexual change, or rather the way sexual change is perceived. In retrospect, the sexual tradition, as a set of concepts and intellectual interventions, laws and social practices, marital and family organization, and diverse patterns of life, can be seen as a sustained effort to channel and discipline the imagined powers of sexuality. Great efforts have been made by the architects and mechanics of the sexual tradition to order and regulate the swampy sexual landscape. It has been well tilled and carefully cultivated by expert hands. Barriers have been put up against the chaos, disorder and disease of the city. Brave and well-intentioned settlements have been constructed to embody a new pattern of sexual and family life. Dams have been built here, rivers canalized there, to reshape 'the forces of nature'. But in vain. What we call 'nature' cannot be so easily appeased. Now the dams are full to overflowing; the rivers are bursting their banks (I make no apology for the male sexual imagery, which seems to me to be central to the sexual imaginary I am describing). Parts of the flood plain have already been overwhelmed. The landscape is being transformed, as familiar buildings go under, or the waters lap their historic foundations. New features appear: an island where once there was a crossroads, a shelter near where children once played. A flood threatens all we can see. There is a certain mood of tired fractiousness in the air, even a hint of civil war, in some areas. An anxiety about contagion is abroad. Where once there seemed order, there is now a pervasive fear, not so much of disorder as of formlessness: an amorphous vista of murky and uncertain waters and a re-shaped landscape which we must learn to navigate without reliable maps. This is the metaphorical landscape on which the struggle over values is being fought.

We live in a world of uncertainty, where good guides and firm guarantees that we can reach any particular destination are in short supply, and where the goals themselves are cloudy and indeterminate. Nowhere is this uncertainty more acute than in the domain of sexuality, which has been the subject in the recent past of apparently endless panics, controversies, anguished moral-izings, and the rebirth of the value issue. It seems a long time since a British Prime Minister (Harold Macmillan, in the early 1960s) could say with insouciance that morals and values were best left to the bishops. Today, the question of values has reached the centre of the political and cultural agenda, with sexuality as the magnetic core. Illegitimacy and the future of the family; surrogate parenthood and embryological research; teenage preg-nancy and the 'age of consent'; divorce and the fate of marriage; violence and explicit sexual imagery; sex education and child sex abuse; sexual diversity and sexual identity; the changing claims of women and the 'crisis of masculinity'; the balance between individual freedom and collective obligations; disease and sexual health; these and other topics have become the focus of public agonizing and personal anguish, the major theme of social policy debates, and the lodestars of drifting politicians in search of a coherent but eternally elusive 'big idea'.

It is not that sexuality has ever been absent from social, cultural and political debate. On the contrary, it is perfectly accurate to say that anxiety about the sexual has, like mysterious creatures scuttling under the floorboards, implicitly shaped many of our public debates for a long time, from the fear of national or imperial decline at the end of the nineteenth century to the structuring of welfare provision from the 1940s to the present (see Mort 1987; Weeks 1981/1989). What is new, however, is the way in which worries about changing sexual behaviour and gender and sexual identities have become the explicit focus for debates about the current shape and desirable future of society. And if, as I believe, we can no longer rely on pre-existing narratives to shape our hopes for the future, if above or beneath the social and the historical there is nothing, then what we believe to be desirable counts. 'An existence without a script written in advance', suggests Zygmunt Bauman (1992b, p. 94), 'is a *contingent* existence'. The debate around sexual values is a response to a growing sense of our contingency, where nothing but uncertainty and death is certain.

THINKING THE EROTIC

If sexuality is, as I believe, about choice rather than destiny, then the issue of what we choose and how and why we do so becomes central to the debate. In the current ethical fog, choice has become a lodestar, but there are as many choices as there are human subjects. My own choices demand a few comments before I launch into the argument proper. So a touch of intellectual autobiography might be useful here, to outline why I have become centrally concerned with questions of values.

My own research and writing about sexuality have been shaped by a rejection of what have come to be known as essentialist arguments, and an attempt to elaborate what has generally, though inadequately, been called 'social constructionism', and which I prefer to call a historical approach to the erotic (see Weeks 1991). The basic assumption has been that it is deeply problematic to think of sexuality as a purely natural phenomenon, outside the boundaries of society and culture. We have all too readily believed that sexuality is the most natural thing about us, that our drives are fixed and inherent, that our identities are dictated by that nature and those drives, and that a history of sexuality must therefore be no more than an account of reactions to those basic biological givens.

Over the past twenty years most of the assumptions behind those positions have been profoundly challenged, building on a century of challenges to essentialist modes of thought (Weeks 1985). Through anthropology and social analysis we have strengthened our awareness of the relativity of sexual norms. From Freud we can derive (though sadly most interpreters have not) insights into the tentative and always provisional nature of gender and sexual identities. From the new social history we have become aware of the multiple narratives of sexual life. After feminism, lesbian and gay politics and the theoretical challenges of Michel Foucault (1979) we are increasingly sensitive to the subtle forms of power that invest the body, and make us simultaneously subjected to and subjects of sex. All these influences in turn feed into the deconstructionist project and the postmodernist critiques which question the fixities and certainties of post-Enlightenment humanism, rationalism and progressivism (Lyotard 1984). With the philosophers of deconstruction we have become alive to the contingency of human arrangements, the finity and delicacy of our placing in a world without intrinsic meaning but clamorous with multiple and conflicting meanings (Rorty 1989). With the theorists of postmodernity we have become more aware of the pain and challenge of moral choice (Squires 1993; Bauman 1993).

As a result we increasingly recognize that sexuality can be understood only in its specific historical and cultural context. There cannot be an all-embracing history of sexuality. There can only be local histories, contextual meanings, specific analyses. Eve Kosovsky Sedgwick has usefully suggested that rather than speak any longer about essentialism versus constructionism, which has led to a tired and repetitive (and perhaps incomprehensible) internal debate among students of sexuality, we should think in terms of universalistic and particularist positions (Sedgwick 1990). Universalistic arguments assume a common experience throughout time and history. Particularist arguments on the contrary want to understand the specifics of any sexual phenomenon: the histories and narratives which organize it, the power structures which shape it, the struggles which attempt to define it (see Plummer 1995). That is fundamentally my position.

Much recent writing on sexuality has been concerned with three interlocked issues. First, there has been a new sensitivity to the sexual identities that we take for granted as given and fixed, but which any careful historical reading show to be culturally specific. Lesbian and gay identities are the classic examples of this: these are widely seen now as products of a specific, if complex history (see Stein 1990; Vance 1989). This in turn has produced a sharper, though still grossly inadequate, interest in the historical evolution of the dominant form of sexual organization, heterosexuality (Sedgwick 1990; Katz 1995). Second, there has been a concern to examine the social regulation of sexuality: the forms of control, the patterns of domination, subordination and resistance which shape the sexual (Foucault 1979). Finally, scholars have explored the sexual discourses which organize meanings, and especially the discourse of sexology which has been crucial, if not alone, in proclaiming the 'truth' of sex (see Weeks 1985).

The core of the historical argument has been that we can understand sexuality only through understanding the cultural meanings and the power relations which construct it (see Foucault 1979 as the *locus classicus*). This does not mean that biology is irrelevant, nor that the body has no role (Giddens 1992). Nor does it mean that individuals are blank pieces of paper on which society writes its preferred meanings. Take, for example, homosexuality, the subject of many of my previous writings. To say that lesbian and gay identities have a history, have not always existed and may not always exist, does not mean that they are not important. Nor should it necessarily be taken to imply that homosexual proclivities are not deeply rooted. That question is in any case irrelevant to the argument. The real problem does not lie in whether homosexuality is inborn or learnt. It lies instead in the question: what are the meanings that this particular culture gives to homosexual behaviour, however it may be caused, and what are the effects of those meanings on the ways in which individuals organize their sexual lives. That is a historical question. It is also a question which is highly political: it forces us to analyse the power relations which determine why this set of meanings, rather than that, are hegemonic; and poses the further question of how those meanings can be changed.

Many contemporary writers on sexuality have been concerned, therefore, with tracing the genealogy of our present sexual arrangements and identities, seeking the elements of confusion and opportunity that order our current discontents and political aspirations, surveying the sexual battlefields which make the current situation so morally and politically fraught.

There are, however, difficulties with this theoretical approach. Many people seem to need a sense of belonging which they conceive as rooted in the imperatives of nature or of all time. They fear that if identities and the values associated with them are conceived of as historically contingent then they will lose all solidity and meaning. When the British gay film maker Derek Jarman was asked in a radio broadcast whether his homosexuality was learnt or inborn, he replied that it was inborn – and then added that at least he hoped so, because otherwise he would have no basis with which to challenge moral conservatism. This position has underscored recent efforts to discover a 'gay brain' or a 'gay gene' (LeVay 1991; Hamer et al. 1993). Better to fall back on the truths of science than to confront the challenge of clarifying why we value what we do.

This points to a real problem, which goes far beyond questions of identity, and embraces all aspects of sexual ethics. Social constructionism has no political belonging. It does not carry with it any obvious programme. On the contrary, it can be, and has been, used recently as much by sexual conservatives as by sexual progressives. In the attempt to ban the 'promotion' of homosexuality by local authorities in Britain in 1987–88, culminating in the passing into law of the notorious Clause 28 of the Local Government Act, the bill's proponents explicitly argued that homosexuality could be promoted and learnt – hence the bill's justification (Smith 1990). Of course, the logical corollary of this is that heterosexuality could equally well be learnt, and is in fact promoted all the time by the institutions of our culture. But as Carole Vance (1989) has pointed out, by and large heterosexuality has not been subjected to the same vigorous enquiry as homosexuality. Very few people are interested in tracing *its* social construction. It is still regarded as the natural norm from which all else is an unfortunate perversion.

Against the uncertainties of constructionism, then, many seek the certainty of nature or of received tradition. Might it not be better, the argument seems to go, to assert that lesbians and gays are a permanent and fixed minority of the population, like a racial minority, and to claim a place in the sun as a legitimate minority on that basis? Or, for those of a more conservative disposition, the argument appears to be: is it not preferable to base values on some objective or universal standpoint to counter the vagaries of 'subjectivism' and the terror of relativism (see Scruton 1986)?

These positions are tempting because they offer certainty instead of doubt, fixity rather than the anguish of personal decision, but they are, I believe, fundamentally wrong, because they rely on absolutist positions that cannot begin to deal with the complexities of value choices. In the case of Clause 28, and similar moral and political flurries, the arguments of one side cannot be bested by mirror-image arguments from the other: this is natural/this is unnatural; this is good/this is evil. What is at stake in such positions cannot be resolved by appeals to reason, science, truth or tradition precisely because all these terms are contested. What is actually happening is that different moral and ethical positions are being staked out, and in a moral civil war theoretical viewpoints alone cannot promote a particular outcome. They have meaning only within specific contexts, in particular power relations, and in the arguments over time embodied in ethical traditions. So their effectiveness in the end is not dictated by their truth but by the meanings they glue together. Sexual values are important not because they are either rooted in the 'natural' or some revealed truth or foundational given, but because they provide the basis of social and cultural identification which makes possible a meaningful individual and social life, and, where appropriate, moral-political struggles.

That puts squarely on the agenda the question of values (see essays in Squires 1993, including Weeks 1993a). What the historical approach to sexuality has achieved is to make us more aware of the complexity of forces that shape the social, and to sensitize us to the power relations that organize the meanings by which we live. This historical process is generally concealed behind the veil of ideology which works precisely by making us believe that what is socially created, and therefore subjected to change, is really natural, and therefore immutable. But why should we believe that of all social phenomena, sexuality is the least change-able? On the contrary, it is probably the most sensitive to social influence, a conductor of the subtlest of changes in social mores and power relations. If that is the case, then we need to be clearer than ever before of the values that motivate us, and the choices we have to make. Sexuality, as Foucault (1984a, p. 129) put it, is not a fatality. It is a possibility for creative life. And in creating that life, we need above all to be able to affirm and validate our values.

WHOSE VALUES?

Speaking of values is a way of describing the sort of life we want to lead, or think we should lead. In a world without a given or necessary meaning, where the foundations of many, if not all, of the legitimizing discourses which separate truth and falsity, good and evil have been shaken or have collapsed, then how we want to live requires a clarification of what is at stake. Values provide a series of principles from which we can try to deduce goals, and then develop ways of life and appropriate political responses. Values help us to clarify what we believe to be right or wrong, permissible or impermissible. They should also, I believe, enable us, in a complex and pluralistic world, to ensure that what we think is right is not necessarily what other people think is right, and to find ways of living with difference in a tolerant and demo-cratic fashion.

That is not, unfortunately, quite how the debate about sexual values has gone. In the recent past we have been besieged by value-laden arguments – largely from the political and moral right, but also from popes and preachers, ayatollahs, religious revivalists and fundamentalists of various hues – which instruct us how to live and whose moral entrepreneurs do their best to make us conform to *their* values. Phrases such as 'family values', generally encoding a series of hostile responses to changes in family life and sexual behaviour, the impact of feminism and the insurgency of positive lesbian and gay communities and identi-ties, have tended to hegemonize the debate, usually throwing the liberal and radical left on to the defensive. The traditional left, fearful of confusing morality with the excesses of moralism, have often nervously evacuated the field. When they have not, as in recent recuperations of communitarian traditions, they have tended to move towards a moral conservatism which prioritizes 'rebuilding the family' and traditional neighbourhoods as an antidote to social collapse (for example, Etzioni 1993). The debate on 'values' all too often has a dangerously reactionary ring.

Yet despite the 'murderous certainties' (Bhatt 1994) of many of these Messianic prophets of purity and moral renaissance, the overwhelming feeling in our culture is of moral confusion rather than of moral certainty. The 'fashionable madmen', as W. H. Auden called them in his love poem 'Lullaby', parade their fantasies of a final reconciliation between our desires and their will, yet we actually live with a confusing plurality of values and choices, some particular to specific groups or communities, some aspiring to universality, but each rooted in different traditions, histories, theoretical and political trajectories, an apparent cacophony of competing and contradictory hopes and dreams, and ways of life. The oceans and continents of value, as Fekete (1988, p. 1) says, though much travelled 'remain almost uncharted in any way suitable for the navigational contingencies of postmodern itineraries'.

Is it possible, then, without surrendering to fundamentalisms of one sort or another, to find democratic principles and values which can help us to navigate the swampy landscape around us, to develop a set of minimum common standards by which we can evaluate and measure legitimately different ways of being? I believe the answer is yes, but only if we start rethinking values by exploring in a positive manner the sexual and moral diversity that causes so much dread, and by finding within them certain common elements. I am with Foucault (1989, p. 330) in believing that the search for a form of morality that would be acceptable to everyone, in the sense that everyone must bend a knee to it, would be 'catastrophic'. Rather than imposing an artificial order on moral confusion, we have to learn to negotiate the hazards of social complexity, moral pluralism and sexual diversity; to establish key principles or guidelines to measure difference; and to learn how to live with the challenge of uncertainty.

This book is an attempt to explore that challenge. I do not claim that it covers all the ground that could or should be covered. I do not, for example, attempt to explore the complexities of parenting, or the challenge of ageing or disability, or the whole array of possible variables which affect day-to-day existence. My purpose is more modest: to establish a framework within which we can think through the challenges of everyday life. The erotic, and the relationships which focus on it, offers a glittering mirror which can reflect back to us the dilemmas of individual choice in an age of uncertainty.

With this in mind, the first chapter, 'Living with Uncertainty', surveys the shifting sexual terrain, the opportunities and threats which shape our sexual lives. The AIDS epidemic has become for many emblematic of the threats, the fearful harbinger of disaster, the poisoned fruits of a 'permissiveness' run riot. I prefer to see it, on the contrary, as a natural disaster, which nevertheless casts a sharp spotlight on many other changes which are sweeping the sexual landscape: changes in patterns of sexual identity, and an 'unfinished' revolution in sexual mores and the arrangements of intimate life. In the response to AIDS we can also see the promise held out by the transformations of intimate life (Giddens 1992) for what I call a 'radical humanism' which respects and validates different ways of life, different choices, alternative forms of responsibility and love. In the second chapter, 'Inventing Moralities', I set out some of the principles of this position: the challenge of sexual pluralism, what this implies for the meanings of 'care' and 'responsibility', autonomy and authenticity, and the implications of radical toleration and solidarity for exploring and sustaining rather than fearing sexual diversity. The third chapter, 'Necessary Fictions', looks again at the politics of sexual diversity. Dissident sexual identities, in particular, I suggest, are troubling. They also 'cause trouble' for the would-be certainties of sexual life. Yet in the two key elements of radical sexual politics, what I describe as 'the moment of transgression' and the 'moment of citizenship', we see something more than the special pleading of 'sexual minorities'. There are possibilities here, I argue, for rethinking radical and pluralistic politics, which is why, despite the trouble, a politics of collective identity appears necessary.

Chapter 4 moves from the public arena of politics to the private arena of 'The Sphere of the Intimate'. Where should the boundaries between the public and private be drawn?; what are the main components of private life?; and what rights of everyday life can we distinguish to protect the intimate from the encroachments of an imperialistic public? This is, indeed, a 'tour of perplexities', because sexual desire, and the erotic economy it produces, can never entirely be a private matter, which is a major reason why the intimate sphere may always be a battlefield of sorts. Yet it is also the site for the most precious of human qualities, those concerned with love, care and responsibility for life in its finitude. The last chapter, 'Caught between Worlds and Ways of Being', takes up the themes of love and death to tease out the new possibilities of human relationships in the shifting landscape of sexuality.

Several themes recur in these chapters. One I have already referred to, the impact of the AIDS crisis. This is not a book about AIDS, but it would be impossible for me to escape its threatening presence, both because as an individual I have experienced its devastating effects on friends and on the communities to which I feel closest; and as a social scientist because I recognize its twin impact as a symbolic focus of sexual anxiety and as a material factor in the redefining of sexual values and personal relationships. I see in the AIDS crisis a redefiner of the social, a whirlwind which devours, but also a storm which illuminates and reshapes.

If AIDS is the challenge, the hope of the new lies in the everyday experiments in sexual life which are transforming personal life. These are often muddled and confusing, marked by the uncertainty which governs public and private life today. But they also contain within them evidence of care, mutuality, responsibility and love which make it possible to be hopeful about our human future. The essential point I want to insist on is that these virtues are not the prerogative of any particular type of relationship, least of all a mythical and heavily mythologized traditional family. They exist in many forms of life, many ways of being, that need to be nurtured and valued for what they are, not feared for what they are not.

The third theme, which in a sense underlies the whole texture of the arguments of this book, is democracy, a difficult word to apply to the sexual sphere, perhaps, but a vital one if we are to achieve a revaluation of erotic life. If the book does nothing else, it will I hope indicate the importance of valuing the sexual under the light of a new democratic imaginary, where choice and diversity become the benchmarks not of a consumerist paradise but of a mature radical and pluralist democracy.

1

Living with Uncertainty

━━━━►∞◄━━━━

> MARTYN: One of the problems of AIDS is its unpredictability. It is
> like going on a journey without a map.
> TONY: The unpredictability is stressful. Ours is a life of uncer-
> tainty.
>> From an interview with Martyn, a person living with
>> AIDS, and his partner Tony.

> Uncertainty rocks the cradle of morality, fragility
> haunts it through life.
>> Zygmunt Bauman, *Postmodern Ethics*

LIVING WITH AIDS

'To speak of sexuality and the body, and not also speak of AIDS',
B. Ruby Rich has written, 'would be, well, obscene' (quoted in
Crimp 1987, p. 14). I can only concur. Since the early 1980s
AIDS, HIV disease, has haunted the sexual imaginary, embodying
the danger and fear that trails in the wake of the body and its
pleasures. Even as the epidemic becomes 'normalized' in large
parts of the world, it becomes endemic in others, casting a
shadow over the changes that are transforming the sexual world.

I am fully in agreement with those people who refuse to see
'AIDS' as a metaphor for anything (Sontag 1989). It is, as AIDS
activists have long put it, 'a natural disaster', though one helped

along by prejudice, discrimination and less than benign neglect. It is not a judgement from God, not 'nature's revenge' on any group of people, not a symbol of a culture gone wrong. HIV disease is an illness, or set of illnesses, like any other, and in a caring and rational world it would be confronted with all the compassion, empathy and resources that other major health crises demand.

But that is not, of course, how it has always been seen. As the baroque language and the proliferation of metaphors surrounding it suggest, HIV was not responded to like any other virus. The fact that the epidemic was first identified in the early 1980s in the gay male communities of North America, a population that was already subject to marginalization and political and cultural attack, not despite but because of the vibrant growth of those communities in the previous decades, radically shaped the initial response.

The identification of such a health crisis coincided dreadfully with the growth of a moral climate which sought a return to 'traditional values', while attempts were simultaneously being made to transform economic and social policies in the direction of a new individualism and against welfare traditions. This meant that few resources outside those available in the communities at risk were directed at the crisis until the epidemic was almost out of control. As the epidemic spread to other marginal communities and groups, especially the poor, the black and drug users, and barely seemed to touch the 'normal', heterosexual population in most Western countries, even as it was beginning to devastate the poorer countries of the globe, the association of AIDS with the perverse, the marginal, the Other, the disease of the already diseased, gave a colour and stigma to those affected which has persisted, even as community-based organizations, governments, with varying degrees of energy and enthusiasm, and international agencies struggled to contain the spread of infection. Enduring efforts to separate the 'implicated' from the 'immune' (Goldstein 1991), the 'guilty' from the 'innocent', spoke to a culture which feared the impact of sexual change, social complexity and moral diversity. During its first decade AIDS did, therefore, become a symbol: of a culture at odds with itself, of a global issue that evoked a multitude of local passions, moralities and prejudices, the epitome of a civilization whose values were uncertain, where pleasure marched with disease and death. As John Greyson put it in his music-video parody of 'Death in Venice' (quoted in Crimp 1987, p. 268):

> The ADS epidemic
> Is sweeping the Nation
> Acquired dread of sex
>
> Fear and panic
> In the whole population
> Acquired dread of sex.

The person with HIV or AIDS must live with the resulting uncertainty all the time: the uncertainty of diagnosis, of prognosis, of reactions of friends, families, loved ones, of anonymous and fearful or hate-filled others. Everyone else must live with the uncertainty too: the uncertainty bred of risk, of possible infection, of *not* knowing, of loss.

Uncertainty breeds anxiety and fear: about the past, and for the present and future.

> Uncap the rads and fill the room with fear.
> Enormous rooms require enormous fear.
> (Lynch 1989, p. 72)

Yet the truth of AIDS is that its impact is not predetermined, but haphazard. There is no straightforward correlation between lifestyle and HIV infection. The virus itself, though potentially potent in its effects, is itself a relatively weak one. People who 'do risky things' do not necessarily fall ill. As yet ill-understood co-factors (way of life, general health, incidence of poverty and other diseases) may ease the way; but a high element of chance determines who will get HIV, and then who among these will succumb to opportunistic diseases. 'Contingency' is a hallmark of the AIDS crisis.

Chance, accident, contingency: these are more than characteristics of a particular set of diseases. They appear as markers of the present. Things happen to us, without apparent rationale or justification. The hope of modernity – that we could control nature, become the masters of all we survey – may be brought to naught by random happenings in countries of which we know or care little – or by a microscopic organism unknown until the 1980s.

Yet though events may appear accidental and unexpected, the ways in which we respond are not. They have a history – in fact, many histories. AIDS may be a modern phenomenon, *the* disease of the *fin de millennium,* but it is a remarkably historicized phenomenon, framed with histories that burden people living with HIV and AIDS with a weight they should not have to bear.

There are histories of previous diseases, and response to diseases, which provided a rich source of comparisons between the impact of syphilis in the nineteenth century, and AIDS today (Fee and Fox 1988, 1992). There are histories of sexuality, especially the unorthodox sexualities, and histories of the ways in which sexuality has been regulated, telling a tale of power, the institutionalization of the heterosexual norm and the marginalization of the perverse (Foucault 1979). There are histories of racial categorization, of development and undevelopment, which have constructed racialized minorities of the poor and disadvantaged, a Third World in the heart of the cities of the First World, as well as a developing world battling against poverty and disease (see West 1993). There are histories of moral panics focusing on the vulnerable, of punitive interventions to contain the infected, of various forms of oppression of those who do not conform to the norms, and of resistance (Weeks 1991). We are overwhelmed with histories, and with the lessons they could, but usually do not, teach us. But they have one thing in common. These histories are histories of difference and diversity.

Despite the common viral and immunological factors, HIV and AIDS are experienced differently by different groups of people. The suffering and loss felt by gay men in the urban communities of large Western cities is neither less nor greater than the suffering or loss of the poor in the black and hispanic communities of New York, or in the cities and villages of Africa, Latin America or South East Asia; but it is different, because the histories of the communities affected are different. As Simon Watney has written (1989, p. 19):'Wherever we look in the world, it is invariably the case that people's experience of HIV infection and disease faithfully duplicates their socio-economic situation *before* the epidemic began'. We can find here a key to the power of AIDS. It is a syndrome that can threaten catastrophe on an unprecedented scale. But it is experienced, directly or empathetically, as a particular, historically and culturally organized series of diseases. AIDS is both global and local in its impact, and this tells us something vital about the historic present in which we live.

The impact of, and response to, AIDS forcefully reminds us of the complexities and interdependence of the contemporary world. Migrations across countries and continents, from country to town, from 'traditional' ways of life to 'modern', in flight from persecution, poverty or sexual repression, made the spread of HIV possible. The modern information society, global programmes, international consultations and conferences, makes possible a world-wide response to threatening disaster.

Yet the very scale and speed of this globalization of experience produces, as if by a necessary reflex, a burgeoning of culturally and politically specific responses, as well as new identities, new communities and conflicting demands and obligations. In becoming aware of the global village, we seem to need to affirm and reaffirm our local needs, histories and loyalties. Identity and difference: these provide the site of many of the most acute political, social and cultural debates today.

We can see in the AIDS crisis, and in the response it has engendered, several tendencies which cast a sharp light on wider currents and concerns. First, there is a general sense of crisis, a 'sense of an ending', generated by rapid cultural and sexual change, which many have seen AIDS as reinforcing. AIDS did not *cause* this pervasive mood – on the contrary people with HIV have had to endure the consequences of it – but the epidemic rode in on the overwhelming waves of change, and we have to confront the results. AIDS, it has been argued, demonstrates how we as a culture '. . . struggle and negotiate about appropriate processes to deal with social change, especially in its radical form'

(Nelkin et al. 1991, p. 3). And we find that process painfully difficult.

Second, following from that, AIDS reminds us of the complexities of contemporary identities. It was the rise of new sexual identities and communities in the 1960s and 1970s, especially those of lesbians and gay men, which dramatized the fundamental reorientation of sexual ways of being that was taking place. The association of those identities with the threat of disease and death only served to underline the sense of sexual uncertainty that was already manifesting itself in a revival of moral absolutisms and cultural counter-attacks. Uncertainty about who and what we are feeds into wider anxieties and fears.

Third, related to this, AIDS speaks to an 'unfinished revolution' in sexual relationships: a collapse of the settled certainties of family life, an explosion of different lifestyles and life experiments, a potent but incomplete democratization of relationships, and an acute tension between individual desires and collective belongings. Not surprisingly, AIDS, as Seidman (1992, p. 146) argues, has become a principal site to struggle over sexual ethics, and to clarify the meaning and morality of sex.

But finally, these very changes, which seem to many to illustrate the final collapse of the enlightened hopes of modernity, have produced new solidarities as people grapple with the challenges of postmodernity in profoundly humane ways. HIV and AIDS mark you. They have also provided the challenge and opportunities for creating new sensibilities, forged in the furnace of suffering, loss and survival. Out of the pain, rage and anger has come care, mutuality and love, a testimony to the possibilities of realizing human bonds across the chasms of an unforgiving culture. Here we see, I believe, the real possibilities of a radical humanism, grounded in people's struggles, experiences, particular histories and elective traditions.

A SENSE OF AN ENDING?

In an influential book Frank Kermode (1967) wrote of 'the sense of an ending' that shadowed western thought and its fictions.

A looming sense of an ending does appear to haunt many of our cultural assumptions as we approach not only the culmination of the century but also the end of the millennium. Old certainties disappear, or lose their meaning; new ones clash as we attempt to reconstruct a sense of what a common value system could be in the face of cultural fragmentation (to put it negatively) and (more positively) the apparent diversity of human goals. Faced by the apparent contingency of values, many seem to want to give up the struggle altogether as they assert the impossibility of agreeing on anything of ultimate significance. Others speak as if we are dancing on the rim of a volcano, with the only hope a firm yanking of the guide ropes, and a tighter disciplining of our unruly desires.

As Susan Sontag has said, in the countdown to the millennium, a rise in apocalyptic thinking may be inevitable (Sontag 1989). But it is not simply the imminence of a symbolic ending that feeds our anxieties. Apocalyptic thinking, Giddens (1991, p. 4) suggests, is a characteristic of the late modern world because it introduces risk which previous generations have not had to face. Faced with the breakdown of old traditions which related trust and values to a strong sense of place and belonging, traditions which securely locked us into the certainties of gender, family, morality and nation, individuals have been thrown back on themselves, which has involved hazards of individual choice and interpretation of meanings. Morality, Bauman argues, has been increasingly privatized and, like everything else that shares such a fate, 'ethics has become a matter of individual discretion, risk-taking, chronic uncertainty and never-placated qualms' (1992a. p. xxiii).

In such a world we are vulnerable to waves of anxiety highlighting our contingency. The opposite to trust as a basis for social life, as Giddens (1990, p. 100) points out, is not mistrust but angst and dread. It is not surprising, therefore, that fear looms over our actions. Hutcheon evokes the threat of a 'recessionary erotic economy' (1989, p. 141), brought about by a terror of disease and a fetishization of fitness, and others have observed the ways in which fitness and health have become a new focus for a sense of self and a harnessing of the resilience of the body

(Coward 1989, p. 126). We live, Linda Singer (1993) has argued, under the 'hegemony of epidemic', requiring us to avoid risk, and adopt a 'new sobriety' in our personal conduct. This is more than a simple extrapolation from the AIDS epidemic, but a response to a wider sense of crisis, and explanatory modes, shaped by a new language of contagion. We speak of 'epidemics' of child sex abuse, teenage pregnancy, pornography . . .

The more culturally conservative, on the left as well as the right, suggest that we are living through a progressive demoralization of society, with every index of social order, from civility to the breakdown of stable family life, streaking off the graph. We seek simple solutions in scapegoats. Unmarried teenage mothers become not only a symptom of sexual change but a cause of social ills, from housing crises to crime (Murray 1994). Faced with a 'panic-culture', a sense of living at the 'edge of the world', enticed and repelled by the 'pleasures of catastrophe' (Kroker and Kroker 1988, pp. 13ff), there is a temptation to seek a total solution. An epidemic of whatever kind, whether of genuine disease or of presumed moral debility, seems to require at the least a managerial response, a mobilization of an effort to control. The new fundamentalisms, whether secular or religious, Christian, Hindu or Islamic, try to move the furniture of our minds into a new shape, where absolute truths are wedded to moralistic proscriptions and prescriptions (Bhatt 1994). Or in the absence of anything obvious we surrender to that 'modern, wilful' kind of nostalgia that seeks refuge in myths of stability, harmony and golden ages, somewhere in our childhood or just below the horizon of historic memory (Robertson 1990). Back to basics indeed!

Given the very real uncertainty that swims alongside our every action, and the assertive certainties that seek to cure doubt, how can we measure what is actually happening? Are we really at the end of time?

'Endings' are of course largely fictions, attempts by human minds to impose some sort of order (however apocalyptic) on the chaos of events. A century, after all, is only an arbitrary time-frame; it is unlikely that events will so gather as to fall readily within its boundaries. But the imminence of a new period, however invented, may dramatize a sense of impending change, and even come to portend disaster. The crises of the *fin de siècle*, Showalter (1991, p. 2) argues, 'are more intensely experienced, more emotionally fraught, more weighted with symbolic and historic meaning, because we invest them with the metaphors of death and rebirth that we project onto the final decades and years of a century'. It is, perhaps, no accident then that our contemporary sensibility produces strong sympathies and pre-occupations with the political, cultural and philosophical movements of the turn of the last century (Harvey 1989, p. 285).

Myths, metaphors and images of sexual crisis and apocalypse have marked both the nineteenth-century *fin de siècle* and our own. Just as the decades since the 1960s have been attacked for their endorsement of sexual permissiveness and licence, so the 1880s and 1890s were seen by the novelist George Gissing as decades of 'sexual anarchy' (Showalter 1991). In both periods, all the laws governing sexual identity and behaviour seemed to be undergoing rapid transformation, as the boundaries between men and women were challenged and stretched, as family life seemed to be under threat, as sexual dissidence achieved an unparalleled verbosity, as the sexually 'perverse' invaded the arts and literature, and as the fear of sexual disease taunted the imaginary of private and public life.

As AIDS opportunely offered a metaphor for twentieth-century lapse, so syphilis and other diseases haunted sex, marriage and the family in the nineteenth century (Mort 1987). The child sex abuse scandals of the 1980s and 1990s immediately evoke memories of the discovery of 'the maiden tribute of modern Babylon', child exploitation and prostitution in the 1880s. Divisions in the feminist movement today about pornography echo the late nineteenth-century splits over prostitution and moral purity (Walkowitz 1993).

Inevitably, issues of sex and gender intersect with other social categorizations. Fears of racial diversity today play on themes of racial superiority and racial decline prevalent in the last century (Hall 1992). Anxieties about the sexual habits of the young and the poor (often also the black) and overpopulation in the Third

World recirculate anxieties from the last century about the promiscuous sexuality of the newly urbanized masses.

All these anxieties revolve around questions of boundaries, that separate one group of people from another, and identities, that merge them: the boundaries between men and women, the normal and the abnormal, adults and children, the civilized and the uncivilized, the rich and the poor, the enlightened and the masses. In periods of flux and unprecedented change the boundaries begin to dissolve, and identities are undermined and reformed. And in sexuality above all these dissolutions and mergings are most acute, as the great *causes célèbres* of sexual history reveal. Oscar Wilde, the object lesson in the perils of sexual transgression in the 1890s, not only breached the codes of sexual respectability by leading an increasingly dangerous homosexual life, he also broke the barriers of class by indulging with working-class youths (Dollimore 1991; Sinfield 1994). Sexual abuse of children in the 1980s was more than an imposition of unwelcome adult power over children; it also suggested a fundamental undermining of the boundaries between, and responsibilities of (usually) male parents for their offspring (Campbell 1988). Sexually transmitted diseases are the most successful dissolvers of boundaries: they do not admit of barriers of class, race, gender or age, which is why the AIDS crisis was so able to draw on the language of earlier epidemics for much of its initial imagery – with similar apocalyptic effects (Sontag 1989).

Such similarities make it relatively easy to assume that the two endings, of the nineteenth and the twentieth centuries, are identical. But to see the late nineteenth century as a mirror-image of the twentieth would be mistaken. There are common elements but also important differences, which help us to see what is distinctive about our current sense of a sexual crisis. In a brilliant essay in self- and historical reconstruction, *Who Was that Man? A Present for Mr Oscar Wilde*, the playwright and novelist Neil Bartlett (1988) attempts to forge connections between his generation of gay men, those of the embattled but selfconscious and confident urban subcultures of the 1980s, and that of Wilde and his contemporaries in the 1880s and 1890s. He discovers that much is obscured because of the lack of evidence, the silences of a history which has marginalized Wilde's (and his) experience. Certain languages, rituals ('camp', cruising for sexual partners, the disruption of sexual orthodoxy) unite the different generations. But more fundamental are the distance and the differences. Identity is sought and glimpsed; it is the essential gesture of reconciliation with our collective and individual pasts; but it is also elusive. So much has remained at least similar, if not the same; so much has changed. We live in a different world.

We are here on the terrain of what, for want of a better term, I shall call postmodernity. 'Postmodernity' is clearly a relational term defined by something that came before, or at least is passing, 'modernity'. It carries with it that sense of an ending which we have already noted. We can debate its implications endlessly, as many have done, and doubtless will continue to do. Are we, as Giddens (1990) argues, simply witnessing the juggernaut of modernity gathering speed, causing a radicalization of modernity, sweeping away the barriers to change, but leaving us prey to radical doubt? Or, as Bauman (1990) suggests, are we watching the sleek ship of modernity finally receding into the distance, its mission achieved, but casting us adrift in its wake?

The images are graphic, and strikingly different, yet both are suggestive of a period of radical transformation. However we characterize the age, there can be no doubt of its sense of fundamental change with all its resulting uncertainty. This sense of change, of indeed being on the edge of time, has been compounded by the weakening of the legitimizing traditions and master discourses of high modernity. The twin processes of a secularization of moral values, and of a gradual liberalization of social attitudes, especially towards what has traditionally been seen as 'the perverse', have begun to dissolve the old verities (Weeks 1993b). The narrative comforts of the Christian tradition have long suffered the corrosive effects of scepticism and critique, creating the space for fundamentalist revival alongside liberation from superstition. Now even the 'Enlightenment project' of the triumph of reason, progress and humanity, the sense that science and history were leading us inexorably to a more glorious future, has been subjected to searching deconstruction, and its roots have been shown to be murky. Reason has been reduced to a rationalization of power, progress has been seen as the tool of white, Western expansionism, and humanity as the cloak for a male-dominated culture which treats women as other. The universal aspirations and foundational givens of modernity have been radically challenged (see essays in Weeks 1994).

My point here is not to intervene in the wider debates about postmodernity but to trace the parallels between these and recent challenges to the dominant discourses of sexuality, especially of sexual progressivism. The rationalistic triumphalism of the nineteenth-century sexologists is itself now under assault. A number of feminists have seen the science of sex as little more than a tattered cover for the reaffirmation of male power, imposing a male-oriented 'sexual liberation' on women (Jeffreys 1990). Foucault (1979) has famously challenged our illusions concerning the very notion of sexual 'liberation', and by many others sexual liberalism has been denounced as little more than a new garb for the incessant process of sexual regulation and control (National Deviancy Conference 1980). Alongside these there has been a radical undermining of the original bases for the enlightened hopes of the pioneers of sexual reform at the end of the nineteenth century, and which by the mid-twentieth had come to dominate sexual thinking, even among the most conservative: the triumph of science (Weeks 1985). In his presidential address to the Congress of the World League for Sexual Reform in 1929, the pioneering sexologist Magnus Hirschfeld declared that 'A sexual impulse based on science is the only sound system of ethics'; he proclaimed on the portals of his Institute for Sexual Science the words 'Through Science to Justice' (see Weeks 1986, p. 111). Part of that hope died as the Institute's books burned under the Nazi torch. Much of the rest faded in the succeeding decades as sexual scientists squabbled over their inheritance and disagreed over everything from the nature of sexual difference, female sexual needs and homosexuality to the social consequences of disease (see Bullough 1994).

Behind this was the more subtle undermining of the sexual tradition which had been defined in the nineteenth century, in sexology, medico-moral practice, legal enactments and personal life. The narrative of sexual orthodoxy has been vigorously challenged, to be complemented if not replaced by a number of new historical narratives, many by those hitherto disqualified by the would-be science of sex. As Gayle Rubin (1984) has famously put it, a veritable catalogue of types from the pages of Krafft-Ebing has marched on to the stage of social history, each new sexual subject claiming its legitimacy and place in the sun. If the hallmark of the nineteenth-century pioneers of sex reform and the sexual sciences was a belief in the efficacy of science and the revelation of the laws of nature, the characteristic note of modern sexual activists (despite an occasional dabble in sociobiology or genetic determinism) is self-activity, self-making, the questioning of received truths, the contestation of laws which elevate some and exclude others. Scientific sexology has been challenged by a grass-roots sexology; reform from above by community organization from below; and a single narrative of sexual enlightenment by a host of separate histories, from women, lesbians and gays, racial minorities and others (see Plummer 1995).

What we are seeing in these developments is a profound weakening of sexual modernism. The sexual order, with its fixing of sexual identifications under the banner of Nature, Science and Truth, has all but gone, reflecting a fundamental shift not only in theory but in what theory is attempting to grasp. The contemporary sexual world appears as irrevocably pluralistic, divided into a host of sovereign units, and a multiplicity of sites of authority (Bauman 1992a, p. 35), none of which can claim a firm foundation. There is no longer a hegemonic master discourse telling us how we should behave, and those clamant moralities which attempt to fill the vacuum may have their listeners, but cannot affirm an ultimate legitimacy. In this turmoil of discordant voices, sexual behaviour, sexual identity and sexual mores have increasingly become matters of choice, at least for those who have the freedom to choose. We can choose whether and how to give birth or to terminate pregnancy; we can select the sex of the child, even its colour, and not too far into the future, some propose, its sexual orientation. There is greater freedom of choice than ever before about the age of first sexual experience, whom we do it with, how often, in what sort of relationship. We can choose how we wish to identify ourselves, and what our lifestyles should be. Even gender, apparently the most reliant of natural divisions, is now seen as more an elective masquerade than a necessary given: is it possible, Denise Riley (1988) asks, to inhabit a gender without a feeling of horror? At the end of it all, we can choose the conditions of our dying. Existence itself has become a choice (Melucci 1989, p. 110). Choice has become the ruling morality both of the political right (at least in economic matters) and of the liberal left.

The idea of choice is deeply embedded in the liberal ethos of western societies, but under the conditions of postmodernity it has assumed a new significance. As Bauman (1992a, p. xxii) argues:

> The ethical paradox of the postmodern condition is that it restores to agents the fullness of moral choice and responsibility while simultaneously depriving them of the universal guidance that modern self-confidence once promised ... Moral responsibility comes together with the loneliness of moral choice.

Yet how, and with what criteria, we should choose is less clear. Is it surprising then that a sense of an ending, the closure of narrative certainties, presages ethical confusion?

THE SELF AND IDENTITY

The radical individualism that appears the dominant theme of our age, in sexual and ethical values as much as in economic, is an ambiguous phenomenon. On the positive side it undermines the solidity of traditional narratives and relations of dominance and subordination. A discourse of choice is a powerful dissolvant of old verities. In the 1980s, as New Right administrations in the USA and Britain attempted to combine a radical emphasis on a free economy with a social and moral conservatism, it was noticeable that the individualism of the first constantly seeped into and fundamentally undermined the second. By the 1990s, it was clear in both countries that the loosening of the bonds of sexual authoritarianism associated with the 1960s was continuing, even accelerating, despite haphazard attempts at moral rearmament. The most successful high priests of Radical Right politics in the West, President Reagan and Margaret Thatcher, presided over probably the greatest revolution in sexual mores in the twentieth century, despite their best endeavours (Weeks 1993b). Individual freedom cannot stop at the market; if you have an absolute freedom to buy and sell, there seems no logic in blocking a freedom to choose your sexual partners, your sexual lifestyle, your identity, or your fantasies, even if these involve pornographic indulgence and the most elaborate forms of autoerotic ritual.

But the negative side is a sexual libertarianism that brooks no barrier to individual satisfaction, that makes individual pleasure the sole yardstick of sexual ethics. The vast expansion of choice, in part the creature of a new global sexual market offering a wonderland of consumer glitter, with everything from sexual holidays to designer drugs, opens up but simultaneously undermines the possibility of individual development and social cooperation (see Wilson 1985). It makes possible escape from the prison house of dying and repressive traditions, but it places a new, sometimes unbearable, burden on those who are the victims of careless and selfish choices. This provides the bare strand of truth in the jeremiads of cultural conservatives about a prevalent 'narcissism' in contemporary behaviour (Lasch 1980, 1985). The cultivation of the self, men and women as artists of their own lives, can be a valuable aim; when it is pursued without care for the other, without a sense of mutual responsibility and common belonging it can lead to an ethical desert.

We are in danger of becoming 'disembedded', rootless, thrown back on our fragile selves when what we need is a sense of the indissoluble links between individual freedom and social belonging. Carol Gilligan has noted as a paradoxical truth of human experience that 'we know ourselves as separate only insofar as we live in connection with others, and that we experience relationships only in so far as we differentiate other from self' (1982, p. 63). In striving for that balance, however, we need to escape the imprisoning limitations of the essentializing individualism of which we in the West are heirs.

For Thomas Hobbes, at the beginning of the modern period, it was convenient to think of 'men' as if they were mushrooms, fully sprung out of the earth, and 'come to full maturity, without all kinds of engagement to each other' (quoted in Benhabib 1987, p. 84). Even as a speculation necessary for the establishment of the social contract, this was radical stuff, but its vivid evocation of the autonomous self was to become a founding assumption of the liberal tradition. Central to this founding myth is a supposed unity of the self, and a disembodiment of the autonomous individual from any entangling social involvements. Implicit in it also is an assumption that the contracting individual was male. The founding moment of the social contract, as Carole Pateman (1988) has argued, was a fraternal pact, a masculine act of birth, a male replica in the public/political sphere of the ability which only women possess in the private sphere.

The sexual tradition was complicit with these cultural assumptions. If in the past two hundred years, as Foucault (1979) has argued, sex has become the 'truth of our being', it is precisely because the erotic has been conceived of as the core of an essential self, a – sometimes *the* – defining element of our unique individuality. The paradox is that this essentializing of our sexual natures has gone hand in hand with a hierarchical ordering of sexual norms (cf. Rubin 1984). In the triangle of sexual discourses, it has been the male definition of heterosexual normality which has been at the apex, with female sexuality and the perverse at the base. Sexuality has been trapped in the coils of power in its diverse, polymorphous but often highly structured forms. Choice was limited because only normal men had the real freedom to choose their sexual tastes.

Developments during the twentieth century have fundamentally questioned this picture, challenging, in theory as well as cultural practice, the idea of the unitary individual, with a nature given destiny. Freud's uncovering of the contingent self, constantly undermined by unconscious wishes beyond the merely rational, the fragments precariously welded together in only-ever partial resolution of inevitable conflict, is only one among numerous attempts to displace the sovereign, gendered and sexualized individual in theory (Weeks 1985). Now we have become more accustomed to thinking of the fractured self, not so much one thing or another as 'more or less' the same person you were ten years ago. For theorists of postmodernity, the subject is no more than a 'nodal point' in a series of language games, characterized by diversity, conflict, the difficulty of finding a consensus within ourselves, let alone others (Lyotard 1984).

The speculative deconstructions of the self are themselves shaped by a radically contingent world, where the solidity of everyday life itself dissolves into fragmented experiences. If it is true that the unity of the person has always been constituted in and through everyday life (Heller 1984, p. 7), what must we expect of the changes that are remaking it, as old fixed points begin to break away before our eyes?

We can no longer hunger for the sovereign self, with his (usually his) earth making will. Instead we search out the possible identities with which we can feel at one. And there are so many of them! Class and national identities, religious identities, gender and sexual identities, racial and ethnic identities, consumer identities. And none of them is straightforward, for we are simultaneously shaped by all these influences, each of them making differing claims, pointing to different priorities, offering sometimes radically conflicting ways forward.

Identity has become more of a process than a given, offering a choice of beings rather than the truth of ourselves. The unity of the human life, as Alasdair MacIntyre (1985) has suggested, is the unity of a narrative quest. We have to work at it (cf. Giddens 1992).

Of course, none of the choices is absolutely free. They are constrained and limited by relations of power, by structures of domination and subordination. Even when we are apparently most free to exercise our choice, as consumers on the market, we are trapped within cords of gold. Raymond Williams (1989) has described the process of 'mobile privatisation', and the localized and narrow identities around consumption it gives rise to, ever subject to the whims of the economy and our purchasing power. Other identities, around gender, sexuality, race, are often the product of imposed histories, neat categorizations devised for the purposes of social regulation as much as individual choice.

Nowadays, as Melucci has argued, 'the social attribution of identity invades all areas traditionally protected by the barrier of "private space" ' (1989, p. 123). Identities are drawn into the mesh of economic need, social discipline and cultural conformity.

Some identities, however, are a product of struggles, battles against definition by others, and for self-definition. This is the case above all in relation to contemporary dissident sexual identities, especially lesbian and gay identities. And it is around these that the social movements and communities of identity have evolved. These movements and communities are largely networks of small groups submerged in everyday life. Though frequently erupting into the public domain with major interventions (for example, campaigns for abortion, equal rights, against anti-gay legislation) their focus has been the local or functional group, loosely connected confederally with others, forming a community of interests. But within such groups and networks there is an experimentation with and practice of alternative frameworks of sense, producing different definitions of self, which sometimes contrast with, and sometimes mesh into, the consumerized identities being shaped and reshaped alongside them. The result has been profoundly influential in reshaping our thinking about the private sphere. The links between the social and the personal are constantly being defined and redefined, while at the same time the power relations in the domains of everyday life are being made visible, and the spaces for individual inventions of self are being expanded.

But in this they are only the more visible signs of an even more profound change. The fragility and hybridity of modern personal identities forces everyone in highly developed societies to engage in experiments in everyday life: to define themselves, their identities and their needs against a shifting landscape. The transformation in relations between men and women during the twentieth century, however limited and constrained it has been in some areas, is a strong marker of this. Women's claims to sexual autonomy represent the strongest undermining of the traditional narratives of the sexual order. It is not surprising that this has also produced signs of a 'male backlash', and 'flight from responsibility' (Ehrenreich 1983). Not only is a sense of self being remade, but there is also a fundamental unsettling of relationships.

This concern with the self and identity is more than a preoccupation of the politically and sexually marginal. It is an aspect of what Giddens (1991) calls the 'reflexive project of the self' which he sees as fundamentally characteristic of late modernity:

> In a post-traditional social universe, reflexively organized, permeated by abstract systems, and in which the reordering of time and space realigns the local with the global, the self undergoes massive change. Therapy, including self-therapy, both expresses that change and provides programmes of realizing it in the form of self-actualization. On the level of the self, a fundamental component of day-to-day activity is simply that of *choice* (Giddens 1991, p. 80)

We have no choice but to choose. What and how we choose is, however, a problem. Faced by a cacophony of options we can opt for the monadic, solipsistic way; or we can choose a being with others. The first returns us to the most extreme manifestations of the individualistic tradition. The second forces us to think about the limits of choice, that human interaction where free choice impinges on the freedom to choose of others. This is the postmodern ethical dilemma at its most stark. How, and with whom, and with what traditions, we identify becomes critical.

The postmodern recognition of the instability of the self, of openness in the choosing of identities, seems to many to reduce everything to flux: there are no fixed boundaries between people, only arbitrary labels. Identities are relativized, and therefore it seems to some diminished. Yet we cling to them. In a world of constant change, people apparently need fixed points, points of alignment. Identities, personal and social, are both precarious and essential, historically shaped and personally chosen, affirmations of self and confirmations of our social being. We construct narratives of the self in order to negotiate the hazards of everyday life, and to assert our sense of belonging in an ever more complex social world. But that puts on the agenda the sort of lives we want to live – and in a world of multiple ways of life this question can become a powerful focus of uncertainty.

SEXUALITY, RELATIONSHIPS AND THE DEMOCRATIC IMAGINATION

Modernity, Giddens (1992) has argued, is a post-traditional order in which the question 'how shall I live?' has to be answered in day to day decisions about who to be, how to behave, what to wear, what to eat, and, crucially for this discussion, how we should live together, whom we can love. As the energies of postmodernity gather pace, undermining settled patterns and old certainties, so these questions come more and more to the fore, and nowhere more so than in what I shall call the sphere of the intimate, the domain of 'private life' and its infinitely malleable and promiscuous partner, the erotic.

Intimacy in its modern form, as Giddens (1992) suggests, implies a radical democratization of the interpersonal domain, because it assumes not only the individual being the ultimate maker of his or her own life, but also equality between partners and freedom to choose lifestyles and forms of partnership. This theme of democratization, and its dilemmas, is crucial to our understanding of changes in sexual mores. There are two key areas where it is especially significant: family and/or domestic arrangements; and sexuality and love.

We are currently in the midst of a sometimes fevered debate about the family and domestic arrangements. Among conservatives this takes the form of a lamentation at the decline of the family, a hallowed theme hardly new, as we have seen, to this *fin de siècle*, but given a new wind because of transparently dramatic changes to its form, and because it has become an easy symbol for wider changes. Among liberals and radicals, on the other hand, the 1960s theme of finding alternatives *to* the family has given way to a recognition that there are 'alternative families', differentiated in all sorts of ways: by class, ethnicity, life-cycle and so on, and by deliberate choice of lifestyle. We may anguish over some of these forms, and attempt to determine what is best for childrearing and social stability (two parents seem to be preferred over one, heterosexual parents are generally favoured over homosexual), but broadly, and with varying degrees of reluctance, there is a general recognition on the liberal left that domestic diversity is with us to stay.

The problem is that while we may recognize the fact of diversity, we have yet to forge a language or set of values by which we can measure the legitimacy of all these forms. 'Commuter-marriages', relationships carried out at a distance as partners stretch the bonds of intimacy by constant travel (and surely the best neologism in this area), are apparently acceptable; homosexual partnerships, however domesticated, regularly are not, despite the growing recognition of 'partnership rights' in a number of countries (see chapter 4 below). The furore in the late 1980s over 'pretended family relationships', that other neologism for lesbian and gay relationships (Weeks 1991, chapter 8), showed that at least in the United Kingdom the boundaries of acceptability may indeed have expanded, but not that far.

And yet one of the most remarkable features of domestic change has been the emergence of common patterns in both homosexual and heterosexual ways of life (see Bech 1992a and b; see also chapter 4 below). Contemporary lesbian and gay relationships, in principle at least, are freely chosen by autonomous individuals, and have to be constructed afresh each time (cf. Weston 1991). They survive only as long as they offer a satisfactory framework for fulfilling the domestic, emotional and/or sexual needs of the freely contracting partners. Of course, there are always all sorts of inequality, of income, age, ethnicity and so on that structure these relationships, but in principle they are partnerships between free agents, carrying little historical baggage, except (a big exception I admit) that of public opprobrium.

Heterosexual relationships, by contrast, remain – in the well chosen words of Clark and Haldane (1990) largely 'wedlocked', despite the secular decline in marriage rates and the massive rise in cohabitation. In Britain, for example, most people still marry at some stage, often when children arrive, and regularly remarry when they (frequently) divorce. Even cohabitation is marriage-like, and the majority of children born outside marriage are registered in the name of both partners. Whatever the changes that have transformed the institution, most of us live or have lived in families, and we remain wedded to familial language. Recent surveys in the USA and Britain reveal a surprising conservatism in domestic and sexual arrangements, at least in the majority white populations (Laumann et al. 1994; Wellings et al. 1994). Yet alongside this continuity there are profound changes rattling the doors. The rise in divorce (a third of marriages expected to end in divorce), the prevalence of premarital sex (the vast majority of partners now have had sex before marriage), the gradual fading away of the stigma of illegitimacy (a spiralling number of births outside marriage), the rise of one-parent families, (90 per cent headed by women), even the judicial recognition that there can be rape in marriage (Weeks 1993b): all these are familiar facts, but their implications are often misunderstood. It does not necessarily imply 'a breakdown of the family' as our more conservative commentators used to see it. As has frequently been pointed out, the divorced very often remarry, and remarry. There is a constant effort to 'make a go of it'. But the underlying ideology is changing.

People try to make a go of it, sometimes several times over, for a variety of reasons, but the central drive is the search for a satisfactory relationship as a key element in personal affirmation. Marriage becomes more and more a relationship entered into and sustained only for as long as it delivers emotional satisfaction from close contact with others, from intimacy (Giddens 1992). Of course, as Janet Finch (1989) and others have pointed out, there are still many obligations which hold relationships together, especially children, and these are structured along lines of gender more often than not, and it is still true that most marriages do not end prematurely in divorce. But increasingly choice of involvements is the key, and the reasons for choice are the hopes, often dashed but resilient, that the new relationship will deliver the goods. And these goods are emotional involvement and satisfaction.

In other words, marriage is entered into less as a status transition (though it remains that) and more as a sign of commitment. But in that it is only a more symbolically potent form of the commitment that lies at the heart of many other forms of relationship, including non-heterosexual.

Marriage today embraces elements of what has been called a 'pure relationship' (Giddens 1992). Pure relationships are sought and entered into only for what the relationship can bring to the contracting partners. They are inevitably mediated through a host of socio-economic and gender factors. They often survive through inertia, habit and mutual dependency, as well as because of the web of obligations that are negotiated through the relationship. But the principle is that the relationship survives only as long as the commitment survives, or until a more promising relationship offers itself. The pure relationship depends on mutual trust between the partners, which in turn is closely related to the achievement of the desired level of intimacy. If trust breaks down, so in the end does intimacy, and the search for a better arrangement renews. This involves a high degree of instability. There is a new contingency in personal relationships. But the emphasis on personal commitment as the key to emotional satisfaction also has radical implications. For commitment implies the involvement of consenting, more or less equal individuals. The pure relationship implies a democratization of intimate relationships: the emphasis on individual autonomy and choice provides a radicalizing dynamic that is making possible the transformation of personal life.

Two things are important here. First, the relationship, whatever its form, marital or non-marital, becomes the defining element of the sphere of the intimate that provides the framework for everyday life. Second, it is the focus of personal identity, in which the personal narrative is constructed and reconstructed to provide the provisional sense of unity of the self that is necessary in the world of postmodernity. The pure relationship is both a product of the reflexive self, and a focus for its realization. It offers a nodal point for personal meaning in the contemporary world. It is here that sexuality and love are important, because they provide some of the prime sites for the attainment of meaning today.

Since the nineteenth century at least, Foucault (1979) and

others have argued, there has been a constant attempt to tell what you are by telling the assumed truth about your sexuality. The great polarities that we take for granted in speaking about social and personal life, male/female, heterosexual/homosexual, were assumed to be located in fundamental divisions within our sexual natures. We are now more aware that these divides, that we so easily assume are inbuilt and natural, personal to us, are in fact deeply historical and social. In part these definitions have been impositions, a complex effect of the play of power. In part they have been the result of a long process of internal struggle, negotiation and self-definition (see Kern 1992).

Giddens (1992), in partial challenge to Foucault (1979), has argued that sexuality has the importance it does in the contemporary world not because of its significance for the control systems of modernity but because it is a point of connection between two other processes: the separation of experiences into discrete categories of existence, which has led to the privatization of death as well as of sexuality (in fact it made the emergence of sexuality as a discrete area of life possible); and the transformation of intimacy which has democratized sexual relations, and opened the way to the pure relationship. Although presented as antagonistic theories, however, these positions are not in practice incompatible. The very fact that sexuality has been bound up with structures of domination and subordination, for women, the sexually transgressive and the colonized, internally and externally, has inevitably meant that the sexual has been a prime site for the struggle for a sense of self and identity. Those struggles in turn have contributed to the democratization of relationships. Inevitably, then, our sense of our self, the meanings we attach to our lives, are closely shaped by our sense of our sexuality. Sexuality may be a 'historic construct' (Foucault 1979) but it remains also a key site for the construction of personal meaning and social location.

But in the process the meaning of sexuality has itself changed. For long locked into the history of reproduction, it has now to a large degree floated free of it, a process that was well developed long before the Pill promised a once and for all technological fix (Wellings et al. 1994). It continues to evoke images of sin, for many, violence, for children and women particularly, and perhaps for all of us, power. It is still linked with the threat of disease, re-evoked by the presence of the HIV epidemic. It is, as Carole Vance (1984) put it, a site of danger as well as pleasure. But in a complex process, its meanings have expanded. It has become for most what it always was in theory, polymorphous or 'plastic'. In principle, at least, the erotic arts have been opened up to all of us, via a thousand sex manuals on the joys of sex, a flourishing trade in sexual representations, and an explosion of discourse around the body and its pleasures. Sexuality has become an arena for experimentation. This is closely related to the question of relationships, because if commitment, intimacy, trying again, are keys to modern private life, so is their attainment through sexual satisfaction, which increasingly means the exploration of the erotic, in ever more exotic and intricate patterns. There are, of course, many types of relationship without sex, and a lot of sex without relationships. But it is not an accident that intimacy as a term is closely related to sexual activity. Modern intimacy is closely linked with the exploration and satisfaction of sexual desire.

Where does that leave love? It is easy to talk about sexuality without love, and love without sexuality. But it is clear that love also is increasingly something that is shaped contingently, as a focus for intimate relationships. Love, like sexuality, has become more fluid, less a prescription for eternal devotion, more a matter of personal choice and self-making, a mode of communication rather than an eternal truth (Luhmann 1986). Its meanings are made for and in specific circumstances. That does not mean that it is less important; on the contrary, its very mobility, its poten-tiality for transcending the divide between autonomous indi-viduals, makes it an ever more vital ingredient of social as well as private life. But we cannot assume its form; it must be nego-tiated afresh each time. Love, Bauman (1993, p. 98) argues, is insecurity incarnate.

These changes are affecting men and women alike, but their impact is highly gendered. Giddens (1992) has argued that women are in fact in the vanguard of change, and there are certainly many signs of a new ability among women to take control of their lives and commitments: most divorces, for example, are initiated by women. Changes in sexual mores may have sexualized women's bodies to an extraordinary degree, though often exploitatively; they have also opened up unprecedented spaces for autonomy and self-actualization. Yet the pragmatics of independence are always hazardous. In their study of young women's attitudes to their bodies and sexualities in the context of the risk of HIV and AIDS, Holland et al. (1994) show how the assertion of female sexuality remains geared to the exigencies of male needs. The potential for autonomy is there, but so are the constraints:

> Sex connects bodies and this connexion gives women an intimate space within which men's powers can be subverted and resisted. If women can recognize and capture this space, they can negotiate relationships with men which upset the gender hierarchy and so are potentially socially destabilizing. We suggest that few young women recognize and capture this space because they lack a critical consciousness that they are living a disembodied femininity. Where women do have a critical consciousness of the embodiment of their sexuality, and are comfortable with desires of their own, men's power can be directly threatened . . . which might help explain the prevalence of male violence in sexual encounters (Holland et al. 1994, pp. 34–5).

Research such as this indicates that sexuality remains a battleground, where the meanings of sexuality and love are still fought over, even in those parts of the world where sex-talk is most open and explicit. And yet it also suggests that even in the most resilient interstices of male privilege the potential for change, for renegotiation of relationships, is apparent.

Like all developments these shifts and changes in personal relationships are highly uneven in their impact. They are the cutting edge, and their effects are transforming intimate life, but they are working through the residue of deeply sedimented traditions. Not only are the changes highly gendered, there are different patterns in different communities. In their study of mixed race relations in Britain Alibhai-Brown and Montague (1992) illustrate the complexities of choice where racial and ethnic identification intersect with sexual attraction and love.

Inter-racial relations are scarcely new, but they have always of necessity had to negotiate the hazards of group norms and shifting, yet institutionalized patterns of prejudice and discrimination. Increasingly they also have to live with the reassertion of more exclusive collective identities among racial and ethnic minorities, leading to reinforced social taboos against exogamy. The rise of fundamentalist commitments among these minority communities, affirming translocal loyalties to Islam or Hinduism or other all-encompassing belief systems as an aspect of passionate group loyalties, is regularly associated with concerns with the gendered and sexualized body, as if the essence of identity can be asserted only through bodily purification (Bhatt 1994). Yet at the same time, as Alibhai-Brown and Montague argue:

> ... just as there are many Asian and Black Britons who would now argue against mixed relationships, there are also many others whose lives have been enriched and transformed by them and who see this as a new dawn. It can no longer be assumed, as it once was, that white values would dominate – that the Black or Asian partner would turn 'white', give or take an occasional ethnic headscarf, or sari at the office Christmas party, which was commonplace in the previous two decades ... Nothing is taken for granted (1992, p. 15).

'Nothing is taken for granted.' This is becoming the leitmotif of sexual manners as individuals struggle, pragmatically, to define their needs in the fluctuating circumstances in which they live their sexual lives. Bauman (1993, p. 98) argues that there are two characteristic strategies for coping with the potential flux in relationships that now opens up, what he describes as 'fixing' and 'floating'. Fixing takes place when the potential openness of 'confluent love' (Giddens 1992) and sexuality is set firmly in place by the demands of duty. 'Floating' is what occurs when the arduousness of the constant negotiation of the terms of the relationship leads to our 'cutting our losses', starting again, ever hopeful that this time we will get it right. Neither is particularly appealing. The first, at its most extreme, would seem to prefer an empty shell to the creativity of a living relationship. The second can result in what Bauman (1993, p. 106) describes as a 'de-ethicized intimacy', where responsibility to others, especially children, is lost in the pursuit of personal satisfaction. These are not, however, the only possibilities. The democratization of sexuality and relationships that is now on the cultural agenda, only partially realized though it may yet be, creates the space for rethinking the ethics and values of personal relationships, for exploring what we mean by terms like responsibility, care, concern and love. This is the challenge of the transformations of sexuality now taking place. In this postmodern world it is unlikely that we will ever rid ourselves of the spectre of uncertainty, but its presence might help us to realize that living without certainty is the best spur there is to thinking again about what we value, what we really want.

TOWARDS A RADICAL HUMANISM

In this chapter I have attempted to survey some of the changes which are transforming personal relationships and our ideas of sexuality. I have explored three areas where I saw this taking place: in a sense of an ending, in changes in our concepts of the self and identity, and in the democratization of everyday life. Many have claimed to see in such changes the threat of dissolution, fragmentation, amorality. I, on the contrary, prefer to see the possibilities of something more hopeful, a new humanism which respects diversity and the maximization of individual choice while affirming at the same time the importance of the human bond.

The AIDS crisis, in all its frightening impact, bearing the burden of fear of disease and death in the wake of pleasure and desire, seems to many to embody the downside of the transformations of sexuality in recent years, a warning of the dangers of things 'going too far'. Yet in many of the responses to it we can see something else: a quickening of humanity, the engagement of solidarity, and the broadening of the meanings of love, love in the face of death.

In the past couple of hundred years, death has become a taboo subject; like sexuality it has been separated off from everyday life, hidden from view, and like the erotic it has inevitably returned to haunt us, providing the horizon of our thoughts. Norbert Elias has suggested that in refusing to look 'the finitude of individual life, . . . the dissolution of one's own person' directly in the face we are losing something from our lives (1985, pp. 33–4).

I want to suggest that the exclusion of death as an essential part of life is itself undergoing a profound challenge, not least because of the impact of the HIV/AIDS epidemic. A sense of the contingency and uncertainty of life has been brought to many people, many of whom are very young, by the threat of premature illness and death. But it has also produced something else: a sense of the meaning that can be brought to life by the threat of death. I quote from an article subtitled 'Memories of Life with a Person with AIDS':

> Paul's death, and AIDS generally, was not a good thing. It was not romantic, it was not heroic, it was not kind. We shared it, and I discovered, to quote Gerda Lerner, that it is 'like life – untidy, tangled, tormented, transcendent. And we accept it because we must. Because we are human' (Interrante 1987, p. 61).

That sense of our humanity being reaffirmed through the experience of death is I believe a profoundly transforming experience, a democratizing experience also, which gives new meaning to our experience of, and need for, human relationships in all their diversity.

Diversity, Feyerabend (1987, p. 1) argues, is beneficial while uniformity 'reduces our joys and our (intellectual, emotional, material) resources'. But a growing perception of the very different ways of being human, and sexual, that now exist has fed into a sense of crisis, and a search for some approximation to uniformity. Sontag (1989, p. 78) has detected in the response to AIDS a punitive desire, 'the desire for stricter limits in the conduct of personal life'. But this is more than a reaction to a threat of viral contamination, as I have sought to demonstrate. It is a response to the collapse of old certainties, and the recognition of our contingency. As boundaries become more fluid and dissolve, the numbers desiring to police the guard houses grow, on both left and right.

. The value debate is happening because of this sense of uncertainty. It seeks to draw lines, demarcate boundaries, set standards, confirm hierarchies of value. It is an important debate because it forces us to think of limits, and articulate a sense of what is right or wrong, appropriate or inappropriate. But it is doomed if it seeks firm guarantees, or new and detailed maps to enable us to negotiate the murky highways and byways ahead. The very desire for guarantees that values are eternal and secure in some objective heaven is, as Berlin reminds us, 'perhaps only a craving for the certainties of childhood or the absolute values of our primitive past' (1984, p. 33).

But if the first condition of a radically democratic society is, as Laclau (1990, p.125) argues, to accept the contingent and open character of all its values, and to abandon the fruitless search for a single foundation, that does not mean we should abandon the effort to articulate and clarify the values that do inform our behaviour. There can be agreement on the importance of valuing, even if the conclusions we come to are different. The responsibility for valuing lies not in some Platonic heaven of eternal certainty, but in human action and creativity – in us, with all our uncertainty.

So where to begin? I suggest the starting place is with those everyday experiments in living to which I have already referred, and in the invented moralities that shape them. The changes that are transforming our sense of ourselves and our relationships are unsettling and anxiety making, but they are also deeply creative. George Eliot concludes *Middlemarch* with the thought that:

> ... the growing good of the world is partly dependent on unhistoric acts; and that things are not so ill with you and me as they might have been, is half owing to the number who lived faithfully a hidden life, and rest in unvisited tombs (1966, p. 896).

If we could listen more carefully to those 'unhistoric acts' of simple human bonding, disinter those 'hidden lives' of unspectacular experimentation, and pay greater respect to human inventiveness in the face of adversity and radical change, we might be happier than we appear to be at the moment to live with the certainty of uncertainty.

2

Inventing Moralities

What is good, is something that comes through innovation.
The good does not exist, like that, in an atemporal sky, with
people who would be like the Astrologers of the Good, whose
job is to determine what is the favorable nature of the stars.
The good is defined by us, it is practiced, it is invented. And
this is a collective work.

> Michel Foucault, interview with Michael Bess
> at University of California, Berkeley, 1980

... to say that we invent values means neither more nor less
than this; that there is no sense in life *a priori*. Life is nothing
until it is lived; but it is yours to make sense of, and the value
of it is nothing else but the sense you choose.

> Jean-Paul Sartre, *Existentialism and Humanism*

To declare that existence is absurd is to deny that it can ever
be given a meaning; to say that it is ambiguous is to assert
that its meaning is never fixed, that it must be constantly
won.

> Simone de Beauvoir, *The Ethics of Ambiguity*

THE CONTINGENCIES OF THE EROTIC

The erotic is inevitably, and probably eternally, caught in the web
of value debates, trapped in the domain of moral agonizing,
ethical debate, personal choice and collective decisions. What is
less inevitable is that the sexual itself should be the measure

of value, the yardstick by which actions, individuality, personal relationships and the state of the culture can be judged.

We have long been used to the idea that morality and sexual behaviour have a peculiarly intimate relationship – to the extent that 'immorality' in the English language almost invariably means sexual misbehaviour, and 'moral', to a lesser but still potent extent, implies adherence to certain agreed norms of behaviour, and types of activity. In Western cultures, at least, as encoded in the Christian traditions, sexual activity has had a special relationship to notions of valid behaviour, of truth. A 'morality of acts' long enshrined a sexual hierarchy which told us which types of erotic activity were appropriate or inappropriate, right or wrong. These activities in turn defined the type of person we were: moral or immoral, innocent or guilty, normal or perverse. They signalled the essence of our being because the erotic embodied some notion of fundamental truth. It spoke in its own name, infiltrating our bodies, structuring our fantasies, undermining our will.

During the past two millennia there have been significant shifts in the way the culture has enshrined sexual desire: a deep cesspit of sinful urges (it is better to marry than to burn), the sanctifying force in relationships, a dynamic energy that requires repression, and as the transforming power that requires 'liberation', to name but a few (see Davis 1983). As the power of religion and the absolutism of faith, revelation and tradition declined, by the early twentieth century they were increasingly replaced with a new absolutism based on scientific truth, which often refigured many of the inherited truths – about the relations between men and women, about the spectrum of sexual variations – but nevertheless remained wedded to some notion of an essential truth about human sexual nature being locked in the mysterious recesses of the body (Weeks 1985). The truth of sexuality has been seen as a key to individual and social truth.

Two key developments have undermined this. The first has been the transformation of sexual and gender relations over the past generation. The changes have been uneven, often contradictory and chaotic. But they have been important in opening new spaces for individual choice and many different ways of life, and in their relativizing of sexual mores. The second has been the growing understanding of the ways in which the erotic, far from shaping the individual and the social, is profoundly constructed by historical forms and relations of power. In their pioneering work of sociological deconstruction of sexuality, *Sexual Conduct*, John Gagnon and William Simon suggested that:

> we are victims to the needs of earlier societies. For earlier societies it may not have been a need to constrain severely the powerful sexual impulse in order to maintain social stability or limit inherently antisocial force, but rather a matter of having to invent an importance for sexuality (1973, p. 17). ·

The discourse of historical 'invention' was subsequently taken up and developed within a plausible theoretical framework by Michel Foucault (1979) and a host of other writers; and the rest, as they say, is history. We are now increasingly accustomed to thinking of 'sexuality' as a fictional unity of disparate bodily and mental processes, of identities as historically constituted, of gender as a social imperative rather than merely a biological given, and of the erotic as complexly intertwined with the webs of power and domination. All this is today a fairly familiar and widely accepted narrative, and I fully endorse it – indeed, I have contributed to it (Weeks 1981/1989, 1985, 1986). But it is still necessary to go a step further, and tease out its implications for thinking about the sexual. There are two which are particularly important.

In the first place, if sexuality has no intrinsic meaning, if it is neither good nor bad in itself, if, on the contrary, far from being a measure of meaning it embodies the imprint of a vast range of social meanings, like sedimented layers of rock, then the value systems built around it have to be understood as both historical and contingent. They are historical in the obvious sense that they are products of history, in all its complexity (not History in all its simplicity). They are contingent in the sense that they do not embody any master plan, either of God or Man. They are, to a greater or lesser degree, arbitrary human arrangements, products of innumerable social and ideological struggles, and hence of

shifting relations of power, of patterns of domination and subordination, of historical settlements and individual and collective
resistances.

The second implication, usually overlooked, follows from the
first. If sexuality does not speak its own truth, if not only what
we define as good or bad, moral or immoral sexual behaviour,
but the structure and meanings of sexuality are historically contingent phenomena, then a clarification of what we want and
value, as individuals and as cultures, matters. If, as some argue,
we are in the midst of a moral civil war (e.g. Hunter 1991),
then we need to be able to clarify what side we are on, and why.
And if we can no longer believe in a simple morality of acts, if
we are no longer able to hear the Word of God, or follow the
Laws of Nature with any certainty that we know what they are, or
accept any other foundational givens, then what we do and how
we do it are issues of profound concern. The world may have no
intrinsic meaning, sexuality may not speak its own truth, the
guides we have may be riddled with confusions and misleading
or wrong directions, the meaning of sexuality may be clouded in
ambiguity, but meanings are not absurd. They have, however, to
be constructed, or 'invented', from the fragments of history and
experience that swim around us (see Mackie 1977).

There are many constructions, many inventions, none of which
in themselves embodies a final and unchallengeable truth. My
underlying assumption, indeed, is that finality is impossible, and
even undesirable. There is no magical solution for our sexual
dilemmas, either in a new objective morality or in a redemptive
resolution of all conflict. It is more a question of charting the
possible paths, clarifying choice, and learning to live with our
irreducible diversity. Such a position, it should be scarcely necessary to add, embodies its own set of values, speaks from its own
tradition or traditions. One thinks from a tradition, Laclau (1990,
p. 219) argues, for 'traditions are the context of any truth' (see
also MacIntyre 1985, 1988). My aim in this chapter is to chart
the principles, stemming from certain traditions, which might
enable us to steer through the ethical dilemmas posed by sexual
diversity. I shall look in turn at the question of 'invention', the
difficulties of sexual choice, the meanings of autonomy, and

the perspectives for toleration and solidarity. In the process the traditions with which I align myself should become clearer.

THE PATHS OF INVENTION

To speak of the 'invention' of 'right' and 'wrong' is to open a magical box of fears, and supreme among the terrors is that of 'subjectivism' (Mackie 1977), the reduction of all values to individual whim. That is indeed a danger, but it is not my intention. My purpose is quite different: to suggest that we in fact live in a world of values, that human beings are value making and value bearing subjects, that values form the substratum of individual and social existence. We cannot live without values. These values embody notions of what is good and appropriate, or what is not so good, even evil, and inappropriate, and are organized in the various ethical traditions of which we are heirs. The problem is not our lack of values, but the hierarchies in which they are trapped, which claim truth, concepts of right and wrong, as their exclusive prerogative. To say that these notions must always be contextual and relative is not to abandon our ability to measure and judge actions. It is simply to say that we need to be clear why we are making the decisions we do make, what values inform our practices. Only in this way can we engage in the endless conversation about values, different values, that is the human lot.

The paths of invention are many and varied, so where to begin? The quotations that open this chapter provide a useful starting-point for my own argument. Though Foucault and Sartre speak from different theoretical traditions, and certainly make uneasy bed-fellows (see McNay 1992, 1994), they both pose the question of invention in a radically challenging fashion, and we can draw from them several useful ideas, not necessarily either new or original, but succinctly summarized. First of all, there is the emphasis on the idea of the 'good' as a human creation, not a gift from science, or an imposition from without (though it can be presented as the first, and can become the second). Following that, there is the emphasis, in Foucault at least, on the collective

origins of our notions of the 'good'. They are not simply ema-
nations of the minds of philosophers. They are given meaning,
and validated by traditions of belief and practice, reviewed, reconstructed and reinvented through collective experience, products
of human agency. And as there are many traditions and collectivities, so there are many notions of the 'good'. But third, there is
the clear suggestion that despite the apparent meaninglessness
of the world in the abstract, meanings are not only possible but
necessary, meanings to be won, meanings that embody a principle, that of innovation and change.

With regard to sexuality Foucault's arguments are clearly the
most relevant. The context in which Foucault made his comment
is illuminating. It is taken from an interview he gave at the
University of California at Berkeley towards the end of his life
(Foucault 1988a), and is important because it signals a crucial
moment in the work of a thinker generally associated with postmodernist critiques (whether that is a just description of Foucault's work is another matter). His discussion of the basis of
morals represents, I would argue, a shift from 'deconstruction'
to what we can, for want of a better term, call 'reconstruction',
a move from usefully tearing apart the presuppositions of Western
thought to reveal their (often dubious) origins and multiple
meanings, to beginning the arduous task of 'deconstricting', the
freeing of sexuality from its encrustations of myths and prejudices, and thereby to reinvent the erotic.

The American philosopher Michael Walzer (1987, 1988) has
explored the problem of 'invention' in some depth. He distinguishes what he terms the 'path of invention' from two other
tendencies in moral philosophy, the 'path of discovery' and the
'path of interpretation'. The path of discovery, Walzer argues,
assumes that moral principles are out there, somewhere in the
heavens or nature, waiting to be discovered by detached and
dispassionate philosophers. It is, in the domain of sexuality, perhaps the most seductive path of all, for it assumes that truth –
the truth of our bodies, the truth of our instincts or genes, or the
truth of revelation – can be known, and transmitted to others.
Its characteristic form of power is executive, the laying down of
the Law as embodiment of truth, and as such has powerfully

shaped Western modes of thought around the body. While most legal systems in the West have sought systematically to separate the legal from the moral, so that law becomes an ebodiment of what is socially acceptable rather than morally pure (hence a progressive liberalization of the laws on marriage and divorce, birth control, abortion, censorship, homosexuality), a nostalgia for the absolute lingers in the Christian moralism of much of the New Right, and in the neo-fundamentalism of militant Islam and Hinduism.

Its prophets *know*, because holy writ tells them, or philosophical lucubrations reveal it, that certain things are right, and certain things are wrong, because they are rooted in the truths of human nature – a binarism that happily often conforms to the fixed hierarchy of gender and sexual normality that are embodied in the particular cultures for which they speak. Unfortunately, such truths rarely address the diversity of sexual values which appears as a greater truth of our time, except through execration, and what Jacqueline Rose (1988, p. 20) has described as the 'retributive violence' of ethical absolutism.

The search for the truth of morality, Walzer argues, ignores the fact that the everyday world *is* a moral world, and 'we would do better to study its internal rules, maxims, conventions, and ideals, rather than detach ourselves from it in search of a universal and transcendent standpoint' (1988, p. ix). This is his preferred 'path of interpretation'. Discovery is not necessary, Walzer suggests, because we already have what the discoverers claim to find: we already inhabit a rich world of morality, for values and morality are the very essence of social life. The task of the 'connected' moral critic is to evoke the shared moral values, by telling a 'plausible story' about which values ought to be fundamental. These values may have been invented in the past, but are now embedded in thick communal traditions.

The problem of invented traditions, Walzer goes on, is that they make truths, they seek to provide what God and Nature unaccountably forgot to provide, a universal corrective for all the different social moralities. They have attempted to provide a goal, an end – whether justice, political virtue, goodness, or some other truth; this has demanded the bending of human wills, energies and desires into a preconceived ideal, where unorthodoxy or resistance have been the ultimate sins. The results, whether (to take just two of the most obvious examples) in the terror waged by the most ardent advocates of the French revolutionary morality, or in the enthusiasm to make 'homo Sovieticus' the 'new Soviet man' in the wake of the 1917 Russian Revolution, have been universally disastrous.

So a moral code or value system, invented (or 'legislated', the characteristic governmental form) by others for our own good, must be avoided at all costs. But that leaves room for believing that the term 'invention' in a weaker sense may be of some value. As Walzer concedes, the weak sense of invention comes close to his own preferred approach of interpretation and connectedness. It stresses the importance of human creativity, of basing values in lived experience, and of exploring the variety of human possibilities already apparent to us. The invention of coherent sexual narratives need not involve the legislation of rigid ways of life for others; in practice, today, it is more likely to embrace the creative redeployment of fragments of history and experience into a plausible story. Richard Rorty argues that a full 'de-divinisation' of truth claims (whether of executive injunction or legislative power):

> would, ideally, culminate in our no longer being able to see any use for the notion that finite, mortal, contingently existing human beings might derive the meanings of their lives from anything except other, finite, mortal, contingently existing human beings. (1989, p. 45).

That involves listening to what James Joyce in *Ulysses* called the shout in the street, which in this context means the sexual stories and possibilities inherent in the innovations and experiments in living that alarm the morally conservative, but provide the possibilities of creative life for many others: 'If the word of God can no longer be heard, we can start giving our own voices a new dignity' (Laclau 1990, p. xiv).

There are many voices, and many plausible stories that can be told, many of them created or invented in the struggles of everyday life. The effectiveness of sexual stories, Plummer (1995) suggests, depends on an ability to tell them, and an audience to listen to them. In recent years we have witnessed the construction of a mass audience for many hitherto implausible narratives, emanating from private worlds and communities of support and identity. The task is not to order or legislate them away, but to interpret them, and to explore ways of them speaking together, in a civilized conversation about the body and its sexualities.

That, however, requires a shift in our thinking about morality: away from a morality of acts, which locates truth and rightness or wrongdoing in particular practices, and the expression of certain desires, and towards an ethics of relationships, and choice of relationships, which is intent on listening to how we engage with one another, and respond to one another's needs as fellow human beings.

This I take to be part of the task Foucault undertook in *The Use of Pleasure* (1984/1985) and *The Care of the Self* (1984/1986), the last, posthumously published volumes of his *The History of Sexuality*. A digression into this body of work is relevant here. In these works Foucault is seeking a way of placing the 'search for truth' into a different perspective: one that breaks with the agonizing religious or philosophical search for the truths of morality, with the nineteenth-century search for truth in the body, or the Freudian unravelling in the twentieth century of the mysterious whisperings of unconscious desire. 'The problem is not to discover in oneself the truth of sex but rather to use sexuality henceforth to arrive at a multiplicity of relationships' (1989, p. 204).

In order to understand how we moderns saw ourselves as subjects of sexuality, it was first necessary, Foucault argued, to show how Western man had become the subject of desire. To do this he attempted a new genealogy of 'desiring man', from classical antiquity through the first centuries of Christianity (1985, 1986). Although the break was not sudden or absolute, Foucault detects a decisive difference between the ancient and the Christian era. The fundamental issue for the ancients was not the tortured agonizings over the sins of the flesh, or the conflict between desire and truth, the body and morality, in order to achieve an inner purity of being. It was the problem of excess, which threatened the ordered pattern of those meant to rule, and which posed a danger for the proper conduct of free adult men.

The dangers of excess lurked in a superficially similar set of issues to our own preoccupations: with the body, the relations of men and women, men and men, men and boys. Like us post-Christians, the ancients were faced with the task of elaborating an ethic that was not founded in religion or any *a priori* justification. Unlike us, however, heirs of Christianity, they did not attempt a codification of acts which made sex itself the bearer of values and moral anxieties, nor attempt to submit individuals to external moral laws. As Rajchman (1991, p. 90) puts it, 'ancient ethics was not a strategy to normalize a population, nor a matter of abstract inner obedience to universalizable rules'. It was instead an attempt to shape an 'aesthetics of existence', an art of life through which excess was balanced by temperance, pleasure by self-discipline. The ancients were constructing rules of conduct which did not derive from a central truth about sex, but from the set of relations in which the free man was embedded: dietary matters, the rules of the household, and erotic relations (particularly between men and boys).

I cite this argument not because it is necessarily telling the full truth about the ancients, which is not my concern here, but for what it tells us about Foucault's contemporary project. He is not, clearly, suggesting that the ancients offer a model for our own dilemmas. Theirs was an ethics for free men, from which women, children and slaves were notoriously excluded. His intended task is two-fold. First, he seeks to problematize the Western preoccupation with the truth of sexuality, and our willingness to seek, and then subordinate ourselves to external laws of morality. No aspect of reality, he says elsewhere, should be allowed to become 'a definitive and inhuman law for us' (1988a, p. 1). But second, he is making a crucial distinction between morals and ethics, in order to explore how we can ourselves seek a contemporary ethics. For Foucault, 'moral' refers to a prescriptive code one must follow on pain of internal or external sanctions. It is represented by the Christian codes, and by the invented codes of the Enlightenment. Its defining characteristic is its externality and the fact that it is above the individual. Ethics refers to the kind of person one should aspire to be, the type of life one is encouraged to lead, the practices which are invented to turn us into moral beings, into the right sort of person. We might have escaped the ethical codes of the Christian era, but we have not freed ourselves from imprisoning ethical codes, which are in some ways more insidious because they are grounded in the 'so-called scientific knowledge of what the self is, what desire is, what the unconscious is' (Foucault 1982, p. 214).

The contemporary challenge therefore is not to seek a new morality but to invent practices which eschew the models of domination and subordination, sin and confession, the natural and the perverse: practices which are 'practices of freedom'. This involves a struggle against the normalizing pressures of modernity which obscure unfreedom, a lack of autonomy, behind a screen of individualism. Here Foucault does find a model in the ancients. They were not free of moral dilemmas, but they were free to establish a relationship with themselves, to achieve an existence where they could aspire to beauty, pleasure and power, through an aesthetics of existence. That, Foucault suggests, is also our current challenge.

The significance of this argument is that it displaces the binarism which has dominated radical thinking about sexuality since the nineteenth century: the repression/liberation model. If sexuality has no meaning in itself, and its historical genealogy is as an apparatus of power, discipline and regulation as much as self-creation and resistance, then to argue for the liberation of sexuality has no meaning. We can find no redemption in sexuality itself. Foucault makes a useful distinction between relationships of power, which exist at all time, and relations of domination, which are congealed forms of power. We can have liberation from the latter, but what then emerges are possibilities for the development of practices of freedom: 'Liberation opens up new relationships of power, which have to be controlled by practices of liberty . . . In the order of sexuality is it obvious that in liberating one's desires one will know how to behave ethically in pleasurable relations with others?' (Foucault 1988b, p. 4). For Foucault, the problem is then 'to try to decide the practices of freedom through which we could determine what is sexual pleasure and what are our erotic, loving, passionate relationships with others' (1988b, p. 3). Freedom is a process not a given, a practice not a goal: 'the *practices* of freedom are what people try to make of themselves when they experience the existence of freedom in the history that has formed them' (Rajchman 1991, p. 110).

The emphasis on practices of freedom is a useful one, for it directs us to think about what sexual freedom could mean for contemporary men and women (see Watney 1994; Grimshaw 1993). But there are as many interpretations of freedom as there are systems of domination and subordination. The task is not to determine what freedom in general is, but what the historically possible forms of liberty can be. For Foucault, the apparatus of sexuality is at the heart of the workings of power in modernity. Through the various axes of sexuality (relations between men and women, adults and children, sexuality and reproduction, and the normal and the perverse) the intricate patterns of domination and subjectification have been formed and congealed. It follows that practices of freedom are developed against the forms of domination. They are necessarily oppositional, and their aim is to challenge the taken for granted, the given, and to develop new forms which ask 'what is desirable?'

This oppositional style operates on two levels. First, through its mode of analysis, political genealogy, it exposes the socially determined nature of sexuality, and by surveying this particular battlefield contributes to freeing the body from the regulatory patterns of the culture, particularly those forms which delimit individual liberty, such as institutionalized heterosexuality. Foucault requires us to question what is, in order to understand what can be. Second, it challenges us to discover new realms in which bodily pleasures can be explored, to test the limits of subjectivity through erotic experimentation and experience, constantly to reinvent oneself as a sexual and ethical being. This in turn involves the development of ways of life which encourage innovation and experiment, which dissolve the certainties of the past and the present in the shaping of alternative ways of being.

Does this mean that anything goes, returning us to an easy (and inevitably male-dominated) libertarianism, as many of Foucault's critics (see, for example, Soper 1993) suggest? Foucault (1982) makes a distinction which is relevant here between freedom of sexual acts and freedom of sexual choice. True to his general outlook, he is against the former because it could permit acts which cause harm. He is, however, in favour of the latter because it opens up possibilities. That of course leaves open such questions as which acts are indeed harmful; which acts open up new, positive possibilities; and which choices are valid and which are not. Foucault's controversial views on rape, which he seeks to redefine as an act of power rather than sexual violation, is an example of how the displacement of the sexual itself can confuse the arguments, as feminist critics have pointed out (see McNay 1992, MacCannell and MacCannell 1993). There is, as McNay notes, a crypto-normatism in Foucault's thought on issues such as this which assumes that freedom of choice in itself will lead to free subjects.

Sexual diversity may be a fact, but living with it poses often intractable problems. Foucault's general position, while fundamentally complex, is nevertheless clarifying, I would argue, when it invites us to think hard about what the practices of freedom could be: what is meant by choice, what does sexual autonomy involve, how can we live together in difference? We may not find the answers in the body of Foucault's work, but we can see there some of the most critical questions. The challenge for us is not so much to find answers that will be applicable in all circumstances but to pose the questions in a way which will help us, in Hannah Arendt's words 'to think what we are doing' (1958, p. 5). And the first question we need to ask concerns the limits of diversity and choice.

DIVERSITY AND CHOICE

The contemporary sexual landscape is haunted by a double-headed spectre: the irredeemable diversity of sexualities, the fact of otherness confronting us in all our dealings with individuals and collectivities; and the necessity of choice. In a very important sense these spectres have been at the heart of sexual debates for generations, and have shaped the various discourses around the sexual in profound (and usually contradictory) ways. What I believe is new is that the carapace of moral (and subsequently) scientific certainty that held diversity in check, and delimited choice, has now cracked, probably irreparably. A rich variety of exotic plants have broken cover through the cracks, and the profusion seems to increase rather than diminish as (or even because) our moralists (the enthusiastic horticulturalists of the sexual landscape) attempt to scythe them down. Cut off one head, and half a dozen more suddenly bloom. But which of these plants are flowers, and which weeds; which are sweet smelling, and which bear poisoned fruit?

There is no longer, I have suggested, any readily generalizable answer to such questions in moral treatises, scientific textbooks, or legislative codes, try as people might to uncover them. The collapse of the old moral certainties has gone too far. Rather we need to clarify the values which might help us to decide which forms of diversity are life enhancing, and which are profoundly inhumane, which choices are free and informed, and which are enforced. We can do this only by broadening our approach. Just as sexuality is a deeply social phenomenon, bearing the impress of complicated histories, enforced moralities and the infinite play of power, so we must focus our choices about sexuality and the body in a wider political and ethical framework. The variety of sexual possibilities to which the body is heir are in themselves neither good nor bad. Sexuality has no intrinsic meaning, it cannot speak its own truth because its manifestations can only ever be culturally mediated. But because of its malleability it can express a variety of human potentialities. The erotic offers a space of possibility for exploring, and positively affirming, the different ways of being human.

Our sexual codes increasingly endorse, often wearily, the fact of sexual diversity. The challenge is to endorse the value of diversity without surrendering to absolute relativism, a relativism which abandons any attempt to achieve certain agreed minimum standards of human values and conduct. This is fraught with difficulties. Milne, for example, in arguing for a 'qualified and limited version of moral relativism' (1986, p. 147) cites the

example of purdah for women in Islamic cultures. He agrees that
this severely restricts women's choice, but appears to argue that as
these restrictions are moral in Islamic societies, they do not
constitute a violation of the human right to freedom. While we
may concur that human rights must be interpreted contextually,
and that women should have a right to choose to enter purdah,
with all its restrictions, if they wish to do so, it is difficult for a
Western liberal or radical to endorse the customary entrapment
of women in situations from which they have no legitimate exit.
'Custom is "King of all" ', Feyerabend writes, 'but different
people obey different kings' (1987, p 42). Yet kings, as we know,
lose their thrones, or at the very least become constitutional
monarchs, bound by rules and institutional checks and balances
which ensure plurality and freedom of choice.

In other words, an endorsement of diversity cannot stop at the
boundaries of a culture, however deeply its norms may be rooted
in apparently self-sustaining traditions. It must become part of
the culture too if variety and genuine choice are to be guaranteed. On the other hand, there is an equal danger in elevating
freedom of choice into the only moral value, into a position that
says that all options are equally worthy because they are freely
chosen, and it is the very act of choice which conveys worth.
This is what Charles Taylor (1992) describes as 'soft relativism',
because it eschews any attempt to evaluate different options.

The truth is that freedom of choice is often difficult, especially
in sexual matters, because of the delicate relationship between
desire, emotions and social norms. A battered wife or an abused
child do not choose the circumstances in which they live, or in
which they are subject to abuse. They may have a theoretical set
of choices – to leave the domestic hearth, to go to a refuge or,
in the case of children, to appeal to others or run away. But
we know that in practice such choices are difficult. Loyalties,
commitments, dependency and fear all block the free play of
choice. Moreover, choice has consequences with which we have
to live: women living in poverty as single parents, children in
institutional care, separated from those who may actually love
them . . .

Some issues illuminate the dilemmas acutely, as is now the

case with abortion. For long a symbolic issue in many Western countries, especially the United States, where it has become a mark of vitriolic political loyalties, by the early 1990s it had become a global problem. The International Conference on Population and Development, held in Cairo in September 1994, demonstrated that 'choice' had become inextricably tangled with questions of development and underdevelopment, poverty and the power of capital, as well as religion and who had the right to exercise control over a woman's body (see Panos 1994). Abortion has become a moral and political battlefield on a global scale, and because reproduction is an issue that is simultaneously individual and social, it has collective consequences. A 'woman's right to choose' is confronted by appeals to the rights of the foetus, which cannot choose, and by the norms and values of a culture, which may or may not provide access to abortion.

In her essay entitled 'More than a "woman's right to choose?" ', the feminist writer Susan Himmelweit (1988) dissects the dilemmas of choice for women in these circumstances. While endorsing women's freedom of choice, she pinpoints three problems with the liberal ideology in which this is customarily encoded. First, there is a need to recognize that choices are always made in specific economic, cultural and political contexts, and it is necessary to understand how that context is formed. The range of possibilities and the choices of others may profoundly affect the individual choices that can be made. Second, in many situations, the individual finds herself in a position where real choice is an illusion, where circumstances force a choice, particularly for those who are subordinate in society, imposing a responsibility without real freedom. Third, the experience of having to make a choice may structure a situation in an undesirable way, forcing it to be subject to a timetable of rational decision making, when in other circumstances it might be experienced in more desirable or spontaneous ways. Choice may then become an unwelcome burden, a burden which it is impossible to refuse.

Himmelweit herself argues for unrestricted access to abortion as an aspect of reproductive freedom. It is a woman who nurtures the foetus, a potential human being, and it is inevitably her final responsibility whether to continue a pregnancy or not. But it is also the responsibility of society, she suggests, to have some notion of the circumstances in which abortion is a reasonable course of action, or not, and to work towards a situation where choices can be made with a full awareness of the consequences for all concerned. We should be moving, Himmelweit goes on, away from a position on abortion based on a woman's right to choose, to one that guarantees unconditional access to abortion on more broadly humanitarian grounds, based on a woman's care and responsibility for the foetus, and a full awareness of the circumstances in which difficult choices have to be made by the woman:

> A recognition of the active involvement and interdependence of mother and foetus would provide a secure foundation for a humanitarian claim for abortion on demand, based on the welfare of both mother and foetus (Himmelweit 1988, p. 53).

Two principles emerge from this discussion. The first is the need to secure a situation in which choices are tempered by a wider system of values which allow free discussion of the hazards and problems of choice – and provide the necessary circumstances for the individual to make a truly free, informed, yet still difficult choice. In this example, the overriding principle is the importance of social norms which recognize that women's caring responsibilities may lead to a variety of different decisions, and that, without abandoning the ultimate freedom of women to make the final decision, 'there is a public responsibility to create the conditions in which women will choose courses of action that are seen as desirable' (Himmelweit 1988, p. 53). Choices are individual, but they have social and political contexts and consequences, and it is important to debate what they are. Freedom to choose is always a freedom in specific situations, and choice has to be guided by a commitment to self *and* others.

The second principle follows from this: the importance of recognizing the *significance* of choice. 'Soft-relativism self-destructs', Taylor (1992, p. 37) has said, because it cannot determine what is significant. Significance implies a social relationship, an evaluation of what is important, and therefore an ethical position, the creation of a 'horizon of intelligibility' which helps

us to make meaningful choices, fully aware of the likely consequences for ourselves and others of making certain choices.

A simple celebration of choice ignores the fact that choices can
be painful, and involve significant social struggle. A strong
example of this, which Taylor pursues, is the question of choice
of sexual identity, constructed around sexual preference. It has
long been apparent that there is no necessary connection
between, say, homosexual activities and lesbian or gay identity
(see chapter 3 below). Homosexuality exists in a variety of worlds
from the situational homosexuality of, for example, the all-male
prison, to the casual and non-defining, and often guilt-ridden
activity of the married man, the closet homosexual. To come out
as lesbian or gay (and even more definitively, as 'queer') can,
however, in certain circumstances be more than an individual act
of affirmation. It is a political act (see Weeks 1985). In the
sexual politics of the 1970s, 'coming out' was a defining political
statement for a generation of openly homosexual people, signify-
ing a rejection of institutionalized heterosexuality, the existing
patterns of domestic life, the various forms of prejudice, discrimination and oppression that existed, and against this proposed an
assertion of different ways of being (see Altman 1971/1993).
Western cultures, in the event, proved more accommodating than
radical theorists had anticipated, and a broadly 'live and let live'
atmosphere has developed in many western countries, especially
in the larger urban areas. But intolerance remains, and the
muted tolerance that has developed does not always signify
acceptance. In these circumstances, simply to say that to be lesbian or gay is no more important than the colour of one's hair,
that it is just one lifestyle among many in the hypermarket of
contemporary consumerism, is subtly to downgrade the original
goal, which was to assert the equal value of the homosexual
choice, and the often painfully difficult paths to asserting recognition for that (see Taylor 1992, p. 37).

The discourse of choice has meaning only because some
choices are more difficult and some are more significant than
others. An endorsement of sexual pluralism and choice does
not, therefore, rule out judgements of superiority (Taylor 1992,
p. 105). On the contrary, it frequently requires it, for otherwise

the choice is worthless, an empty vessel. A radical pluralism requires something more than a glorification of choice: it needs a shared idea of what constitutes meaning and significance, in a way which allows maximum individual freedom of choice within a consensus on what constitutes acceptable behaviour.

This puts the charge of moral relativism, often launched against those who speak for diversity and choice, into a different perspective. No one believes that every position is as good as any other, yet, as Laclau (1990, p. 104) observes, to believe there is truth outside context is 'simply nonsensical' (see also Geertz 1984). Finding a balance between meaningful individual choice on the one hand, and agreed cultural standards of judgement on the other is a peculiarly fraught business. Heller (1987, p.43) argues that a sense of justice protests against an extreme cultural relativism, for if different ways of life cannot be compared, ranked and graded in any way at all there can be no justice. Yet justice does not require that we all behave in the same way; there can be a plurality of goods within a notion of the shared good.

So the key issue becomes: what are the norms by which ways of life can be ranked? Heller (1987) proposes that only those actions including domination, coercion, force and violence should be compared and ranked at all. That is because they limit the two fundamental principles that constitute a minimum universal standard: the right to life and the right to liberty. Actions which enhance life chances and extend freedom can be seen as universal goods; those which inhibit them are bad.

If we accept this, as I do, then it is apparent that individual freedom of choice can not be an absolute. It is inevitably shaped by the contexts and meanings which allow autonomous individuals to choose. This, however, requires that we have some idea of who the choosing subject is, or could be, what autonomy means in the contemporary world.

AUTONOMY AND AUTHENTICITY

Morals used to be regarded as too important to be left to mere human beings, Bauman (1993) has suggested; now they can be left to no one else. Liberating morality from the carapace of artificially constructed ethical codes involves the 'repersonalizing' of it, the recognition of the central responsibility of the autonomous subject: 'Moral responsibility is the most personal and inalienable of human possessions, and the most precious of human rights' (1993, p. 250). The profoundly moral nature of the individual, Bauman argues, precedes the social. He quotes Levinas: 'Responsibility is what is encumbent on me exclusively, and what humanly, I cannot refuse' (1993, p. 77).

That on the surface is a radically individualistic position, and apparently elevates personal autonomy and responsibility above all else. But if we recognize, as we must, that the individual can realize his or her freedom only with and through others, then the balance between our personal autonomy and our responsibility to others becomes the central issue. Rorty (1989, p. 43) has described individual life as the always incomplete, yet sometimes heroic, reweaving of a web of relationships, a web without end which time lengthens every day. In this web we find ourselves through finding others, for as Taylor notes: 'self-fulfilment, so far from excluding unconditional relationships and moral demands beyond the self, actually requires these in some form (1992, p. 73).

There is no individual goal or essence to be realized except through our involvement with others. That is the burden and the challenge of individual freedom and responsibility.

As I observed earlier (chapter 1), although the principle of autonomy is common to the debates of both left and new right (see Held 1987, pp. 270–1), there are profound differences between them in the meaning and implications of the term. Cohen (1992, p. 181) has made a useful distinction, which he sees as a mark of these different meanings, between the celebration of 'individualism' and the promotion of 'individuality'. The former is the philosophical underpinning of market economics and modern consumerism. The latter emphasizes the significance of individual freedom and personal discretion, and opens the way to the wider expansion of life chances, implying what Held calls 'democratic autonomy':

Individuals should be free and equal in the determination of the
conditions of their own lives; that is, they should enjoy equal rights
(and accordingly equal obligations) in the specification of the
framework which generates and limits the opportunities available
to them, as long as they do not deploy this framework to negate
the rights of others (1987, p. 290).

The discourse of equality, of equal opportunities to pursue one's
choices and life chances without blocking the equal rights of
others points to a political programme of social transformation.
It also has profound implications for thinking of sexuality and
about the relations of power and domination in which it is
embedded. Autonomy implies several things simultaneously: freedom to evaluate and justify conflicting values and obligations;
the right to make certain personal decisions; and a goal for
personal development. It embodies a set of aspirations by which
we can judge our own actions, and those of others. Autonomy
can never, however, be absolute: 'The ethics of just procedure is
the ethics of *optimum* freedom. It is *not* the ethics of absolute
freedom' (Heller 1987, p.259). Relative autonomy, therefore, is
the human condition. To ask for more than this is to end up
with something less. The more we liberate ourselves from all
norms the more we are in danger of becoming unfree, of undermining the real autonomy of the self. Democratic autonomy puts
the obligation on the individual to express his or her desires in
ways which respect the claims of the other, in forms which are
moral for that individual, and which acknowledge and attempt
to deal with the inequalities which inevitably intrude between
social actors.

The concept of autonomy, even if it can only ever be relative
and contextual, embodies hopes and dreams that are inherent
in the transformations of everyday life during the past century
(see Giddens 1992; and chapter 1 above). Above all it expresses
the hope for meaning, often sought in sexual relationships.
Taylor detects in contemporary individual and moral relativism
a simplistic version of something more valuable than narcissism
or hedonism: a quest for self-fulfilment which contains a model
ideal, that of authenticity (1992, p. 15). And the erotic has

become one of the major sites for seeking and finding a sense of the truth or authenticity of experience. As Kern (1992) has indicated in *The Culture of Love*, a move towards authenticity in sexual relationships, in the context of growing autonomy and choice, has been a key development in the twentieth century. We know the limitations of that, and the uncertainty to which the flux of sexuality gives rise, but the aspiration towards personal fulfilment in and through erotic relationships has become a central dynamic of the culture.

A model ideal involves a picture of what a better or higher life would be, where better or higher are defined not in terms of what we happen to desire or need, but as representing a standard of what we ought to desire. Following Heidegger, Kern (1992) argues that 'inauthenticity' signals a passivity before life, waiting for a fate that will happen to us willy-nilly. 'Authenticity', on the other hand, indicates a willingness to anticipate the future resolutely, to grasp our present and future as our own responsibility in the light of changing circumstances – a position that is close to that of Giddens (1992) on the need to 'colonise the future' in the context of growing reflexivity. We have to make the future, or the future will surely overwhelm us.

That suggests that the meaning of authenticity is itself something that has to be fought for, and constructed. On a simple level authenticity generally implies being true to oneself, to one's own desires and wishes, and implies a fixity of the self that cultural trends have combined to undermine. This is the burden of Foucault's critique of the existentialist use of the term as represented by Sartre:

> I think that from the theoretical point of view, Sartre avoids the idea of the self as something which is given to us, but through the moral notion of authenticity, he turns back to the idea that we have to be ourselves – to be truly our true self (quoted in McNay 1992, p. 171).

In this form the idea of authenticity has had a powerful influence on the discourses of sexuality, and especially of those which promote sexual change. It would be difficult, writes Dollimore, 'to overestimate the importance in modern Western culture of transgression in the name of an essential self which is the origin and arbiter of the true, the real (and/or natural)' (Dollimore 1991, p. 39). For many the erotic remains the absolute touchstone of authentic selfhood, of realizing the true, uncorrupted self (see Evans 1993). It also offers ways of escaping an entrapping or imposed self. In his essay on the revulsion against sex produced by the AIDS crisis, 'Is the rectum a grave?', Leo Bersani mounts a passionate defence of promiscuous desire, especially among gay men, as a way of freeing the self from normative imprisonment:

> Gay men's "obsession" with sex, far from being denied, should be celebrated – not because of its communal virtues, not because of its subversive potential for parodies of machismo, not because it offers a model of genuine pluralism to a society that at once celebrates and punishes pluralism, but rather because it never stops re-presenting the internalized phallic male as an infinitely loved object of sacrifice. Male homosexuality advertises the risk of the sexual itself as the risk of self-dismissal, of *losing sight* of the self, and in so doing it proposes and dangerously represents *jouissance* as a mode of ascesis (1987, p. 222).

If the self is an imposition, a prison which limits free choice, then the escape from, or perhaps better, a transcendence of the self, has its appeal. Our culture has all too readily justified erotic activity by reference to something else – reproduction or the cementing of relationships usually – and has ignored the appeal of the erotic as a site of freedom, joy and pleasure. As Avedon Carol (1993, p. 152) comments: 'It shouldn't be so difficult to acknowledge sex as a source of physical pleasure that should be stimulating and satisfying to all participants ... whether within relationships or on a casual basis, as an all-for-all mutual exchange of pleasure'. Pleasure, joy, happiness are desirable goods, and the erotic is a prime source of them, for men and women, homosexuals and heterosexuals alike (see Segal 1994). But pleasure as an end in itself seems a limited goal if it ignores our complex involvement with others. To say that is not to prescribe any form of relationship: it is neither an appeal for the restitution of family values, nor an advocacy of monogamy or permanency. It is not the form (whether legal or illegal, socially sanctioned or consciously transgressive) but the content, the meanings we attach to the actions we undertake in the name of the erotic with which we should be concerned. A generalized *jouissance* that forgets the other, that ignores the social context and mutual responsibilities of erotic transactions comes dangerously close to recuperating the essentialized self in the very act of rejecting it (see MacCannell and MacCannell 1993, p. 230). Authenticity, if it is to have any useful meaning in relationship to sexuality, must involve more than either a realization of a putative true self, or a dissolution of the self in the pursuit of polymorphous pleasures. It requires some perception of the meaningfulness of our practices of freedom; what we exercise them for. The autonomous self does not exist outside time and context. It has to be created.

This is the focus of Foucault's critique of Sartre. He counterposes to what he sees as the essentialism of the Sartrean notion of authenticity the idea of creativity, a task not of realizing the self but of making it: 'From the idea that the self is not given to us, I think that there is only one practical consequence: we have to create ourselves as a work of art' (quoted in McNay 1992, p. 351). We need, Foucault is suggesting, to delineate an aesthetics of existence in which autonomous individuals become the artists of their own lives, in which the body and its pleasures become the focus for transcending the limits of the existing apparatus of sexuality. This is clearly related to a wider move in Anglo-American philosophy towards the 'aestheticization of the ethical': that aesthetic considerations are, or should be, paramount in determining how we choose to lead or shape our lives, and how we assess what a good life is. Rorty, for example, explicitly advocates the aesthetic life as the ethically good: a life motivated by the 'desire to enlarge oneself', the 'desire to embrace more and more possibilities', expressed in the aesthetic search for novel experiences and novel language (quoted in Shusterman 1988, p. 338). With Foucault, erotic experimentation and the forging of new patterns of relationship become the main focus for the elaboration of an aesthetics of existence, and of ethical values.

This provides a clear enough position to validate many hitherto tabooed practices and desires, and has been used as such. So homosexuality provides space for inventing new forms of relationship, sado-masochism offers opportunities for pushing desire to the limits, to explore power and responsibility (see Weeks 1985). What Giddens (1992) calls 'polymorphous unperversity' or 'plastic sexuality' has, as we have seen, become not so much the practice of the perverse few as the arena of experimentation for the many. The erotic has become a key site for that constant process of discovery and remaking, of starting all over again, which has been a powerful trend in Western (especially American) life for several centuries. Yet there is an ambiguity in the emphasis on self-creation, which Frances Fitzgerald (1987) – in search of those experiments in living which have ever been part of the American dream – acutely noted in her travels in America during the early 1980s. The stress on individual transformation embraces not only a search for sexual free space, especially in gay urban enclaves, but also a space for the self-appointed elect, the born-again religious whose toleration of others (especially the sexually different) may be extremely limited. The dream of a proliferation of cities on the hill, created by artists for life, all too often comes to naught because of the power of the small towns on the plain, their moral certainties crushing all but the true believer.

So, though endorsing artistry for life might be appealing in many ways, there are significant problems with simply doing so. Individuals make themselves in many different ways. There is a danger, as McNay (1992, p. 172) notes, of a covert return of the philosophy of the subject which Foucault is consciously attempting to undermine, with the consequence that contemporary individualism is not so much undermined as celebrated. Feminist critics have criticized Foucault for concentrating on surfaces in his celebration of the artist for life, and for ignoring the social determinants that limit autonomy, especially for women (e.g Grimshaw 1993, p. 60). There is certainly a 'gender- blindness' in Foucault's work which makes many commentators wary of embracing it fully (Soper 1993), though such criticism often ignores the fact that Foucault is elaborating a model to be developed by free subjects, an ethical goal, not describing current practices embodied in gendered hierarchies.

There is, however, a broader criticism that can be made. The real danger is that the artist for life will lack the ability to feel for others in their needs, will want to lead a life of meaning for him- or herself, without asking whether the same is possible for others. Foucault himself (1988b) argues that 'care of the self' must involve care for the other, but without clear regulative principles for ensuring that, there is an obvious danger that the creative self becomes an artist for him- or herself alone.

Authenticity as a goal necessitates something more, and here the work of Agnes Heller is valuable. In her book *Everyday Life* Heller counterposes what she describes as the aristocratic style of the aesthete to the democratic search for a *meaningful* life:

> In the meaningful life . . . the role of conscious conduct of life is
> constantly expanding, leading the individual on in confrontation
> with new challenges, in perpetual re-creation of life and person-
> ality, coupled with safe-keeping of the unity of that person and of
> the chosen value-hierarchy (1984, p. 268).

Meaningfulness involves the recognition that the self is indeed a creative self, but creativity can be fully realized only through values which acknowledge at the same time our responsibility to others. Social developments, as Taylor (1992, p. 77) puts it, have given rise to an age of responsibilization. How this responsibility is exercised may ultimately be an entirely personal and individual matter, but the regulative principle must be one's sense that each individual's actions are given meaning through mutual involve-ment with others:

> If the end of the individual is self-determination, then the higher
> purpose to which the individual is committed is likely to be the
> self-determination of others. Put the other way round: aiming at
> the self-determination of others is the very purpose behind the
> individual's self-realization which is never to the detriment of
> the person's self-determination (Heller and Fehér 1988, p. 36).

This suggests the need, as White (1991, p. 137) argues, to reform-ulate the principles of pluralism in terms of 'a sense of responsi-bility to otherness'. A radical pluralism, in sexual as well as other matters, requires that we recognize that justice demands not only the avoidance of unnecessary pain to the other but the fostering of care and responsibility for the other. This is not the same as subsuming one's own needs abjectly to the needs of others, because similarly the other's self-determination depends on his or her recognition of responsibility for you. But though reciprocity is a good, responsibility and care for the self and the other cannot depend on one's expectation of return. The responsibility is yours alone (see Bauman 1993). An action is good if it is done without expectation of return: 'a person is good if he or she prefers to suffer wrong than to wrong others' (Heller 1988, p. 174), to suffer injustice rather than inflict it.

Care and responsibility are unexceptional terms, and few are likely to disagree with them as principles. But when combined with an acceptance of the values of diversity and autonomy they can carry us a little further along the road towards a postmodern sexual ethics. They imply, for example, that the commitment must be not to a paternalistic care but to a 'lightness of care' (White 1991) which recognizes the limits of others, and the necessity to limit your own actions. Care requires a drawing in of others to your interpretative frame, a willingness to hold open a space in which difference can unfold in all its peculiarity and specialness. Responsibility to oneself, for others, and for other-ness involves a hesitancy to place, and an avoidance of excessive control. It means respect for individual choices, and for the dignity of each individual.

This emphasis on responsibility, care and respect as prime regulative values clearly has analogies with 'difference feminism' which has explored care and responsibility. Gilligan (1982) is the best-known example in the distinction she draws between an ethic of responsibility and an ethic of justice. An ethic of justice emerges in the work of contractarians, Kantians and Habermas, and constitutes an ethical-political world around concepts of autonomous subjects who balance claims and rights according to universal principles. An ethics of responsibility, on the other hand, emerges from the experience of connectedness, compassion and sensitivity to context. Gilligan broadly equates these positions with masculinity and femininity (see Larrabee 1993), but they are not necessarily gendered concepts. On the contrary, they may be seen as fundamentally complementary.

But this requires knowledge of or 'curiosity' about the other. Foucault elevates curiosity to one of the prime elements of his ethical position, while Rorty sees curiosity as a primary virtue, the opposite of cruelty, a main characteristic of which is 'incuriosity' (White 1991, p. 92). Curiosity takes the form of a close-grained concern for the details of the lives of others, an openness to other lives which is the precondition of respect and toleration of difference.

Care, responsibility, respect and knowledge: these are more than minor virtues. They speak for a system of values in relationships which make individual autonomy possible while encouraging diversity to flourish. I shall return to these themes in more detail in the final chapter of this book. My purpose here is to assert that in thinking of the erotic we need, if we are to escape the moral chaos of unbridled individualism, to relate individual desires to a context which takes account of the other, that allows individuality to develop to its fullest possible extent with others. That is not to be prescriptive about any particular set of sexual practices, or any pattern of relationships. In fact, my assumption is that these values are relevant to all forms of erotic life, and provide yardsticks by which we can measure the significance of the decisions that only autonomous subjects can make. Practices of freedom require that we know what freedom is for.

All this presupposes a wider system of social values, and to conclude this chapter I want to look at two interrelated themes which will help us to explore these: toleration and solidarity.

TOLERATION AND SOLIDARITY

The contemporary sensibility which rejects any foundational truths and delights in otherness requires a reformulation of sexual toleration. Toleration is central to the liberal tradition, and a necessary prerequisite for the attainment of just treatment of minorities, and those who transgress the norms of a culture. A 'live and let live' culture has alleviated the worst oppressions of past periods, and who can deny that it is better than its alternative, the reassertion of moral authoritarianism and of absolute standards of behaviour. But the liberal tradition suffers from a basic flaw. Toleration is not seen as a good in itself, but for what it leads to. It is essentially a negative value.

The roots of toleration lay in the religious conflicts of the seventeenth century, and the concept reflects at best an uneasy truce between communities of believers who might otherwise slaughter themselves (Mendus 1988; Mendus and Edwards 1987). It usually reflected a reluctant acceptance by the majority or strongest grouping that they could not obliterate the faiths of others, but had to live with them as best they could. Toleration did not signify approval; on the contrary, it usually meant (mutual) disapproval. It is a stand-off position, assuming incompatibility, and the problematic status of difference. It is a pragmatic response to the murderous consequences of pursuing truth at all costs.

The concept of toleration espoused by Mill in the nineteenth century is more absolute, based on a concept of respect for the individual and his or her diverse ends: the only concept of freedom which deserved the name was that of pursuing our own good in our own way, as long as we do not attempt to deprive others of theirs, or block their efforts to achieve it (Mill 1859/ 1975). But even for Mill, the icon of modern liberalism, diversity is to be tolerated as a means to an end: intellectual advance and moral progress, and the pursuit of individual truth (Canovan 1988). 'All silencing of discussion is an assumption of infallibility' (Mill 1859/1975, p. 24), and a belief in infallibility is the enemy of truth. But behind this, as in later advocates of communicative openness (Benhabib and Dallmayr 1990), there is a stark assumption that discussion will lead to rational agreement on truth, and differences will dissolve in a universalistic harmony. Difference is either a means to an end (the pursuit of truth), or a problem to be overcome (in the achievement of a new universalism). It is not seen as a good in itself.

Sexual toleration remains broadly within the bounds of such definitions. Its most famous encoding in the Anglo-Saxon tradition was in the Wolfenden Report on prostitution and homosexuality, published in 1957, and the legislative changes that flowed from it (Wolfenden 1957, Weeks 1977/1990; Warnock 1987). Legal conservatives argued that a shared morality binds society together. The law must, therefore, enforce what the majority prefer (Devlin 1959). If they abhor homosexuality, then homosexuality can be justifiably criminalized. Against this, H. L. A. Hart (1963), representing the Millian tradition, argued that the law must balance the harm done by an action against the harm done by making it illegal. If a law was unworkable, as the law on homosexuality was widely seen as being, and if it infringed personal liberty, then the balance of argument suggested a liberalization of the law, as a marker for a greater degree of toleration (see Warnock 1987).

This latter position triumphed in the sexual reforms of the 1960s, and continued to shape debates on sexuality subsequently in the 1970s (on obscenity) and 1980s (such as on human embryo research). It remains, despite a resurgence of moral absolutism, the dominant moral and legal framework. The difficulty is that it does not endorse diversity in any way. It sees it as a problem of social order or individual discipline. It was noticeable that the British reforming sex legislation of the 1960s did not positively endorse abortion or male homosexuality previously regarded as crimes. They were reluctantly decriminalized in certain limited circumstances (Weeks 1981/1989).

A positive fostering of diversity as a good in itself demands something more than this. A reluctant acceptance of diversity perpetuates inequalities, domination and prejudice. Nor can a strictly limited toleration in these circumstances enhance the pursuit of truth in a Millian sense. For if there is no final truth to be sought, if we are inevitably faced by contingency, then what matters most are relations between free people in which their diversity is respected for what it is, and where they can communicate their needs openly in democratic discourse. This is the position to which Hannah Arendt was moving in her commitment to unending discourse (Mendus 1988; Canovan 1988), and is central to the position of the exponents of a 'new' or 'radical' toleration.

A radical toleration is not merely negative, but positive: 'it is now no longer true that toleration involves merely leaving others alone, or refraining from persecuting them. On the contrary, it requires creating opportunities for others and going out of one's way to assist them' (Mendus, 'Introduction' to Mendus and Edwards 1987, p. 14). It involves the fostering and recognition of diversity. A radical toleration based on the value of equal life chances recognizes all human needs except those which use other humans as a mere means, that is involving oppression and domination. From this viewpoint, all forms of sexuality with these exceptions can be regarded as good and worthy of respect. That does not mean that they cannot be criticised. But they can be criticized only if they are granted recognition first, and if the criticisms follow the rules of civilized discourse. As Heller and Feher put it: 'other people's alternative ways of life are our concern even if we do not live them ourselves . . . It implies an active relation to the other without violating the other's negative freedom, the freedom from interference' (1988, p. 82).

To care for difference becomes an affirmation of our limits, and our need for others. This is the only way we can be at home with homelessness, 'a way we sensitize ourselves to the sublime of everyday life' (White 1991, p. 129; see also Jowers 1994).

Radical toleration assumes a social system which is open to the acceptance of the positive merits of difference, and has procedures for the adjudication of them. This points to the wider value of solidarity for only a sense of a wider belonging can put a break on the absolutism of difference. As Bauman notes: 'One may go a step further and propose that tolerance as such is possible *only* in the form of solidarity: that is . . . a practical recognition of the *relevance* and *validity* of the other's difference, expressed in a willing engagement in the dialogue' (1992a, p. xxi).

In the contemporary world, then, difference becomes the starting-point for reflection, discussion and action about constructing solidarity. Solidarity, as Arendt argues, is the public equivalent of compassion (Canovan 1988, p. 193). It implies care and responsibility for others, a belief in the dignity of the other, an ability to learn about others, and a willingness to support those groups, movements and other collectivities which are intent on reducing the level of violence and domination in private relationships as well as public institutions (see Heller and Fehér 1988, pp. 84ff). It implies too a recognition of equality and interdependence, and a commitment to resolving disputes democratically, through discourse rather than open warfare.

This is the basis of a radical humanism, and of the minimum human standards to which it appeals. In recent years, as we have seen, humanism has been subjected to searching criticism, not least because of its in-built assumptions about who the unitary human subject was: essentially male and heterosexual (see Riley 1988, p. 9). Even the language we continued to use until very recently to express our sense of solidarity with others, that of fraternity, assumes a non-gendered subject which marginalizes women. Fraternity, as Phillips (1984) notes, embodies a male alliance. But a rejection of specific historical constructions of humanity need not involve a rejection of the validity of human-ism: it only means that we need to recognize that its validity has been constructed through particular discursive practices which are now open to renegotiation and change.

From this point of view, radical humanism can be seen as a 'regulative ideal' rather than a metaphysical concept: 'as a harbinger of an open-ended polymorphous future for what may emerge, through its own practical self-institution, as a human family' (Fekete 1988, p. xv), the creation of Humanity as a project of political construction, not something that has always been there waiting to be recognized (Laclau 1990, p. 245). The con-cept of humanity as the 'essential cluster' is not based on anything fundamental in human nature, as Kant thought. Ideas of humanity are imaginary foci, which inspire thinking (Rorty 1989, p. 195), a 'handy bit of rhetoric':

> Solidarity is not discovered by reflection but created. It is created by increasing our sensitivity to the particular details of the pain and humiliation of other, unfamiliar sorts of people. The progress of human solidarity is the ability to see more and more traditional differences as unimportant when compared with similarities with

regard to pain and humiliation. Ability to feel pain is all we have in common, but that can be the core around which solidarity is built (Rorty 1989, p. xvii; cf. Walzer 1987, p. 24).

But it is necessary to ask whether an awareness of pain and humiliation are enough to generate a radical humanism which realizes solidarity. Concern for others can take many forms, some of them more limited than others. Take altruism, generally seen as a universal good. Blum (1980) defines altruism as concern for the good of another person for his (sic) own sake, or conduct motivated by such a regard. That is, it is equal to benevolence (though apparently in Blum a male benevolence), and suggests care and concern for the other. But altruism is an ambiguous concept. It can be withdrawn (Marquand 1990, p. 9), or it can be enforced, as in the compulsory altruism of family life (Finch 1989). In certain situations, as in the 'new altruism' of the 'AIDS industry', as dissected by Patton (1990), it can suggest a sympathy and concern which actually falls short of empathy and identification. In practice, radical humanism requires something more than this, something more like the mutual involvement and identification suggested by the term 'community'.

The word community, the novelist James Baldwin (1986, p. 122) states, 'simply means our endless connection with, and responsibility for, each other'. Community, in fact, is one of the few words which never has negative connotations (Williams 1989, p. 112), and is used promiscuously in a host of political constructions, from the left and the right. It attempts both to express social realities and offer an aspiration. In the form of contemporary communitarianism (Sandel 1982, 1984), the search for community betrays a dissatisfaction with personal existence under abstract liberalism, a revulsion against its coldness and impersonality, its instrumentality and narrow self-interest. In this formulation, the idea of community suggests that men and women should be members and not strangers.

As such it has become a key idea in the postmodern world, coming, Bauman (1989, p. 145) suggests, to replace reason and universal truth in postmodern philosophy. There are no values or ethics that are not community based, argues Laclau (1990,

p. 245), for communities embody certain traditions. A tradition in this sense is 'an argument extended through time' (MacIntyre 1988, p. 120), in which certain fundamental agreements are defined and redefined in terms of differences with those inside the tradition, and with those outside it. Communities have similar qualities.

Communities are not fixed once and for all. They change as the arguments over time continue, and as other communities exercise their gravitational pull. But at the same time, the social relations of a community are repositories of meaning for its members, not sets of mechanical linkages between isolated individuals (Cohen 1985, p. 98). A community offers a 'vocabulary of values' through which individuals construct their understanding of the social world, and of their sense of identity and belonging (Cohen 1985, p. 114). 'Community' suggests embeddedness in a world which seems constantly on the verge of fragmentation.

The spirit of community and the ideal of solidarity are therefore closely related. The difficulty is that a particularist community may undermine the wide sense of community that has to be created to achieve a radical humanism. The strongest sense of community is in fact likely to come from those groups who find the premises of their collective existence threatened (Gilroy 1987, p. 246), and construct out of this a community of identity which provides a strong sense of resistance and empowerment. Unable to control the social relations in which they find themselves, people then shrink the world to the size of their communities, and act politically on that basis (Gilroy 1987 p. 245). The result is a presumptive particularism as a way of embracing or coping with contingency. And as Rosenblum (1987, p. 126) has pointed out, social pluralism and the proliferation of associations do not necessarily mean variety for men and women personally:

> In pluralist societies membership can be ascriptive and stifling. Heterogeneous spheres must not only exist; they must be open and accessible, so that individuals are free to exist as well as enter them and so that immersion in one context does not exclude others.

The challenge is to imagine community without either neo-tribalism (Maffesoli 1988) or self-immolation. The key problem is not whether community but what sort of community, and what sort of identity, are appropriate at any particular time. Foucault distinguishes between three concepts of community: a *given community*, a *tacit community* and a *critical community*:

> a given community arises from an identification: 'I am an X.' Tacit community is the materially-rooted system of thought that makes X a possible object of identification; and critical community sees this system of thought as singular or contingent, finds something 'intolerable' about it, and starts to refuse to participate in it (quoted in Rajchman 1991, p. 102).

In the contemporary world given or traditional communities are losing their moral density as old values crumble and uncertainty rules. The latent sense of community that Walzer (1987) and others detect under the procedural republic of liberalism (cf. Rosenblum 1987, p. 166) may provide the necessary support for a wider sense of solidarity, but in it lurks the danger that the communal values that are discernible will be conservative and exclusive. A critical community, on the other hand, results from a problematization of a given or latent identity. It is open to new experiences and ways of being, which make new subjectivities possible.

A critical notion of community is the precondition of a radical humanism, for it questions what is, and opens the possibility of thinking what could be. And there are many critical communities emerging, shaped around dissatisfaction with what now exists. As Laclau (1990) argues, progress towards a universalization of values therefore has to be based on a plurality of emancipatory projects, on the recognition of difference as constitutive of the humanist project. Difference is the name of the universal humanity to be constructed (Spivak 1991), and must therefore be the starting-point for action. This is similar to Benhabib's 'interactive universalism', which 'acknowledges the plurality of modes of being human, and differences among humans, without endorsing all these pluralities and differences as morally and politically valid' (1987, p. 81).

For radical humanism, universality is not the realization of a true self, or the achievement of a Human destiny. It is the concrete process in politics and morals of diverse groups struggling for autonomy. The postmodern condition can lead to a nihilism, a politics of despair or of self-indulgence. West (1993, p. 19), confronting the nihilism of the African American situation, speaks of the need for a 'politics of conversion'. I would rather stress the importance of a radical humanism, alive to difference, contingency, and the necessary human bond. But the message is common: a need for an ethics of solidarity that has nothing to do with sentimentality or exclusivity. Its task is the development of a sense of agency based on responsibility and care for self and others: 'Doing something in our capacity as "human beings as such", doing it together with others, in symmetric reciprocity, solidarity, friendship as "human beings as such" ' (Heller and Fehér 1988, p. 58); in other words, making the 'human gesture', while affirming that there are many different ways of being human.

There is a major political agenda here which in its broadest form is beyond the scope of this book. There are three areas, however, which are especially relevant for thinking about sexuality. The first concerns the politics of (sexual) identity, community and solidarity. The second is the redefinition of intimate life. The third is the meaning of the discourse of love. These provide the themes of the next three chapters.

3

Necessary Fictions: Sexual Identities and the Politics of Diversity

⎯⎯⎯⎯◦⊃●⊂◦⎯⎯⎯⎯

We live today in societies that are in many ways less 'alienated' than in the past: that is to say societies in which there is greater indeterminacy in our position within them and in which we are more free to decide on movements and identity. They are also societies in which social reproduction depends less and less on repetitive practices and requires the constant production of social myths.
Ernesto Laclau, *New Reflections on the Revolution of our Time*

Human beings are, necessarily, actors who cannot become something before they have pretended to be it; and they can be divided, not into the hypocritical and the sincere, but into the sane who know they are acting and the mad who do not.
W. H. Auden, *The Age of Anxiety*

The prologues are over. It is a question, now,
Of final belief. So, say that final belief
Must be in a fiction. It is time to choose.
Wallace Stevens, 'Asides on the Oboe'

IDENTITY TROUBLE

Sexuality has become a constitutive element in postmodern politics. The politics of the right is preoccupied with sex education,
abortion, the threat of the 'gay agenda', the dangers of single
parenting and the underclass and the need to shore up the
family and its 'traditional' assignment of gender and childrearing
responsibilities. The politics of the left is challenged by the claims
of women and erotic minorities for rights, and faced by the
need to translate its discourse of fairness and equality into an
understanding and endorsement of sexual change. In both directions we see a conventional politics having to confront and come
to terms with an increasing erotic and cultural diversity. Nor is
this challenge limited to the boundaries of the traditional polity.
When the neo-foundationalist rhetoric of 'liberation and purity'
(Bhatt 1995) can mobilize men and women of Asian origin in
the slums of Bradford *and* the villages of Punjab, or when the
universalisms of Roman Catholicism and Islam can attempt to
enter into dialogue on the dangers of abortion and homosexuality, as in the International Conference on Population and
Development in 1994, though with limited success (O'Brien
1994), a new focus has clearly entered into global political discourse: one concerned with the boundaries of identity and the
fact of cultural difference, symbolized by the pleasures and dangers of sexual choice.

In this new and unprecedented situation it is not surprising
that it is the radical agenda of those who extol the virtues of
choice, personal autonomy and the value of diversity who have
become the target of hostile moral attack. The radical sexual
movements that have sprung up since the 1970s have been the
site for some of the most sustained interrogation of values and
ethics during the past generation (Seidman 1992). Questions
about sexual practices, relationships and lifestyles raised by feminism, lesbian and gay politics and to a lesser extent by other 'erotic
minorities', have in turn fed into mainstream culture, in the form
of fashion, representation, sexual techniques, political strategies
and moral debate. The responses to these influences have been
mixed: from stylistic absorption or dialogue to explicit opposition

and outrage. But there has been a sustained common element in the subsequent flurries. In one way or another, they have all raised issues about identity: who we are, why we are, in what ways should we live, how we should love, have sex . . .

The problematic nature of sexual identity has become the fulcrum of wider debates about the meaning and direction of sexual values, and of the politics of the erotic. This is not because of the power of radical ideas alone, or possibly at all; rather the radical questions raised by recent sexual politics have fed into a much wider uncertainty about the stability and fixity of our sexual belongings and identifications, and hence of who we are and should or could be. For this reason, in this chapter I want to explore in some detail this radical agenda, first by looking again at the question of identity, and then by exploring the trouble that radical sexual politics can cause. Let me begin with a personal anecdote.

Several years ago I was a member of a conference panel on precisely this problem of identity. A fellow panellist, Jackie Kay, read as her contribution one of her poems, 'Close Shave' (1991, p. 56). It was a poignant poem of deep but frustrated love and sexual attraction, between a miner, the epitome (in British culture at least) of male strength, communal spirit and family pride (a 'man's man'), and another man, the local barber:

> The only time I forget is down the pit
> right down in the belly of it,
> my lamp shining like a third eye,
> my breath short and fast like my wife's
> when she's knitting. Snip, snap.
>
> It doesn't bear thinking . . .

What doesn't bear thinking is an open declaration of love from a (married) man for another man:

> . . . it's my daughters that worry me.
> Course I can never tell the boys down the pit.
> When I'm down here I work fast so it hurts.

There is, perhaps, little that is unusual or special about the detail of this account: we know of the cost of the homosexual closet on countless lives; we are familiar with the conflicts between desire and duty that flit across all our social adventures. Many of us know what hurts. But there is, I think, something unusual, special, not so familiar yet at the same time deeply representative, about the circumstances in which the poem was written and published. It was submitted for a poetry competition in South Wales, the mythical (though now largely desolated) heart of mining culture. To the surprise of the judges, the person who came forward to receive the prize was a woman. Not only a woman, but a black woman, a feminist; and a black feminist with a rich Scottish accent.

Here for me was a nice metaphor for the complexity of modern identities, revealing in one physical presence a rich diversity of presences, neither one excluding the other. An empathy and subtle identification was expressed across the divides of class, gender, ethnicity and sexuality, while simultaneously a very specific and enabling identity was also asserted: Scottish, black, female and feminist, alive to historical resonances and political alignments, bringing to mind the fact that in the 1984–5 miners' strike in Britain lesbian and gay groups forged an unexpected solidarity with miners in South Wales; and had their support reciprocated in resistance to subsequent anti-gay legislation from the British state (Jackson 1994). Identities and identifications can simultaneously affirm and obliterate differences.

Contemporary identities are, it is now almost commonplace to say, hybrid, made of many fragments of history and of social and personal experience; they are heterogeneous, establishing many possible identifications across the boundaries of many potential differences; they are often political in the broadest sense, making links which defy the neat categorizations of social policy and social science, and challenging settled power relations (Rutherford 1990). Yet they are personally knitted together into narratives which give coherence to individual lives, support and promote social agency, and express certain values: values which we share with those with whom we identify, and which differentiate us from countless others with whom we do not, often cannot, identify.

Because of these complexities, identities are troubling. We search for them, claim them, assert and affirm them, usually with all the passion and personal conviction we can command. They provide a bedrock for our most fundamental being and most prized social belongings. Yet we are often forced to question them, or have them questioned for us, remake and reinvent them, search for new and more satisfying personal 'homes', all the time. As I write, in these turbulent globalized, post-Cold War, 'postmodern' times, questions of identity, personal and collective, are flashpoints for some of the most poisoned and violent disputes across the world: 'intercommunal strife', 'ethnic cleansing', the reassertion of 'lost' or more likely invented national or tribal traditions, have become tokens of our apparent inability to live with diversity, to tolerate the existence of different identities. Simultaneously, new political and cultural identities have proliferated, around race and ethnicity, gender and sexuality, HIV and AIDS, among other collective identities, which have emerged to confirm and promote common human interests, to challenge frozen hierarchies of power and, implicitly or explicitly, to argue for autonomy, diversity and choice. But they in turn generate new types of controversy, around 'identity politics', 'political correctness', the threat to the 'natural order' of sexuality and the like. Not all identities are harmless and enabling. Identities can be battlegrounds. So is the trouble worthwhile?

THE PARADOXES OF IDENTITY

Identities are troubling because they embody so many paradoxes: about what we have in common and what separates us; about our sense of self and our recognition of others; about conflicting belongings in a changing history and a complex modern world; and about the possibility of social action in and through our collective identities. And few identities are so paradoxical as sexual identities.

Sexual identities have a special place in the discourse of identity. They are like relay points for a number of interconnected differences, conflicts and opportunities. For the past few centuries, at least, sex may have been central to the fixing of the individual's place in the culture, but it has not been simply a categorization and placing for a *sexualized* identity (as male or female, normal or pervert, heterosexual or homosexual), rather for a whole set of social positionings. Concepts of national identity have been intricately bound up with notions of appropriate gendered or sexualized behaviour (Parker et al. 1992). The injunctions of nineteenth-century imperial propagandists to the young innocent – to 'be a man' and eschew masturbation, homosexuality or nameless other secret sins, or to embody motherhood and purity for the sake of the race – brought together class, race, gender and sexuality into a potent brew which locked normality and sexuality into a fixed hierarchy that few could escape from even if not so many lived up to it.

The settling of class identities in the first wave of industrialization in the nineteenth century also froze the fluidity of gender differences and sexual behaviour. 'Respectability' betokened more than a middle-class modesty and discretion; it became a way of life where sexual desire and gendered activity were regulated by approved and approvable behaviour (Weeks 1981/1989). Alfred Kinsey was neither the first nor the last to notice the distinct class accents to human sexual behaviour (Kinsey et al. 1948). Similarly, the generation of a racialized 'Western identity', with its distinct sexual classifications and typologies, in turn depended upon the identification of the colonized of the world as distinctly 'other', more primitive, more priapic or blatant, and certainly less 'civilized', which in turn served to confirm 'our' superiority, and the truth of 'our' sexualities.

Unsurprisingly, racial differences have been marked by gendered and sexualized boundaries. Gates (1993, p. 234), for example, notes the ways in which American black nationalism became sexualized in the 1960s 'in such a way as to engender a curious subterranean connection between homophobia and nationalism', so that an assertion of a fiercely heterosexual masculinity became a token of black male belonging, with often dire results (see also Mercer and Julien 1988). Sexuality is woven into the web of all the social belongings we embrace, and that is why the emergence over the past two hundred years, and in a rush since the 1960s, of alternative or oppositional sexualized identities – lesbian and gay, 'queer', bisexual, transvestite and transsexual, sadomasochistic, an exotic parade dancing into history with a potentially infinite series of scripts and choreographies – is seen as subversive by sexual conservatives. They breach boundaries, disrupt order and call into question the fixity of inherited identities of all kinds, not just sexual, which is also the reason, no doubt, for identities being so problematic to those committed to sexual change. If they are asserted too firmly there are dangers of fixing identifications and values that are really necessarily always in flux; yet if their validity is denied, there is an even greater danger of disempowering individuals and groups from the best means of mobilizing for radical change (Weeks 1991).

Identities are paradoxical, and they raise paradoxes. I want to illustrate this by exploring four key paradoxes.

Paradox 1: *Sexual identity assumes fixity and uniformity while confirming the reality of unfixity, diversity and difference*   Many of us in the west like to say who we are by telling of our sex: 'I am gay/straight'; 'I am male/female'. It places us securely in recognized discourses, embodying assumptions, beliefs, practices and codes of behaviour. Yet the truth is rather more complex. 'Possibility and many-sideness', Rosenblum (1987, p. 149) has argued, 'are built into the very idea of identity formation'. This is especially true of sexual identities. Academically and theoretically, we increasingly recognize both the diverse desires, needs and passions of individuals and the diversity of (often conflicting) social obligations and belonging, pulling us in a variety of directions. Is being a member of an ethnic or racial minority community more important than a sexual identification? Do class or community loyalties take precedence over identification with the aims of a political movement such as feminism? Such anguishings have characterized the sexual politics of the past thirty years. We fear the uncertainty, the abyss, the unknown, the threat of dissolution that not having a fixed identity entails. So we often try to fix identities, by asserting that what we are now is what we have really, truly always been, if only we had known.

But consider the realities. We all know lifelong heterosexuals who suddenly come out as lesbian or gay. We know self-identified gays who equally suddenly opt for a heterosexual lifestyle. We also know of many cultures in the world where such questions are meaningless. Where, then, is the essential person? In her book on cross-dressing, *Vested Interests*, Marjorie Garber (1992) tells of the spokesperson for the International Foundation for Gender Education, one Yvonne Cook. Yvonne is a biological male who cross-dresses, and identifies as a woman, as a lesbian. She dates a biological woman who cross-dresses as a man. Which label corresponds to the real her – or him? Here sexual identities seem endlessly fluid, taken up and used rather than realized, a glittering performance or complicated game rather than a truth claim.

Since the nineteenth century the placing of individuals into clearly demarcated sexual categories, and hence identities, has gone hand in hand with the presentation of plentiful evidence detailing the fluidity and uncertainty of desire and cultural loyalties (Weeks 1985). It is difficult to fit neatly into the social categories which define and limit possible identifications. The binary divisions that many of us in Western countries take for granted, between men and women, heterosexual and homosexual, normal and perverse, provide barriers against, in the words of Epstein and Straub (1991, p. 14), 'the uncontrollable elasticity and terrifying lack of boundaries within or between bodies'. They simplify the complexity of desires, they order the potential multiplicity of our identifications. But those barriers are often fragile, inadequate blocks to the flux of contemporary life, and the range of possible ways of being. The repressed usually returns, sometimes in distorted and damaging ways (such as the homophobia of the 'repressed homosexual'), sometimes in liberating and creative ways, in the elective communities where dissident or oppositional sexual identities, at least, are forged and confirmed. Then identities can become enabling. Yet, I would argue, they are still only ever provisional. We can put on a good performance with them.

But we should never believe they are final, or embody some unique truth about ourselves. 'Unfixity', write Laclau and Mouffe, 'has become the condition of every social identity' (1984, p. 85) – and especially, I would add, of every sexual identity.

Paradox 2:   *Identities are deeply personal but tell us about multiple social belongings*   All cultures seem to depend on their members having a secure sense of self, and a placing in the order of things. But there is no reason to think that the modern individual is a reflex product of his or her 'instincts'. Self-identity, at the heart of which is sexual identity, is not something that is given as a result of the continuities of an individual's life or the fixity and force of his or her desires. It is something that has to be worked on, invented and reinvented in accord with the changing rhythms, demands, opportunities and closures of a complex world; it depends on the effectiveness of the biographical narratives we construct for ourselves in a turbulent world, on our ability to keep a particular narrative going (Plummer 1995).

We apparently need a sense of the essential self to provide a grounding for our actions, to ward off existential fear and anxiety and to provide a springboard for action (Giddens 1991; Cohen 1994). So we write into our personal narratives the elements which confirm what we say we are. And here our bodily feelings and presence become central. In a world of apparently constant flux, where the fixed points keep moving or dissolving, we hold on to what seems most tangible, the truth of our bodily needs and desires, or, in the age of AIDS, our vulnerabilities. It is not surprising that the making and remaking of the body then becomes so basic to our assertion of identities. We worry about its health and the forces that can undermine it (smoking in relative private becomes more tabooed than having sex in public, our cholesterol levels more important than our protein intake); we run and do exercises to ward off its infirmity and temporality (even as we collapse from exhaustion, sore feet or painful muscles); we adorn it in clothes that affirm our sense of individuality (but which also provide a badge of our belonging to one subgroup or another, or our enslavement to the whims of the

market-place); we assert the imperatives of its desires and poten-
tiality for pleasure (though they as often wrack us with their
contradictory messages as confirm a single bodily truth). For the
body is seen as the final court of judgement on what we are or
can become. Why else are we so worried if sexual desires, whether
homosexual or heterosexual, are inborn or acquired? For what
other reason are we so concerned whether gendered behaviour
corresponds with physical attributes? Only because everything
else is so uncertain do we need the judgement that our bodies
apparently dictate.

   Of course, the fact of different, and highly gendered, bodies
matters; on the physiological differences of biological men and
women has been built an empire of division. But the body is a
fickle master or mistress: its needs change; it falls prey to want
or plenty; to sickness and physical decay; its sources of pleasures
can be transformed, whether through chance, training, physical
alteration, mental control – or, increasingly, the demands of a
new regime of 'safer sex'. Even the apparently most decisive of
differences between biological men and women, reproductive
capacity, is now subject to major medical intervention and potential manipulation. So in the postmodern world are we not really,
as some speculate, cyborgs, mythic creatures half human, half
machine, beyond gender, sexual categorization and fixed social
positioning? As Haraway put it, 'By the late twentieth century,
our time, a mythic time, we are all chimeras, theorized and
fabricated hybrids of machine and organism' (1991, p. 150).

   The body is no more immune to the power of culture, and its
transforming possibilities, than our mental attitudes or social
identifications. The body, as Giddens suggests, 'in late modernity
becomes increasingly socialised and drawn into the reflexive
organisation of social life' (1991, p. 198). Yet we necessarily use
the body as the focus of our sense of biographical continuity,
while implicitly acknowledging our social belongings and cultural
baggage. The body, marked by gender, race, age, subject to
pleasure, pain and ultimate extinction, is the site for the inscrip-
tion of difference, the battleground for conflicting cultural
meanings.

   The sexual persona, like the whole personality, is, in Connell's

formulation (1987, p.220), a social practice seen from 'the perspective of the life history', and the sources of that personal
history are inevitably cultural. The socio-sexual identities we
adopt, inhabit and adapt, work in so far as they order and give
meaning to individual needs and desires, but they are not ema-
nations of those needs and desires. Indeed they have no necessary
connection at all to the contingencies of the body. The sources
of the narratives that keep us going, that make sense of our
individual peculiarities, are deeply historical, dependent on social
bonds that provide the map for personal meaning and cultural
identification. And those bonds are multiple: we come from
different nations, classes, statuses, religions, racial and ethnic
groupings, different genders and generations and geographical
areas, each of which provides a sliver of experience, a residue of
a personal history, which we try to integrate into our personal
biographies, to shape our individual identity. Sexual identity
involves a perpetual invention and reinvention, but on ground
fought over by many histories.

Paradox 3: *Sexual identities are simultaneously historical and contingent*   The idea that sexual identities are not simple expressions
of bodily truth but are historical phenomena – and therefore
constantly changing – is a relatively recent one, pioneered largely
by feminist and lesbian and gay scholars (see for example, Duberman, Vicinus and Chauncey 1989). Its origins were largely political, demonstrating the historicity and potential ephemerality of
the categories we take for granted as natural and inevitable, even
as their power was acknowledged. Behind this position is a clear
assumption that, as Laclau puts it, 'the constitution of a social
identity is an act of power and that identity as such is power'
(1990, p. 30). Sexual identities embody power relations, products
of imposition *and* agency, and are rooted in many histories.

We still know most about the constitution of Western homosexual identities over the past few hundred years than about any
other, particularly the overarching categorization of heterosexuality and heterosexual identities (but see essays in Peiss and
Simmons 1989; Katz 1995). Nor is this surprising, for the domi-

nant or hegemonic form of any social position becomes the given, the taken for granted, part of the air we breathe, from which everything else becomes a deviation at best or a perversion at worst. As such it tends to escape thorough investigation – though this is now changing. We are increasingly accustomed to seeing sexuality as a spectrum along which lie many potential sexual desires and many different identities. But that easy pluralism obscures the fact that historically sexual identities have been organized into violent hierarchies, where some positions are marked as superior (more natural, healthier, more true to the body than others). The shaping of a distinctive categorisation of 'the homosexual' over the past century or so in the leading Western countries (but not, until recently, others) has been an act of power, whose effect, intended or not, has been to reinforce the normality of heterosexuality. As Eve Sedgwick has put it:

> The importance – an importance – of the category "homosexual" . . . comes not necessarily from its regulatory relation to a nascent or already constituted minority of homosexual people or desires, but from its potential for giving whoever wields it a structuring definitional leverage (1985, p. 86).

The emergence since the eighteenth century, she argues, of an institutionalized homophobia and homosexual panic, brutally separates men from men, but more crucially serves to confirm and consolidate male (heterosexual) power not only over other men but over women, for 'the domination offered by the strategy is not only over a minority population, but over the bonds that structure all social form' (1985, p. 97). In other words, the apparently neutral description of men as either homosexual or heterosexual conceals the intricate play of power, of domination and subordination, which minoritizes the homosexual experience, and consolidates male power in a new, effective pattern. In the same fashion, the categorization, in psychology, sexology and a variety of other social practices, of some women as homosexual and others as very definitely not, breaks the continuum of all women, and hence serves further to consolidate the sexual power of men (Smith-Rosenberg 1985).

The fact that such arguments are still not only controversial in themselves but contested even as a starting-point for debate is a testimony to the power of the categories that have become sedimented in our consciousness during the twentieth century, and to our cultural preference for neat divisions of people and identities: you are either this or that. But the process of trying to divide people into heterosexual or homosexual groups has been a complex one, and one that is, in Sedgwick's phrase, still 'radically incomplete' (Sedgwick 1990, p. 159), especially when they can be seen not to apply in other cultures, or even universally within our own. There are two related points that must be made here.

The first is that the discursive construction of categories of sexual subjects is a constant process, and involves a struggle over definitions on a sexual-political terrain that is ever shifting. The agents of sexual regulation, whether state, churches or other institutions such as those of medicine or psychology are involved in an effort of definition that is never ending, and the reason for this is quite simply that sexual identities, including (perhaps especially) heterosexual ones, are profoundly unstable. Take two recent sexual-political events in respectively Britain and the United States. The notorious Clause 28 of the British Local Government Act passed in 1988 banned the 'promotion of homosexuality as a pretended family relationship' by local authorities. Whatever the political context in which it took place (Weeks 1981/1989), its only rationale could have been an assumption that without such an act, the influence of an activist lesbian and gay movement promoting 'positive images' of homosexuality could radically overflow the boundaries between heterosexual and homosexual, to the detriment of the principles of normality (Smith 1990). In the *Bowers v. Hardwick* decision by the US Supreme Court in 1986 a Georgian man, arrested for having sex with another man in his own home, had his appeal that this was an infringement of his right to privacy overturned. In effect this denied the right to privacy to homosexuals in their sexual behaviour (Brill 1990). This decision, it has been argued:

not only set the constitution's imprimatur on punishment of

'homosexual sodomy' but equated that act with 'homosexuality' and indeed with 'homosexuals' – a group now not only defined but known by its sodomitical essence (Halley 1991, p. 356).

In effect, by identifying certain classes of illegal sexual activity ('sodomy') with a particular type of personage, it ruled such people out of the normal protection of the constitution.

The interesting point about these two separate cases is that the logic of the actions, one by a court, the other by parliament, were justified on quite different grounds. In the American example, the Supreme Court took a radical step towards taking for granted an immutable homosexual essence, defined by particular sexual practices. In the British case, the argument was different: essentially that, because homosexuality was not necessarily inherent, but could be acquired by overexposure to homosexual proselytizing, it was the task of government to limit 'promotion'. But in both cases, despite the contrary arguments, the clear aim and intention was to construct a class of legal subjects denied certain legal protection in order to delimit their rights and claims – in the interests of sustaining a heterosexual value system that was seen as simultaneously natural and inevitable, and fragile and undermined by the homosexual experience.

The second point is that these categorizations and imposed definitions cannot and do not exhaust the actual lived experience of sexuality or the proliferation of oppositional identities. In the case of homosexuality, there is plentiful evidence that cultures of opposition, pleasure and self-identification were emerging before and then against the opprobrious categorizations that emerged in the law, medicine, sexology and so on in the course of the nineteenth century (see, for example, Bray 1982). It is a characteristic of what Dollimore has called the 'perverse dynamic' (1991, p. 160) that a political and sexual ordering is always internally disordered by the very perversities it produces, and sets up against itself. The power to define may have set the limits on what could be said, done or spoken, but those apparently fixed by the definitions nevertheless produced their own resistances and identities. More recently, the emergence of a distinctive identity politics around sexuality has articulated a growing recognition that the power to define itself combines a multiplicity of powers and hierarchies, not only around gender and sexuality, but also around race and ethnicity, class and status, which in turn has produced new frontiers in sexual politics, and new forms of resistance. Sexual identities are enmeshed in relations of domination and subordination, where many histories intertwine. These examples are simply recent ones of the constant historical work needed to mark distinctions in order to sustain what is seen as a necessary, and certainly dominant, order.

Yet if histories (rather than History) and various forms of power relations (rather than a single Power) provide the context for sexual identities, our assumption of them is not determined by the past but by the contingencies, chances and opportunities of the historic present. As I have already suggested, there is no necessary relationship between a particular organization of desire and a social identity. Many people who practise various forms of homosexual activity fail to recognize themselves in labels such as 'homosexual', lesbian and gay, queer, or whatever the available identity is at any particular time, even in the West, where such descriptions and self-descriptions are hegemonic. In other parts of the world, homosexual practices, where they are not banned totally, are integrated into various patterns of relations, without giving rise to Western-style identities, though other forms of identity do of course exist (Herdt 1994).

This has become particularly crucial in the age of AIDS. It has sometimes been said that HIV and AIDS, in its spread across the world, tells the truth about identity, revealing in infection what is concealed in social life. But it is more accurate to say that HIV reveals the truth about often concealed sexual activities. The assumption that evidence of certain practices reveals the prevalence of identities is not only a fallacy but a dangerous one when it comes to health and safer-sex education, because it assumes that people will recognize themselves in social identities that are peculiar to very specific parts of the world. The development in British AIDS work of a well-intentioned label of 'men who have sex with men', is an attempt to recognize that existing labels do not exhaust homosexual activity. Consequently, there are men who often have unsafe sex with other men who do not regard themselves as at risk of a 'gay plague' because they do not see themselves as gay. Campaigns directed at these 'MWHSWM' have, however, been less than successful because they do not address people in terms that they can themselves recognize (King 1993). Most men who have sex with other men, who refuse a gay self-description, probably see themselves as bisexual or even hetero-sexual, or are locked into identifications, such as those of min-ority ethnic groups, where a gay identity is either lacking or tabooed.

Available identities are taken up for a variety of reasons: because they make sense of individual experiences, because they give access to communities of meaning and support, because they are politically chosen (Weeks 1985). These identities can, however, equally be refused, precisely because they do not make sense to an individual, or because they have no cultural purchase. Identities necessarily differentiate. They also have differential weight for individuals and collectivities at different times. The positive assertion of sexualized identities is more likely to be a result of a sense of exclusion, denial or threat than an easy acceptance of one's lot. By and large the heterosexual majority have not felt it necessary, until the challenges of recent years, aggressively to assert their heterosexual identities, simply because they set the norm. It was not until the twentieth century that women asserted their sense of themselves as sexual beings, because while before that women may have been regarded as 'the sex', their sexuality was generally during the nineteenth century not seen as autonomous but responsive to that of men (Bland 1996). Similarly, the differential emergence of distinctive male homosexual and lesbian identities can be related to the separate experiences and histories of men and women (Weeks 1977/1990).

The creation of an identity involves finding a delicate balance between the hazards and opportunities of contemporary life and an identification with some sort of history, an 'imaginary reunifi-cation', in Stuart Hall's phrase, of past and present: 'identities are the names we give to the different ways we are positioned, and position ourselves, in the narratives of the past' (quoted in Gates 1993, p. 231).

The challenge is always one of shaping usable narratives that can make sense of the present through appropriating a particular history. Not surprisingly, one of the first signs of the public emergence of new identities is the appearance of works that detail the 'roots' of those hitherto obscured from recorded or respectable history: history as a way of legitimizing contingency.

Paradox 4: *Sexual identities are fictions – but necessary fictions*
Sexual identities are historical inventions, which change in complex histories. They are imagined in contingent circumstances. They can be taken up and abandoned. To put it polemically, they are fictions. This is not of course how they are seen or experienced, or what we wish to believe. Worse, in the age of uncertainty through which we are currently struggling, to say this often seems a betrayal of what we need most desperately to hold on to, an arid intellectualism which leaves minorities without hope, and the vulnerable defenceless. As HIV disease visibly and remorselessly spread in the male gay communities of the West from the early 1980s, it was the existence of strong lesbian and gay communities and identities which provided the essential context for combating the virus: in providing social networks for support and campaigning, in developing a grammar for safer sex, in promoting a language of resistance and survival. The homophobia that was encouraged by AIDS demanded, and in fact greatly strengthened, lesbian and gay identities; without them, it often seemed in the embattled 1980s, there was nothing. To say that all this was a fiction seemed perverse.

But to say that something is a historical fiction is not to denigrate it. On the contrary, it is simple to recognize that we cannot escape our histories, and that we need means to challenge their apparently iron laws and inexorabilities by constructing narratives of the past in order to imagine the present and future. Oppositional sexual identities, in particular, provide such means and alternatives, fictions that provide sources of comfort and support, a sense of belonging, a focus for opposition, a strategy for survival and cultural and political challenge. Such a view of identity does two things. First of all it offers a critical view of all identities, demonstrating their historicity and arbitrariness. It denaturalizes them, revealing the coils of power that entangle them. It returns identities to the world of human beings, revealing their openness and contingency.

Second, because of this, it makes human agency not only possible, but also essential. For if sexual identities are made in history, and in relations of power, they can also be remade. Identities then can be seen as sites of contestation. They multiply points of resistance and challenge, and expand the potentialities for change. Identities, particularly those identities which challenge the imposing edifice of Nature, History, Truth, are a resource for realizing human diversity. They provide means of realizing a progressive individualism, our 'potential for individualization' (Melucci 1989, p. 48) and a respect for difference.

Frank Kermode (1967) has made a useful distinction between myths and fictions. Myth, he argues:

> operates within the diagrams of ritual, which presupposes total and adequate explanations of things as they are and were: it is a sequence of radically unchangeable gestures. Fictions are for finding things out, and they change as the needs of sense-making change. Myths are the agents of stability, fictions are the agents of change (1967, p. 210).

From this viewpoint, the dominant (hetero)sexual identities in our culture have some of the qualities of myths: they speak for an assumed naturalness, eternity and truth which belie their historical and contingent nature. The radical, oppositional identities which have arisen in and against the hegemonic ones can be seen as fictions: they offer narratives of individual life, collective memory and imagined alternatives which provide the motivation and inspiration for change. In that sense, they are not only fictions – they are necessary fictions. Without them we would have no basis to explain our individual needs and desires, nor a sense of collective belonging that provides the agency and means for change.

The danger is that these historical inventions, these fictional unities, become closed, the exclusive home of those who identify with them. The semi-ethnic lesbian and gay identities that developed in the USA in the 1970s and 1980s (Epstein 1990, Herdt 1992) provide a graphic example of the dangers as well as the opportunities. They provided the possibilities of individual and collective growth, but they also drew boundaries around the homosexual experience. In extreme cases such developments can themselves become barriers to change. But if their historicity, openness, flexibility and conditional nature – fictional qualities – are acknowledged fully, they provide the opportunity for thinking about not only who you are, but also about who you want to become. They reveal the power relations that inhibit change, by making power visible. And once we accept that sexuality takes its form from historically specific power relations, then it becomes possible to imagine new forms of desire which are not blocked by a sense of powerlessness and inevitability. Oppositional sexual identities in their collective form provide vistas for different futures. By interrogating and challenging normalizing and imposed forms of identity, it becomes possible to invent oneself anew.

Identities in this sense are less about expressing an essential truth about our sexual being; they are more about mapping out different values: the values of autonomy, relationships, of belonging, of difference and diversity. They provide continuous possibilities for invention and reinvention, open processes through which change can happen. As Foucault put it, specifically referring to gay identities, but with a wider echo:

> There ought to be an inventiveness special to a situation like ours . . . We must think that what exists is far from filling all possible spaces. To make a truly unavoidable challenge to the question: what can we make work, what new game can we invent? (1989, p. 209).

That, of course, means that sexual identities are more than troubling on a personal level; they also cause trouble on a social level. I agree with Judith Butler's summing up of the paradox of identity:

I'm permanently troubled by identity categories, consider them
to be invariable stumbling-blocks, and understand them, even
promote them, as sites of necessary trouble (1991, p. 14).

It is the necessary trouble caused by the paradoxes of identity
that makes the politics of sexuality so fraught with tensions, but
so important for rethinking the nature of our social and cultural
values.

CAUSING TROUBLE: TRANSGRESSION AND SEXUAL CITIZENSHIP

Sexual identities cause trouble because they transcend the conventional divides between the public and the private, the individual and the social. They are deeply personal and they are
highly political, particularly at the present time, because they
are ultimately concerned with how we should live, what we should
be. So an effective politics around sexuality must simultaneously
address the aspirations of individuals in their private or intimate
lives and the wider public context which shapes the rhythms of
everyday existence. The conventional logic would suggest that it
is the dreams and dilemmas of individual existence which gives
rise to politics. I am going to argue, on the contrary, that it is
much truer to say that the vicissitudes of politics shape identities,
including sexual identities.

There can be no politics without some sense of identity because
it is through a wider identification (with a party, a movement, a
specific goal) that political practice is made possible. But identity
does not give rise to politics in any simple way. Identities are
relational, formed through social relations and politics, so that
powerful political movements give rise to identity rather than the
other way round. The political articulations necessary for any
sort of hegemonic or oppositional project depend on the construction of boundaries that mark the difference between us and
them, which shape wider identifications (Laclau 1990).

A political project is precisely the attempted unification of
diverse peoples and aspirations into a we that can challenge those

who do not share our developing values. In the process new identities are forged, that do not neccessarily obliterate pre-existing identities, but take up key elements and fragments into a new, wider belonging. The coalitions welded together during the 1980s by the New Right in Britain and the USA provide classic examples of this. They forged, under the powerful symbolic unifications of Reaganism and Thatcherism, a cultural, social as well as political identification in which different groups and individuals could recognize themselves, despite their differences (see, for example, Durham 1991; Newburn 1992). Reaganite Democrats in the USA or 'Essex men and women' in Britain may have had little in common historically or culturally with conservative ideologues or stock brokers, but they could identify with an anti-statism, possessive individualis, and rampant consumerism that spoke to their perceived needs and desires. The sexual fundamentalism of some born-again moral authoritarians in the New Right may have sat uneasily with the avid sexual libertarianism generated by the acquisitive materialism of the consumer boom, but at least all members of the political constituency knew which side of the frontier was their own: that territory which spoke for 'normality', and which feared engulfment by the overflowing of radical sexual difference, whether embodied in the feminist challenge, the dissidence of the movements of newly vocal sexual minorities, or the moral otherness of difficult ethnic and racial communities.

To a large extent they were right to recognize the frontier. The radical identity politics that developed from the 1960s was conditioned by the definition of new boundaries, new sites of challenge to the various forms of power that were seen to hold people into subject positions that were no longer acceptable. Black politics, feminism, the lesbian and gay movement, all bore witness to the articulation of new forms of identity and community. They had their roots in existing forms of being, so that the new movements were seen and presented as a sort of 'coming of age' of what was already there. Without a sense of being and belonging that currently existed, and which a reading of history validated, there could have been no new politics of identity. The emergence, for instance, of gay liberation depended on a steady building of a sense of gay community links over the previous generations, just as 'second-wave feminism' saw itself as finishing the thwarted revolution of the 'first wave'. But in truth, such movements were doing more than realizing what was already given. They were articulating something new, developing new social identities:

> Wasn't it an emerging political movement that enabled the enunci-ation of a gay – rather than homosexual or homophile – identity? And wasn't that political movement formed though identification with other political movements? [i.e. civil rights, black power, feminism] (Crimp 1993, p. 314).

Social, and sexual, identities, can only ever be relational, because without a sense of wider involvements, no identity is possible. As Teresa de Lauretis has said, 'It takes two women, not one, to make a lesbian' (quoted in Crimp 1993, p. 313). The function of social and political movements is precisely to make such identifi-cations possible.

The social movements concerned with sexuality that have emerged since the 1960s, the feminist and lesbian and gay move-ments especially, implicitly assume that it is through social involvement and collective action that individuality can be realized. The new movements may be interpreted as a revolt against the forms of subjectification to which the contemporary world has given rise, a challenge to the technologies of power which by defining individuals in particular ways pin them to particular subordinated identities and locations in society. They reveal the complexity of modern social relations, and the intracta-bility of the contradictions and tensions these produce. They simultaneously offer other possibilities.

At the heart of the new movements is a rejection of imposed definitions, and a struggle for social space in which new identities can be forged. There is of course a historic irony in this process. The identities are being shaped on the very terrain that gave rise to domination in the first place. Racial and ethnic minorities historically challenged racist structures by affirming their racial-ized identities ('black is beautiful'). Feminism has historically affirmed the rights of women by asserting the positive qualities of femininity. Lesbians and gays reject the pathologizing of homosexuality by 'reversing the discourse', and affirming pride in being homosexual (Foucault 1979). In the process, as we have seen, there is a search for a hidden history, a narrative structure which seems to express the truth. But a better way of seeing what is happening is to understand it as a social positioning, where difference is asserted as a positive quality rather than an inevitable or naturalized divide.

This poses difficulties in connecting such movements to conventional politics. For the movements concerned with sexuality what matters more than a single set of goals or a defined programme is the symbolic focus of the activities of the movements themselves, their struggle to gain control over the conditions of life. They cannot therefore be judged in terms of their political effectivity in attaining this or that legislative shift, important as this often is. Their ultimate importance lies in their cultural, individual and informal impact on the lives of the individuals who align with them, and are addressed by them as active subjects.

The term 'movement' conveys some of this sense of informality but perhaps suggests too much a cohesiveness in organization which is only spasmodically present. As Melucci (1989, p. 6) has argued, social movements are normally ' "invisible" networks of small groups submerged in everyday life'. They tend to be concerned with individual needs, collective identity, and a part-time 'membership', and constitute laboratories in which new experiences are invented, and tested, in which reality is re-described, and individuals can develop alternative experiences of time, space and personal relationships. They attempt to shape a new 'grammar' of everyday life rather than political programmes.

Their major function, at least in their earliest forms, is to translate actions into symbolic challenges that upset the dominant cultural codes, and reveal their irrationality, partiality and illegitimacy as products of power and domination. So they have a dual role: to reveal the macro and micro forms of domination that constitute modern life; and to demonstrate the possibilities of other forms of life that are not simply prefigurative of some imagined future, but are actually being constructed in the here and now.

So the practical activities of such movements characteristically subvert conventional views of political activities. Consciousness raising, networking, carnivals, festivals, candle-lit processions affirm both a sense of collective being and challenge conventional patterns of life, transmitting to the system a picture of its own contradictions. They illustrate both the complexity of power relations, and the possibility of subverting them.

In this way, despite their informality and *ad hoc* nature, they can in particular circumstances become active participants in the domain of politics. They regularly make demands on the conventional structure of politics, often couched in uncompromising terms. They also lean towards a politics of direct action, avoiding in most cases the forms of representative democracy. Contemporary social movements are frequently unstable both in their composition and strategic thrust, and there can be no *a priori* guarantee of their progressive nature (Laclau and Mouffe 1985, p. 87). Interestingly, some of the neo-fundamentalist movements of recent years are themselves, in the delay in the triumph of their universalist hopes, explicitly redefining themselves as social movements with the same claim to social space, and to difference, as other, overtly progressive groups. Thus Ralph Reed, of the Religious Right in the USA, noted in 1993 that: 'We are . . . learning to define ourselves by who we are not, just as the civil rights movement did in the 1960's . . . our movement is taking on the issues voters care about' (Reed 1993, p. 15; see also Herman 1994).

The political meaning of contemporary movements depends upon their articulation with other struggles and demands. A feminist campaign for censorship of images is often more at home with the extreme right than with progressive politics (Thompson 1994a); a gay fascist group is simply fascist. When aligned to a wider democratizing politics, however, they share a 'radical-democratic ethos' (Lash and Urry 1987, p. 300) concerned with expanding the space for individual and collective growth, and in broadening the basis of the public sphere. They reflect at their most dynamic the complexity and diversity of contemporary civil society.

Such movements are not, it is important to insist again, simply expressing a pre-existing essence of social being. Identities and belongings are being constructed in the very process of organiz-ation itself. They are effective in so far as they can speak a language which brings people into the activities, alignments and subjectivities being shaped, and the most effective language avail-able is the language of community.

Like a movement, which both grows out of, and creates a sense of wider identification, a community must be constantly reimagined, sustained over time by common practices and sym-bolic reenactments which reaffirm both identity and difference (Cohen 1985). A national community may be sustained by allegiance to the flag, national days, the ritual of elections or monarchy, by victories in war, war memorials and military pride, or by the less harmful ephemeral hysteria of athletic competi-tions or the soccer World Cup. A black community may reenact its difference through defence of its territory against racist attacks or the symbolic presence of the police. It may also reenact and celebrate it in carnival, the inversion of the daily humdrum exist-ence where reality is turned upside down, the streets become the property of the oppressed, and the repressed experiences of the community can return, triumphantly for the day. In the same way, the losses of the AIDS community can be mourned and the lives of the dead celebrated through candle-lit vigils and the sewing of memorial quilts. Without such reimaginings a com-munity will die as difference is obliterated or becomes meaning-less before the onrush of history.

Community stands for some notion of solidarity, a solidarity which empowers and enables, and makes individual and social action possible. The sexual movements of recent years have both encouraged and built on a sense of community, a space where hitherto execrated sexual activity and identities have been affirmed and sustained. Such a validation of community has been at the centre of the response to HIV and AIDS by the group most affected in the West, gay men. It has made possible a social and cultural response whose aim, in Richard Goldstein's words, is 'to promote survival, demand attention, and defeat stigma' (1991, p. 37). As Watney has argued, it is also a sense of belonging to some kind of community 'that will always determine the development of a resilient sense of self-esteem which is demonstrably the sine qua non of safer sex education' (1991, p. 13). At the same time, the absence of a sense of community around sexual issues among other groups affected by the epidemic has been a critical factor in limiting the development of a culture of safer sex and personal responsibility. (It is worth noting that only in the wake of the AIDS crisis has the term 'heterosexual community' come into use, a term defined more by its absence of meaning than by its resonant social presence.)

Sexual dissidence is ultimately dependent upon the growth of that sense of common purpose and solidarity represented by the term community. The appeal to the authenticity of one's sexual experience (Dollimore 1991), which has been a symbolic token of many of the pioneers of radical sexual change, becomes culturally meaningful only in so far as it speaks to, and evokes an echo in, the experience of others in a latent community that is on its way to becoming a critical community. With the development of a sexual movement with a sense of its own history and social role, the idea of community becomes a critical norm through which other possibilities are opened up.

There is, however, no necessary unity in the resulting politics of sexuality. The movements of sexual dissidence over the past generation have been marked as much by their fragmentation and disputatiousness as by any underlying sense of unity or purpose. Nor should this be surprising. There is no essential pregiven identity in womanhood or homosexuality, or of any other sexualized category. Divisions of class, race, sexual taste, political alignment and countless other factors have constantly divided the radical sexual movements and the communities of identity associated with them. It is possible to detect, however, two distinct political 'moments' in contemporary sexual politics which indicate the possibilities as well as the dangers: one is the moment of challenge to the traditional or received order of sexual life, a subversion or transgression of existing ways of sexual being; the other is a movement towards inclusion, towards redefining the polis to incorporate fully those who have felt excluded, a move towards full 'sexual citizenship'. These are not absolutely separable moments. On the contrary, they are simply different aspects of the same project. They have, however, had different implications for the politics of identity and sexual diversity, and therefore need to be explored separately.

The moment of transgression

Transgression, the breaching of boundaries, the pushing of experience to the limits, the challenge to the Law, whatever it is, is a crucial moment in any radical sexual project. As an individual act it speaks of a self obscured by an ignoble sexual order. For many this act of defiance is the expression of a buried truth. It is the characteristic stance of the individual resister who says 'Here I am, I can do no other'. As James Baldwin, quoting Walt Whitman, put it in an epigraph for his pioneering homosexual novel, *Giovanni's Room* (1956/1963), 'I am the man; I suffered, I was there'. But even when the social origins of identities and the complexities of desire are recognized, the living-out of individual acts of defiance can challenge the status quo. As Garber says, one of the most important aspects of cross-dressing 'is the way in which it offers a challenge to easy notions of binarity, putting into question the categories of "female" and "male" ' (Garber 1992, p. 10). In the same way, the appearance of self-affirming groups of militant lesbians or gay men in the 1970s disrupted expectations of the natural order of heterosexuality.

The difficulty with transgression, however, is that the limits are always flexible and changing. As Foucault (1963/1977) observed in 'A Preface to Transgression', the crossing of boundaries, a going further than the Law allows, always sets up a new boundary which must be transgressed, leading to a transgressive spiral which is potentially interminable (see also Wilson 1993, p. 110). At one time it seemed transgressive to be open about one's homosexuality. Today, in many circles, people are more shocked to hear that a self-declared lesbian or gay man is having a heterosexual affair. In an age when the singer Madonna can sell millions of copies of well-worn sado-masochistic iconography through mainstream publishers (Madonna 1992), it is difficult to believe that any individual act in itself will shock. What matter more are the critical elements and the various possibilities spelt out in the transgressive transactions, the new niches of possibility that appear, and these depend on the changing social geography of sexuality.

As Teresa de Lauretis argues, homosexuality today:

> is no longer to be seen simply as marginal with regard to a dominant, stable form of sexuality . . . it is no longer to be seen either as merely transgressive or deviant vis-à–vis a proper natural sexuality . . . according to the older pathological model, or as just another optional 'lifestyle', according to the model of North American pluralism. Instead, male and female homosexualities . . . may be reconceptualized as sexual and cultural forms in their own right, albeit emergent ones and thus still fuzzily defined, undercoded, or discursively dependent on more established forms (1991, p. iii).

Homosexuality has become a way of life that for many begs acceptance rather than continuing transgression. Yet as against the continuing norms of the culture an element of subversive otherness clings. Though the different sexual and cultural forms may be notoriously fuzzy, and highly contested within and without, a perverse and transgressive dynamic is still at play, though now not simply as an individual act of subversion but as a collective activity. Witness as evidence of this the appearance in the late 1980s within the lesbian and gay communities of North America and elsewhere of the idea of a new 'queer politics':

> A new generation of activists is here. They have come out into communities devastated by the HIV epidemic and into political consciousness through the struggle around AIDS. But AIDS is not their main focus.
>
> The new generation calls itself *queer*, not *lesbian, gay and bisexual* – awkward, narrow and perhaps compromised words. *Queer* is meant to be confrontational – opposed to gay assimilationists

and straight oppressors while inclusive of people who have been marginalized by anyone in power (Bérubé and Escoffier 1991, p. 12).

The widespread adoption of the term 'gay' in the late 1960s betokened a rejection of the cautious, adaptive and what appeared to the new activists as the apologetic style of the old homophile movement (Altman 1971/1993). Similarly the new queer politics signalled a break with what activists and theorists (so far as they can be distinguished) see as the minoritizing and integrationist strategies of the lesbian and gay politics of the 1970s and 1980s. It emerged, ironically (or perhaps not), at the very moment when that politics was with varying degrees of success attempting to break into the mainstream: in the USA in campaigns to force acceptance of lesbians and gays in the military; and in Britain in partially successful efforts to change laws concerning the age of consent which discriminated against homosexuality.

There is an important history here which it is worth briefly disinterring. The initial impulse of gay liberation in the 1970s was to challenge fixed categories which had restricted the lives of homosexuals. By identifying a dominant order which privileged heterosexuality, it sought through radical acts of subversion and transgression, and the building of a radicalized community, to break the limits of existing categories. In assuming the polymorphous sexual potential of everyone, it endorsed the liberation of homosexual desires in heterosexuals as well as self-identified homosexuals, and looked forward to 'the end of the homosexual', and also, of course, the end of the heterosexual (Altman 1971/1993). The result, however, was the apparent opposite: the consolidation of lesbian and gay identities, and elements of a backlash by those who reasserted the primacy of heterosexuality. In the process, the gay movement became less a universalizing tendency and more the voice of a new constituency. Its politics moved from liberatory to particularist, its defining characteristic less a contestation of what was, and more the expression of a minority status. In the USA especially, as Warner (1993, p. xvii) observes, 'the default model for all minority movements is racial or ethnic', and it was as the equivalent of a newly confident semi-ethnic group that lesbians and gays claimed their rights (Epstein 1990).

Within such a discourse, two developments became inevitable. First, there was an emphasis on asserting a claim to citizenship within existing discourses of minority civil rights. Hence a politics that could put its all into campaigning for access into hitherto restricted occupations, such as the military (Shilts 1993), or into legislative reforms or judicial campaigns that recognized equality of treatment, or struggled for the recognition of gay or lesbian marriages. This was not unimportant, both as a mobilizing effort against discrimination, and as an assertion of presence and hence legitimate identity. It had the effect, however, of potentially reifying an unproblematic collective identity and constituency, when in both theory and everyday life the idea of a fixed or given lesbian or gay identity and community was in flux. For the very emergence of newly self-confident identities reflexively produced, and this is the second point, a profusion of sub-identities – bisexuals, 'boy lovers', gay *and* lesbian sadomasochists, gay radicals and gay conservatives and the like (Weeks 1985); it also produced further challenges to these new identities, on the grounds that they were white, middle class, male, etc., from women, black gay activists, people of colour and numerous others (see Radical America 1993). The dynamo of particularist identities, once started, led in the direction of proliferation, not uniformity, towards separatism rather than unity, towards essentializing rather than redefining difference.

The politics that flowed from this 'ethnicizing political desire' was pluralistic, coalitionist, 'Rainbow' tinted (Warner 1993), but at the expense of fixing both identity and community. The reality of belonging is, I have argued, much more complex and fluid than this, and queer politics attempted to reflect this:

> The queers are constructing a new culture by combining elements that usually don't go together. They may be the first wave of activists to embrace the retrofuture/classic contemporary styles of postmodernism. They are building their own identity from old and new elements – borrowing styles and tactics from popular culture, communities of color, hippies, AIDS activists, the anti-

nuclear movement, MTV, feminists and early gay liberationists. Their new culture is slick, quick, anarchic, transgressive, ironic. They are deadly serious but they wanna have fun (Bérubé and Escoffier 1991, p. 14).

As was the case with their predecessors in the radical sexual politics of the 1970s, there is a dual movement at work: the construction of a new identity, with all the characteristic paradox of asserting similarity and difference; and a challenge to rigid categorizations, by embracing all who would identify with the new politics, whatever their previous sexual identities, preferences or activities. So queer politics embraces not only radical, self-defined lesbians and gays, but also sadomasochists, fetishists, bisexuals, gender-benders, radical heterosexuals, single parents, queer artists, black and white – the list is potentially infinite because the organizing principle is not an assumed sexual identity based on orientation or practice, but identification with the forms of politics and patterns of transgression that define queerness:

> The preference for 'queer' represents, among other things, an aggressive impulse of generalization: it rejects a minoritizing logic of toleration or simple political interest-representation in favor of a more thorough resistance to regimes of the normal (Warner 1993, p. xxii).

Several different impulses can be seen at work here. The primary one, perhaps, is the impact of the AIDS crisis, which, as Crimp notes, 'brought us face to face with the consequences of both our separatism and our liberalism' (1993, p. 314). This was a crisis that acted, in the word used by the French sociologist Pierre Bourdieu (cited in Mort 1994), as a 'developer' in a new and uniquely painful social and cultural conjuncture. Crisis moments force their participants to see a coherence in their sense of the world which ordinary circumstances would not have produced. New positions are marked out, new boundaries are drawn, which follow the logic of a civil war, producing clearly demarcated camps and antagonists. The AIDS crisis dramatized for many of those caught in its wake the pretence of contemporary citizenship, a citizenship that excluded huge numbers of people living with, or confonting the threat of, a ghastly and life-threatening syndrome of diseases. It seemed that belonging depended on good health and orthodox sexual practices. A profound sense of exclusion forced the emergence of a more radicalized sexual politics, in which the ancient stigmatizing term 'queer' could be reclaimed by a new generation of activists, radicalized by the experience of AIDS. The direct action groups Queer Nation in the USA and OutRage! in Britain (Watney 1994) were established as a militant response to a deep sense of alienation from the existing language of citizenship, based as it was on a normalizing notion of belonging.

This development was furthered by the gradual emergence over the previous generation of a 'homosexual diaspora', or perhaps more accurately an 'invisible college' of intellectuals and activists, who were alive to a translocal sense of alignment which went beyond national boundaries. Developments in the USA found echoes among activists in Canada, Britain, Australia: an assertion of a dissident politics opened the way for a new positioning of identity. Each national culture produced its own variation, according to its own rhythms and social pressures. But generally, the emergence of queer politics in turn provided new opportunities for dialogue between those who had found the previous emergence of particularist identities problematic: between women and men, homosexuals and heterosexuals, black and white. The burgeoning of a deliberately transgressive lesbian culture, often playing with a selfconsciously fetishistic iconography previously associated with gay men, and constructing alliances with gay men, provides a vivid example:

PUSSY (Perverts Undermining State ScrutinY) was a feminist anti-censorship sub-group within OutRage!, the queer direct action group based in London. We were a unique combination of activists. Launched under the slogan, 'PUSSY Rules the World' and 'Boy Pussy and Chicks with Dicks Working Together', PUSSY included lesbian members of Feminists Against Censorship, lesbian writers, artists and cultural workers, women sex trade workers, and gay men from OutRage! (Smith 1993, p. 20)

The new queer cinema of the early 1990s provides another example of these tendencies: internationalist in scope, transgressive and contestatory in style, it provided a space for the interrogation of fixed identities (see Arroyo 1993; Gever et al. 1993; and the contributions to Julien and Savage 1994). Henry Louis Gates Jr refers to a key example of this tendency, the work of the British black and gay film-maker Isaac Julien, and his description is apposite. Referring to Julien's film *Looking for Langston*, a lyrical odyssey in search of the meaning of the blackness and gayness of the American poet, and of Julien himself, he writes that its importance:

> is in presenting an aesthetics that can embrace ambiguity; perhaps it is not without its reverential moments, but it is not a work of naive celebration. It presents an identitarian history as a locus of discontinuities and affinities, of shared pleasures and perils (Gates 1993, p. 238).

Both of these examples epitomize the meaning of queerness: a cultural project which explores identity while problematizing it, and which reflects on difficult alignments (men and women, black and gay in these cases) in a new identification which works to transcend them.

The theoretical grounding of this form of sexual politics, which has defined itself as 'queer theory', is perhaps only peripherally related to the activism, but nevertheless embraces the same terrain of subversion and transgression. The lineage comes from the theoretical work of the first generation of lesbian, gay and feminist activists and writers, but whereas that work was largely sociological and historical in focus, queer theory owes as much to literary deconstructionism and Foucault. In its most characteristic form in the writings of Sedgwick (1985, 1990), Butler (1991, 1993), Dollimore (1991) and others (see Warner 1993), its major concerns are with the dynamics of the emergence of the homosexual/heterosexual binarism as evidenced in works of literature or theory. As Mort (1994) has observed, this has the curious effect of reasserting rather than deconstructing the binary divide, and of elevating heterosexuality and homophobia into the principle dynamic of social organization; this happens at the expense of a more nuanced notion of the dispersal of sexuality throughout society that the work of Foucault suggests. In terms of political positioning, however, the identification of 'heteronormativity' (Warner 1993) as the major focus of sexual oppression has the effect of defining the frontier against which a queer politics can be organized. It thus provides a necessary grounding for the conceptualization of a politics of relational identities (Crimp 1993) which can break with fixed and rigid pre-existing identities.

This exploration of queer politics is not intended to demonstrate that this is the only possible response to the cultural crisis generated by the sexual politics of the 1980s and the impact of the AIDS crisis. In fact, the transgressive moment can be seen in a host of social arenas, especially in the communities of people of colour, where women and non-heterosexuals battle for cultural space within their own communities (see Bhatt 1994, 1995). My intention is rather different: to show how identities can be re-formed by new political requirements, and how differences can be realigned in the process. In the long perspectives of history, queer politics may well prove to be an ephemeral ripple rather than a refreshing wave. Queer politics has all the defects of a transgressive style, elevating confrontation over the content of alternatives. Although it seeks to deconstruct old rigidities, it creates new boundaries; although it is deliberately transgressive, it enacts its dissidence through the adoption of a descriptive label which many lesbians and gays find offensive, often seeking enemies within as much as enemies without (see McIntosh 1993). Despite this, it is an interesting phenomenon not only because of what it says or does, but because it is a reminder of the perpetual inventiveness of a collective sexual politics which stretches towards different ways of being. Whatever one thinks of it, it illustrates the continuing construction of identities and of a sense of community which transcends old certainties and divisions, while challenging the orthodox epistemology of sexuality:

Queer culture and politics herald a lesbian and gay sexuality that is SEXUAL, SEXY and SUBVERSIVE – not only of heterosexist

notions of being, but of former lesbian and gay orthodoxies . . .
Queer promises a refusal to apologise or assimilate into invisibility.
It provides a way of asserting desires that shatter gender identities
and sexualities (Smyth 1992, pp. 59–60).

Identity, or the subversion of identity which is its mirror-image,
becomes a way of speaking about what could or should be, rather
than expressing what is.

The moment of citizenship

The above suggests, however, a wide political agenda which transgression in itself can rarely fully articulate. As Elizabeth Wilson
insists:

> we transgress in order to insist that we are there, that we exist,
> and to place a distance between ourselves and the dominant
> culture. But we have to go further – we have to have an idea of
> how things could be different, otherwise transgression ends in
> mere posturing (1993, p. 11).

Yet as Mort (1994) observes, there is a real difficulty with queer
sexual radicalism, and therefore of 'going further'. It speaks most
obviously to the aspirations and possibilities of a relatively narrow
social stratum, largely of the progressive middle class: 'postmodern intellectuals', social and media professionals and the relatively small bands of activists around sexuality and AIDS work.
The radical pluralist agenda, Mort suggests, dramatizes many of
the broader social and personal anxieties experienced by these
groupings, but does not easily address the wider anxieties stemming from a generalization of uncertainty, and the appeal of the
absolute. That does not mean that a radical agenda would not
appeal to a wider constituency, but it does mean, as Mort concludes, that it must be translated into a wider, more widely recog-
nizable, language of politics.

The concept of citizenship has been seen as one possible way
of expressing how, in response to Wilson's appeal, 'things could

be different'. Since the ancient world, citizenship as a concept speaks of the individual belonging to and participating in a wider community, bearing rights against and obligations to that community (Held 1991, p. 20). It invokes membership and involvement, which brings entitlements and duties. It weaves a web of reciprocal claims and responsibilities that seeks to address both the needs of individuals and the requirements of society, operating in the 'hinge' between the complexities of everyday life, and the changing patterns of social institutions and the state (Mercer 1990, p. 68).

The problem is that historically the aspiration to citizenship has encoded a particular version of sexual behaviour and private life into its central discourses. In the ancient world, where it had its origins, we know that civic belonging was the prerogative of 'free men', and excluded women as well as the 'unfree'. Its associated ethical codes, while accepting a form of homosexual practice, were shaped by a social organization of the household which is antithetical to late modern views of freedom of choice and lifestyles. During the nineteenth and twentieth centuries the ideal of citizenship has been progressively broadened to include social as well as civic and political rights – to include basic welfare provision alongside freedom under the law and political representation (Marshall 1963) – but its subject has remained conventionally familial and heterosexual. As Turner notes:

> Citizenship was a major plank of postwar Keynesian reconstruction: it was based on assumptions about full employment, the validity of the nuclear household and the dominance of exclusive heterosexual relations (Turner 1993, p. xi).

The consequence was the exclusion of those who did not easily fit into this pattern. In an age of citizenship, Benton (1991, p. 154) says, there are two sorts of non-citizen: 'those who have never been admitted, and those who are exiled'. Sexual outsiders meet both criteria. While laws regulating sexuality have generally been liberalized throughout the West, there remain key areas where full citizenship rights are denied, even though social obligations remain in place (the US military's exclusion of open and active homosexuals provides one key example; those countries, like Britain, which have different ages of consent for homosexuals and heterosexuals provide another). Not surprisingly, many remain sceptical of the utility of the idea of citizenship. David Evans, in his study of *Sexual Citizenship*, sharply and graphically remarks:

> The history of citizenship is a history of fundamental formal het-
> erosexist patriarchal principles and practices ostensibly progress-
> ively 'liberalized' towards and through the rhetoric of 'equality'
> but in practice to effect unequal differentiation (1993, p. 9).

Others have pointed out the ways in which the language of citizenship can simply become assimilated to a rhetoric of consumer rights, the form of 'belonging' to which contemporary culture is particularly prone (see Cooper 1993).

Nevertheless claims to full citizenship have been a major element of sexual politics since the 1970s, largely in the form of campaigns for rights. If the discourse of transgression as a road to emancipation or liberation is one pole of recent sexual politics, the discourse of rights is the other, and they are complexly intertwined (see Weeks 1991). The early gay liberation movement both gave rise to an emancipatory project *and* to a more vigorous campaign for legal and social rights for lesbians and gays, just as women's liberation propelled a more radical claim to achieving, finally, the rights of women. This apparent divide between an emancipatory politics and a liberal rights agenda remains controversial and contested in all the countries where radical sexual politics have developed (see, for example, Herman 1994, on the Canadian experience), yet in historical perspective it is likely that each moment is necessary to the other. Without a radicalized agenda, the politicization of sexuality would have proved difficult; but without careful lobbying and campaigning, detailed legal change, whether in statute or in the interpretation of the law, will always be impossible. Both moments are essential to the opening-up of space for the social recognition of diverse ways of life, even if the carnival of difference and the sober suits of integration do not always mix.

In their overview of the American response to AIDS Stoddard and Rieman (1991) make a strong case for arguing that the more reactionary proposals for dealing with the epidemic, such as quarantining, have been thwarted because of a much longer-term revolution in attitudes towards rights since World War II. Between 1950 and 1980, they argue, after long and painful struggle, especially over the civil rights of African-Americans, 'American law came to embrace the principle of eliminating prejudice based on factors unrelated to individual merit, and established concrete actions based on bias' (Stoddard and Rieman 1991, p. 243). They are not sanguine enough to believe that this revolution in civil liberties is complete, or that discrimination against people living with HIV and AIDS will nicely fade away, or that legal and political agitation is unnecessary. But there is for them an important general lesson in this: a climate where individual rights are recognized makes it easier to extend those rights to more and more outsiders. It provides both a mobilizing focus for action, especially through the courts, and a language which allows for a widening definition of membership, including the membership of the sick and those discriminated against because of their identification as unpopular sexual and cultural groups.

Rights do not exist in nature. They are products of social relations and of changing historical circumstances and balance of forces, so the claim for rights is always in terms of some rights rather than others. A culture highly attuned to rights discourses, such as the American, opens itself to an ever-widening concept of rights. In a social and cultural tradition like the British, rights-based arguments are more aetiolated (see Watney 1994, chapter 17), and the framework for arguing for sexual rights is consequently less sturdy. The real point, however, is that whatever the formal legal procedures and traditions, an argument for sexual rights is inevitably concerned with expanding or, perhaps better, stretching to the limits, the scope of the rights discourse. By arguing for a more extended definition of rights, we are actually changing the definition of what can be regarded as a right.

In an important sense what the campaigns for sexual reforms have done since the 1970s is to argue for rights in the terms already existing within their particular cultures: to try to force these societies to realize for self-defined sexual minorities what they claim to be the mobilizing ideals of the liberal polity. This is most developed in the USA, but the same principles of activity are evident elsewhere. In Canada, for example, the lesbian and gay movement was able to mobilize strong support around two campaigns in the 1980s: for a 'sexual orientation' amendment to Ontario's Human Rights Code (known as 'Bill 7'), and around a gay couple's claims to be considered members of a family for the purposes of receiving unemployment benefit, the Mossop case (Herman 1994). Though the campaigns had varying degrees of success, both cases became important *causes célèbres*, and effective in affirming lesbian and gay identities during a period of cultural embattlement. In the same way, a discourse of equal rights proved a useful unifying appeal in the effort to equalize the heterosexual and homosexual ages of consent in Britain in early 1994. In such campaigns success or failure is important (the British initiative in fact failed in its ultimate objective, though the age of consent for gay men was reduced from 21 to 18), but perhaps in the longer term what matters most is how successful these efforts are in shifting the terms of the debate, and in broadening the interpretation of rights and citizenship.

All these efforts, while teetering on the edge of something else, effectively used the traditional language and processes of liberal rights claims: the claims of excluded minorities, of equality of domestic arrangements, or of equal rights under the law. These are important rights to claim, and their power and force cannot be underestimated, but they are essentially negative claims: freedom from interference from and discrimination by the law on the grounds of equal status, rather than any attempt to claim a right to be different (see Jeffery-Poulter 1991). Within the terms and processes used, there is little scope for challenging the normative assumptions within the law, legal processes and social practices. Characteristically, such campaigns exclude explicit endorsements of sexual diversity, and the legitimacy of different patterns of domestic life. They usually avoid questions of the social ordering of sexual identities because the idea of a fixed identity (e.g. I was born this way; I cannot change my desires because the law tells me to do so; my relationship with X is just as monogamous as a normal marriage) is politically less challenging, and probably more effective in liberalizing the law. The logic is integrationist.

Most people would probably be quite happy with that, but in limiting the argument to existing notions of citizenship something potentially more challenging can be lost: a recognition above all of the richness that can be realized through encouraging a dialogue between different ways of life, and through developing a language of citizenship based on the fluidity of contemporary identities. Watney, for example, writes that the weak concepts of citizenship currently in circulation in Britain 'involves a clear ranking of priorities within our individual and collective identities, a subjection to political, juridical and regal authority in our sense of who we are' (1994, p. 166). Against this he proposes an 'ethical' notion of citizenship which 'offers the potential for very different processes of identification with one another', based on a validation of our differences as well as our common humanity and need for social belonging.

This is what I take Plummer (1995) to have in mind when he proposes a fourth notion of citizenship, following those based on the elaboration of civic, political and social rights: the idea of 'intimate citizenship'. Intimate citizenship, he argues, is concerned with those matters which relate to our most intimate desires, pleasures and ways of being in the world. Some of these relate back to more traditional ideas of citizenship, but much of it is concerned with new spheres, new arguments and 'new stories': questions around control of our bodies, feelings and relationships; of access to representations, spaces; and about the imponderabilities and hazards of choice. He offers no blueprints, for blueprints are precisely what are not required in the contemporary world. Instead we can begin to elaborate new languages to articulate the new possibilities and conditions in which we find ourselves.

Mouffe's discussion of citizenship (1991) makes a useful distinction between two forms of political logic: a logic of identity for what holds us together in the political field, a logic of pluralism for what makes us different in the sphere of the intimate.

This returns us then to our starting-point: to the possibilities opened up by the fictional natures of identities. Against the fixity of essentialized identity, we can find opportunity in the challenges of many possible identities. In opposition to the absolutisms of ethnicized identities, we can carve out multiple belongings. Instead of the uniformity of a normalized population we may find comfort in the celebration of difference. And in place of the divisiveness of difference we may, with a touch of imagination, discover unity in diversity. But the precondition for this is a politics of citizenship that emphasizes the need for building a wider solidarity based on a recognition of difference, of developing what Parekh aptly calls 'a common language spoken in different accents' (1991, p. 203).

Identification with a wider 'we' is necessary for the creation of a politics which can go beyond the particularisms of narrow group identities. Pluralism and diversity, however, constitute the condition of our intimate lives. As Smith (1994) points out, the theorizations of such post-marxists as Laclau and Mouffe and such radical sexual analysts as Judith Butler meet in the effort to articulate a politics that meets the requirements of both logics. The delicate art of postmodern politics is to balance them, both to problematize identities, and to create new identifications, which allow the free play of individuality and the validation of difference in what could be called a 'community of communities'.

That implies the need for democratic procedures which guarantee the plural subjects the freedom to engage in a continuous dialogue about their respective forms of life (Keane 1989). It involves a process of 'mutual challenge' (Phillips 1994) through which the fluidity of contemporary identities can be negotiated, and different needs and desires translated one to the other (Hollis and Lukes 1982). It requires that the asymmetries of power that inhibit diversity are recognized and challenged. And it necessitates the construction of a wider solidarity in which our difference and our mutual need and respect for one another is affirmed in what Giddens calls a 'life politics', concerned 'not to "politicise", in a narrow sense of that term, life-style decisions, but to remoralise them' (1992, p. 197).

But that wider politics, growing out of and growing beyond

the politics of identity, requires in turn that we explore the values of the intimate sphere, the domain both of transgression and of intimate citizenship. It is here that the life experiments promoted by contemporary sexual movements and communities give rise to claims for the recognition of certain rights of everyday life, the necessary complement of a politics of solidarity, respect and diversity.

4

The Sphere of the Intimate and the Values of Everyday Life

—————=>●€—————

> Things have come to a pretty pass when religion is allowed
> to invade the sphere of private life.
>> Lord Melbourne, on hearing an Evangelical sermon,
>> quoted in G. W. E. Russell, *Collections and Recollections*

> Intimacy itself is often so vulnerable and fragile ... Warfare
> in these most intimate worlds has done the greatest harm to
> the most vulnerable among us.
>> Alida Brill, *Nobody's Business: The Paradoxes of Privacy*

> The authentic plurality of ways of life is the condition under
> which the life of each and every person can be good.
>> Agnes Heller, *Beyond Justice*

SHIFTING BOUNDARIES

It is difficult for us today to recapture fully the aristocratic haut-
eur and disdain in the face of moral enthusiasm expressed by
Lord Melbourne in the early nineteenth century, particularly as
many of us now tend to think that religion is, indeed, properly
a matter for private conscience rather than ostentatious public

observance. But many of us might well nurture a twinge of identification with Queen Victoria's first prime minister as we confront
the prophets of today's certainties, whether they arise out of what
John Stuart Mill called the 'despotism of custom' (Mill 1859/
1975, p. 87) or from the moral absolutism of those who feel
obliged to tell us how we should behave in our intimate sexual
lives. Faced by a modern evangelical fervour, which seeks to
instruct us on what is right or wrong, good or bad, what we may
do, or more likely what we must not do, we too, like the languid
Lord Melbourne, might prefer to affirm the absolute privacy of
the personal sphere. It becomes tempting to try to construct the
'thick walls' (Bauman 1988, p. 92) that might fence off the individual and his or her most personal pleasures and desires from
outside interference, especially when it is guided by militant
moralism and religiosity.

Yet as Brill (1990) and Heller (1987) make clear, such a hope
is easier expressed than realized. Defining what is legitimately
free from external interference and regulation is a hazardous,
fraught and contested task; this is especially the case in a cultural
context in which we are painfully learning to live with a diversity
that we find difficult to embrace wholeheartedly. Intimate citizenship, belonging based on the validation of different ways of life,
different ways of being human, is an ethical goal, not an achieved
reality, a battleground rather than a settled landscape. The
boundaries between the political, social and intimate spheres of
contemporary life are constantly shifting, or being shifted. The
borderlines are extremely difficult to detect, let alone police.
'Good fences make just societies', Michael Walzer (1983, p. 319)
has remarked, echoing the poet Robert Frost. But where we
should stake out the borders between private conscience and
public obligation, or between personal needs and desires and
social norms, is less certain. In the increasingly complex cultural
and moral universe characteristic of our age of uncertainty,
boundary definition is difficult, and boundary conflict is pretty
well inevitable.

Boundary conflicts have, not surprisingly, come to the fore in
recent political discourse, like the grinding of ill-meshed machin-
ery. It has been one of the major achievements of contemporary

social movements, especially the feminist and lesbian and gay movements of the past twenty years, to put on the political agenda issues which have for too long been trapped in the silence of the personal, or excluded for one reason or another from mainstream politics. Questions of reproductive rights, child abuse, violence within marriage, personal health, the validity of different sexual preferences, age, disability, racial and ethnic difference have increasingly become legitimate items of public discourse. At the same time, however, issues which for a long time we took for granted as properly in the public interest – the safety of the streets, education, the welfare of our nearest and dearest, the 'quality of life' – have been progressively 'privatized' by conservative regimes in many Western countries, guided by their own moral and political certainties. Governments dominated by the New Right, whilst attacking welfare systems and a 'dependency culture' in the name of the freedom of the individual, have had little compunction about invading privacy as a condition for individuals receiving means-tested benefits (Bauman 1988), or for ensuring that men who have separated from their offspring exercise their proper responsibilities as parents. In such situations morality and financial prudence go unselfconsciously hand in hand. Debates over the meanings of the public and the private, the political and the personal, are not abstract. They relate to the sort of polity we are, and want to be.

So questions relating to personal behaviour are inevitably relevant to public policy, not just in the conventional sense that the private, usually sexual, morals of politicians or other prominent people have to conform to prevailing standards of public acceptability, but in the wider sense of how, when and why the public has a legitimate interest in private life. My aim in this chapter is to explore the question of values in so far as they relate to the personal or intimate in everyday life. I realize that all these terms are ambiguous: the personal is not necessarily the intimate, for instance, nor is the private in the most basic sense absent from public life. But laying down a framework for intervention, or more optimistically non-intervention, in the sphere of the intimate is an urgent, if tortuous, task.

As a working definition of the area I am concerned with I am going to use that offered by the British political theorist David Held: the sphere of the intimate refers to those circumstances of everyday life where 'people live out their personal lives without systematically harmful consequences for those around them' (Held 1987, p. 293). Such a definition, of course, already begs a number of questions. By defining it in this way, an extension of the classic liberal theory codified by Mill to collective as well as individual lives, the real difficulties are bypassed. If there are no harmful consequences, then surely there can be no case for anyone intervening in the sphere of the intimate. But who is to decide what is harmful and how harmful consequences can be avoided? Who is to guarantee the absence of harm? Who has the right to protect us from ourselves? To state a principle of non-interference, vital though that task is, is easier said than done.

The so-called 'Operation Spanner' case in Britain in the early 1990s illustrates the dilemmas graphically (too graphically, it has to be said, for some people). In December 1990 fifteen homo-sexual men were convicted at the Old Bailey in London for various sadomasochistic (S&M) activities involving beatings and various forms of genital torture, including sandpapering and waxing each others' testicles and passing pins and wires into sundry parts of each others' bodies (see Thompson 1994b). All the activities were carried out in private, all activities were consensual, no one had complained to the police (who secured the arrests as a result of wider enquiries), no one needed medical treatment subsequently, and none of the defendants were even aware that any of their activities were unlawful. Nevertheless, eleven men received sentences of up to four and a half years for assault (later reduced on appeal), and a further twenty-six were cautioned for aiding and abetting assault on themselves, a unique concept. The sentences were handed down by the appropriately named Judge Rant, who made clear his personal repulsion at what had taken place (see Kershaw 1992).

Leaving matters of personal sexual taste aside, the Spanner case is important because it provides a vivid illustration of the dilemmas concerning the limits of sexual choice. On the one hand were a range of consensual sexual activities which explore the complex imbrications of pleasure, pain and power. The search for personal self-expression, even spiritual transcendence, through deliberate pursuit of extreme experiences was undertaken within a ritualized context where the rules were clearly laid down:

> The fact is, S&M is controlled and responsible sexual activity. We have a very highly developed sense of ethics. We have a golden rule that when the bottom [masochist] says enough, the activity stops. The bottom will often use a special word when he or she does not want to go further (quoted in Kershaw 1992, p. 7).

In S&M, it is argued, violence is mediated by an intricate sexual etiquette, pain and mutilation are transcended by intense pleasure, while power and domination are made subservient to erotic play and muted through consent. For the radical sexual activists who organized in Countdown on Spanner to oppose the original judgement, the case raised issues both about the legitimacy of sexual choice, however extreme, and about the right to explore sexuality to the limits. For the liberals who supported them in the resulting *cause célèbre* this became an issue of private space, with the emphasis on the significance of consent in justifying sexual choice, however personally distasteful the activities might appear. The appeals were based on the arguments that the convictions violated the European Convention on Human Rights, which guarantees respect for private and family life. In other words, the campaign, and the appeal, argued for an extension of individual privacy from its traditional locale in the family to other forms of social partnership.

For others, however, 'harm' became the central issue. Speaking for the majority decision on appeal to the House of Lords, Lord Justice Templeman declared that:

> The violence of sado-masochistic encounters involved the indulgence of cruelty by sadists and degradation of victims. It was injurious to the participants and unpredictably dangerous (quoted in Herbert 1993, p. 8).

Consent in these circumstances could not justify deliberate harm to body and mind. For some feminists, the argument was wider.

Violence was violence, power and domination was power and domination, and the pursuit of pleasure and the notion of consent could not justify the breach of the norms of mutual care and respect. They represented surrender to male concepts of sex and domination, and the perpetuation of the power of masculine desire, even when women were consensually involved. As a former indulgee in (apparently heterosexual) S&M put it, 'Should women encourage sick male fantasies? . . . Yes, it is wrong to inflict pain – physical and mental – even with consent' (Page 1993; see also Grant 1993, pp. 234–6). The battle-lines were drawn not so much around a necessary divide between the public and the private as around what could legitimately be regarded as of solely private concern when potential 'harm' was at stake.

Sadomasochistic activities offer a limit-case example of a wider dilemma. For one person's choice can be another's sin, a transgression too far, or manifestation of harm, not only to the individuals directly concerned, but to the body politic. A number of issues in recent years have focused the dilemmas. Does the existence and increasing social presence of openly lesbian parents, for example, inflict harm not only on their children but to the wider notion of the family? (Romans 1992). Does an equal age of consent for homosexuals undermine or 'harm' the institution of heterosexuality? (Healey and Mason 1994). Do unmarried mothers weaken the sense of responsibility of their offspring, leading to crime, civil disorder and social harm? (Murray 1994). Is it legitimate to indulge in private one's taste for explicit sexual representations, if such representations offend, or disgust, or inflict violence on, the wider public, and especially women? (Segal and McIntosh 1992). These disparate issues, and many more like them, have become overheated because they raise almost unanswerable questions about the balance between private behaviour and public obligation, personal desire and social responsibility.

In such a confused debate it becomes more than ever important to try to demarcate the sphere of personal life, and to define the significance and meaningfulness of what goes on there. There has been a good deal written in recent years about 'the public and the private' from the point of view of the personal entering the field of politics, but much less debate about safeguarding and guaranteeing the private – except, significantly, when we talk about the family. And even here, as issues of child abuse or the rights and wrongs of parenting underline, the balance between public concern and private rights is a live one. One reason for the reluctance among sexual radicals to demarcate the intimate sphere is, I suspect, that it has demanded such an effort to change the agenda of politics to embrace issues such as gender and sexuality, that any speculation about the personal sphere runs the risk of reprivatizing vital issues. In a climate where returning mentally ill or disabled people to the community – 'community care' – is a code for placing responsibility with the family, and almost certainly the female members of the family, we would be justified in broadening the meanings of the public at the expense of the private. Similarly, after a long struggle to affirm homosexual relationships by 'coming out', lesbian and gay activists might baulk at 'returning to the closet', to the discretion and silence of the private. As recent slogans of activists around HIV and AIDS have grimly underlined: 'silence = death'.

Yet at the same time, and equally legitimately, many of the same people who seek to politicize what has been too heavily privatized, also wish to affirm their 'right to privacy': against arbitrary interventions of church and state, against sexual harassment and public racism. The agonizing within the lesbian and gay communities about the ethics of 'outing' prominent closet homosexuals suggest that there is a deep respect for the privacy of individual sexual choice, even when that choice is obscured by a public avowal of ostentatious and hypocritical heterosexuality (Gross 1993; see also Signorile 1994; Crimp 1993, p. 308; Brill 1990, pp. 128–32). Implicit in a respect for the discretion of private life, broadly conceived, is an assumption that while the personal is indeed frequently political, that does not mean that all personal choices are legitimately the concern of interested others. As Held (1987, p. 292) argues, there is a real danger in an 'unbounded' concept of politics, which by making politics effectively coextensive with all realms of personal as well as social, cultural and economic life, opens all these areas to public regulation and control. In recent years many have become aware of the need to beware the politician who is so certain of his or her moral righteousness that he or she feels free to pronounce, and act, on all areas of life.

So, whatever the often fictitious nature of the demarcations we make, however shaky the boundaries we draw between the public and the private, the personal and the political, we still have to define the limits of legitimate intervention in the sphere of the intimate. The everyday dimensions of social life may not be independent of political life, but they are, as Carole Pateman argues, still *distinct* from it (1985, p. 174).

We need, then, to try to sketch some of the marks of distinction between the public and the private, to explore the values of the intimate, without surrendering to the ever-present urge to find a form of personal morality that would be acceptable to everyone, in the sense that everyone would have to bend a knee to it. My preferred method, on the contrary, is again, to think what we are doing, and we can best do that, I suggest, by exploring those social 'spaces of self-determination', which have emerged in the wake of the transformation of everyday life in recent years (Heller and Fehér 1988, p. 37). There are two key aspects to this: the efforts to redefine the meanings of private and intimate life, and the attempt to articulate the changing values and rights of everyday life.

LOCATING THE PRIVATE

'Private life', the location of the sphere of the intimate, is preoccupied with the things that matter most directly to us as social beings: home, family, friends, sex and love, procreation and childcare, the rhythms of leisure and relaxation, comfort, sadness and happiness. To name them is evidence enough that these are an inescapable part of social life, shaped by complex forces as much as by personal inclination. But the control we have over these ordinary things, vices as well as virtues (Shklar 1984), the space available to us to shape them to our developing needs, is a fact of history, or of conflicting histories. The public/private divide has been shaped in history, in a long evolution.

Most societies seem to need to make some provision for protecting privacy, though what is regarded as private and intimate may vary (Moore 1984). The differentiation of spheres, however, is a product of a traceable history. The ancient Greeks thought that a man who lived only a private life, or who was not permitted to enter the public realm of politics, or like the barbarian did not have one, was not fully human. Today, we do not think primarily of deprivation when thinking of the private sphere (whatever the oppressions and exclusions that may actually go on there). On the contrary, we seek there the enrichment of our individuality, our humanization (Arendt 1958, p. 38), and the meanings that shape our belongings.

Our concepts of privacy and intimacy are a product of a long process of social differentiation characteristic of modernity (Giddens 1992). In the process the meaning of privacy has changed. In the early modern period it referred to the density of civil society, and all those activities, economic as well as social, which sustained the polity, and needed to be safeguarded against arbitrary interference by state officials: property, markets, families, universities, voluntary bodies. But as the concept of the social as a separate sphere developed, so private life came to designate those areas that needed to be sheltered from society, a retreat for spirits in conflict with the demands of organized political and social life (Rosenblum 1987, p. 66). Following Rousseau, an early explorer of intimacy as a rebel against the perversions of society, the romantics' cultivation of the self sanctified the personal sphere as a domain of sensibility against the conventionality of bourgeois society. John Stuart Mill's appeal for toleration was not so much against the arbitrary powers of the state, as against the tyranny of opinion which threatened the flourishing of individual diversity in private life (Mill 1859/ 1975). In our own day, Isaiah Berlin has offered the most influential elaboration of 'negative freedom' as a defence against any interference with the cultivation of individual creativity: privacy becomes a fundamental human need, which should brook no intervention (Berlin 1984).

In the liberal tradition, then, privacy increasingly came to refer to the personal and the intimate in the most individualized sense. And in the process, the boundaries around the personal have also been redefined. By the nineteenth century, the family had become the privileged focus of personal life, but simultaneously changed its meaning. The family was seen, in early liberal thought, as an institution securely located in private life, meaning life in civil society, an institution primarily for transferring property and for cultivating social values and roles. By the nineteenth century, however, it was increasingly perceived as the domain of personal retreat, the protector against the harsh realities of the outside world, the special domain of women, and the haven and emotional sustainer for exhausted working men (Rosenblum 1987; Kern 1992). In the course of the past century, as Giddens (1992) and others have indicated, it also became the focus of intimacy, for the making and remaking of commitments and relationships that define the late modern sphere of the intimate.

Such at least is one history. It suggests simultaneously that personal life has become the intense focus of our day-to-day existence; that its most intense haven is the family; and that, for many conservative commentators at least, it is embattled, threatened by impersonal forces all around, from state interference to the insidious enticements of consumerism (see Mount 1982). Another history, however, has shown us the family in a different light: less as the harmonious focus for the cultivation of our individuality, more as the terrain of conflict, inequalities, sexual tensions, 'compulsory altruism' and often painful obligations.

I do not intend here to enter into a history of the family. My aim rather is to use the family as an illustration of the difficulty of demarcating the space of the personal and the intimate. For the family, as David Morgan has said, is 'both societal and individual, both institutional and personal, both public and private' (1985, p. 285). It is, therefore, a crossroads of many histories and social influences. Far from being the building block of society, the family is one of its most complex products, a 'series of multi-layered relationships folded over on each other like geological strata' (Connell 1987, p. 121). Nowhere else, it can be argued, are relationships so extended in time, so intensive and dense in their marriage of economics, power and resistance, and yet so vulnerable to the whims of desire and the challenge of self-making.

It may be easier to accept today than in the more libertarian climate of the 1960s that the family is both 'special' and privileged in our culture: special by reason of its moral density, its continuity over time, the responsibilities it evokes; privileged both in the commitments we make it, and in its position in ideology, morality and social policy (Finch 1989). At the same time, as we are now more willing than in the past to admit, the obligations we feel and the work we do for the family are filtered through the gauze of cultural difference and gender inequalities; these obligations are historically constructed, not a simple product of nature.

As Janet Finch (1989) has shown, the shared meanings of the family generate a 'hierarchy of obligations' – to spouse above all, to children, to siblings and others, in which women rather than men emerge as carers. The obligations spring from the accepted common sense of everyday life, and are sustained by a vague public opinion, expressed through gossip, reputation, family pride, scandal and so on. But the point I want to draw out of this analysis is that despite the weight of opinion, and historical tradition, this is a 'negotiated order', not an inevitable or permanent one. 'There is a sense', Finch has argued, 'in which all assistance between relatives must be the subject of negotiations about when it is to be given, by whom, for how long, and on what terms' (1989, p. 55). These negotiations are not between absolutely free agents; they are structured by a host of assumptions, not least those governing the proper responsibilities of women and men. The family is a contested space, where there is room for manoeuvre, but also explicit and tacit limits.

Family intimacy, then, has its limits. The majority may still see 'the family' as a repository of values, as the ideal to which we all aspire. Certainly, politicians see it as a powerful totem around which policies can be developed; and more generally, 'family' remains a word which evokes a warm glow and a sense of 'home'. The alternative languages of belonging are feeble and aetiolated in comparison with the language of family. Yet for some, the pursuit of intimacy may involve escaping from the embrace of its ostensibly natural home, the family. And social differentiation, which has marked off the family as a special institution, has created other social spaces where intimacy may be pursued. As I have already indicated, in the anonymity of cities in western Europe from at least the seventeenth century there developed an increasingly complex male homosexual subculture, with its intricate rituals, argot, modes of recognition and, above all, sexual intimacy (Gerard and Hekma 1988, Weeks 1977/1990; Chauncey 1994). In the romantic friendships of women, or even in the more mundane patterns of female interaction around domestic and reproduction worries, we see a very different but parallel history of intimate involvement, like the male partly in and partly outside the family (Smith-Rosenberg 1985; Faderman 1981; *Feminist Studies* 1992). The history is not necessarily evolutionary or continuous, but in such cultures of intimacy, different from those of the family, we can see precursors of the lesbian and gay communities of the late twentieth century. The emergence of these 'elective communities', communities of choice rather than ascription, has provided a space for the development of personal life – and new types of intimacy, affection and friendship (see Nardi 1992).

Our concepts of privacy have not yet, however, caught up with this social change. Take the 'right to privacy'. Its origins lay not in any concern for fundamental human rights, but in English and colonial American opposition to general warrants to enter and search for broad categories of material. It was part of a general defence against classic abuses of governmental authority. As the means of surveillance have changed – especially the advance of electronic means – the right to privacy has become a more urgent claim, for the protection of the privacy of our individuality as much as our property (Rosenblum 1987, pp. 67–72).

But the right is limited. It has long been applied to family matters, but it has not been extended to lesbians and gays in the pursuit of their sexual preferences. As with all claims to right, the value framework within which rights are formulated is all important. The freedoms of everyday life are constantly governed by a host of assumptions embedded in the practices of public life about what constitutes proper behaviour, and these shape what should be regarded as appropriately private.

Yet at the same time, the private fights back against public definitions. As Agnes Heller has observed in her book entitled *Everyday Life*:

> It is from the conflicts of everyday life that the greater conflicts of society in the main are generated: answers have to be found to the questions thrown up in these conflicts, and no sooner are these settled than they reappear to re-shape and re-structure every-day life anew (1984, p. 47).

'Private life' has generated the social movements, around sex, gender, race, the quality of life, which have significantly changed the political agenda – and in so doing have shifted the boundaries between public and private. They have also, as we have seen, affected the ways in which we try to define our personhood, and our identities – identities which themselves dwell on the borderlines of the public and the private – and have thus begun to change the meaning of what it is to be an individual in society. In the process, as Brill (1990, p. 4) has noted, privacy has moved from a passive claim, to be left alone, to an active right to do and be as you wish, as long as certain conditions are met.

The question then is: what should these conditions be? In trying to respond to this the AIDS epidemic, as in so many other areas of sexual life, provides some key insights. AIDS, as Brill suggests, provides a 'new prism' for understanding privacy: 'Once articulated, AIDS is the pebble in the lake causing ripple after ripple of privacy invasion' (1990, p. 101). But it also offers a way of understanding the new possibilities of intimacy. AIDS, as we have seen, arrived on the scene in the early 1980s, precisely as the conservative reaction against the liberalism and relativism of the 1960s and 1970s was gathering pace. For the moral right it came to symbolize the inevitable effects of a breaching of the old boundaries, and the abandonment of old verities. *The Times* (London), in a notorious leader (19 February 1985), saw AIDS as dissolving the social contract which kept the private and the public separate, 'the trust on which social life is built, the trust which allows us to separate and tolerate private conduct, even of an immoral and exotic kind, from the public business of society'.

By implication, the spread of AIDS justified the imposition of new controls on private behaviour. AIDS, Ronald Bayer argues:

> has represented a challenge to the central impulse of liberal individualism, forcing into the social realm matters that had come to be viewed as of no legitimate concern; it has revealed the limits of the ideology that has provided the wellspring of cultural and political reform (1991, p. 191).

The claims for the absolute rights of the individual to choose his or her sexual behaviour, Bayer is suggesting, came up against the absolute right of society to be protected against the threat of a devastating risk to the reproductive chain as well as the health and well-being of the population as a whole. Questions of the regulation of personal behaviour inevitably became a key policy issue. In practice, in most Western countries at least, attempts were made to balance the rights of the individual and the needs of society, to measure, for example, the individual's right to confidentiality against the community's claim to protection, as in the question of compulsory testing for HIV. In the best practice, not invariably followed, alas, health education and safer-sex advocacy sought to advertise risk without wiping out choice. But this was relatively successful in limiting infection, at least in the gay communities of Western countries, because it tied in with a wider development, the growth of a sense of mutual responsibility among those most at risk. This was a direct result of the broadening of the arena of private space through the construction of sexualized communities where the possibilities of safer sexual behaviour could be easily discussed and developed (King 1993, Weeks 1993c, Segal 1994).

In practice, this meant the elaboration of a sexual etiquette in which the individual actors could attempt not so much to eliminate all risk of coming into contact with HIV, but rather to seek a balance between risk and trust in sexual contacts by a pragmatic adoption of 'safer sex', geared to the specific context of sexual relationships. For example, studies of the phenomenon of 'relapse' from safer-sex guidelines in gay relationships reveal a very complex set of private negotiations between partners taking place. Partners who engage in 'risky' sexual behaviour, such as unprotected anal intercourse, often do so as part of a trade-off between desire, commitment and trust in an ongoing partnership. In the intimacy of the partnership itself, unprotected sex may take place, while casual sexual encounters outside that relationship are governed by the etiquette of safer sex (Hart et al. 1992, Davies et al. 1993; Kippax et al. 1993). In other words, simple injunctions from the public sphere to avoid unsafe sex are mediated through the intricacies of personal experience and values, where choices are made which are relevant to the intimate needs and experiences of the actors involved.

The implications of this are both negative and positive. On the negative side is the perpetuation of risk, of the transmission of the virus, even as, or perhaps because, the risky acts are expressions of trust and commitment. Researchers into the sexual attitudes and behaviour of young women in the context of HIV and AIDS have suggested that an awareness of risk has always to be negotiated through the reality of male sexual power within and outside intimate relations. As Ramazanoglu and Holland observe:

> Although a few young women had reflected very critically upon their experience and set out to change their relationships with men and men's control over them, such reflection was difficult to achieve and very difficult to practise consistently . . . Women's sexuality is contradictory in both contesting men's power, and contributing to its continued success, through women constituting themselves as acceptably feminine (1993, p. 260).

This suggests again that the precondition for successful negotiation of intimacy, and in this case 'safer sex', is the openness that can come only from a sense of mutuality between equal partners, which in turn is predicated on a community of values which validates those principles. The evidence suggests that the continuing stigma against homosexuality (Davies et al. 1993), and the survival of male sexual domination and female 'complicity'

(Coward 1992) perpetuate risk in individual negotiation of sexual banne-
encounters – and hence the continuation of unsafe sexual
activity.

But on the positive side, there is plentiful evidence also that
where intimacy is developed within a culture of individual and
collective responsibility and care, then the sexual imagination
can flourish, even run riot, with a minimum of risk. The culture
as a whole may shiver at telephone sex lines, 'jack-off parties' and
safer-sex orgies, the sexualization of leather and rubber clothes,
computer sex, sex toys, or consensual S&M, which whatever its
other pains and pleasures tends to downplay penetrative sex.
Only a perverse moral imagination could see this 'eroticization
of the whole body' as 'wrong' when compared with the risk of
transmission of HIV through unprotected and unsafe sex; the
epidemic has not so much invented (we live, after all in a poly-
morphously unperverse world) as highlighted the incitement to
sexual experimentation (Altman 1986).

Hart et al. refer to 'the intimacy and coterminousity of public
and private concerns' (1992, p. 230) in the AIDS epidemic. There
is, inevitably, a legitimate public concern in the behaviour of
individual actors in so far as their actions may have public effects.
But as the examples above illustrate, the most obvious responses
– moral injunction and moralistic evaluation – are not necessarily,
perhaps never, the most effective, or ethically valid, approach.
On the contrary, the most effective response is to provide a social
framework within which responsible and active agency and safe
erotic experimentation becomes possible. It is not what you do,
but how you do it that should matter.

Two implications can be drawn from the active concept of
privacy sketched here. The first follows the logic of the emergence of contemporary sexual politics: that no issue relating to
private life should *a priori* be forcibly excluded from public concern (see Young 1987). It is, as I have suggested, from the changing spheres of private life that many of the most important issues
of contemporary politics have emerged. It is vital that the problems generated in intimate life should reach the political agenda
as necessary. But the obverse of this is also true: no issue of
private behaviour should become a public issue if it conforms to

the broad principles and values expressed in the concept of radical toleration. If, as Heller (1987) argues, the key issue is whether it is possible to find a common normative standard by which we can come to terms with different ways of life, then no intrusion into private life can be just if it offends or undermines that standard, and the values that sustain it. Heller argues for a standard based on the two minimum universal values, of freedom and life. Social systems and forms of regulation can be regarded as just in so far as they share common institutions, maximize the opportunities for communication and discourse, and are controlled by the conditional value of equality: 'equal freedom' and 'equal life chances' for all. In a pluralistic cultural universe, there are 'good lives': 'Different ways of life can be good, and can be equally good. Yet a lifestyle good for one person may not be good for another person' (Heller 1987, p. 323).

It follows that the radically different life goals and patterns of life of different people should be beyond formal regulation to the extent that they are based on the conditions of equal freedom and equal life chances.

What does this mean in practice in thinking about the intimate sphere? It involves, I am going to argue, the need to elaborate certain rights of everyday life. The right to privacy can be guaranteed only as part of a wider recognition of certain other key claims, which provide the basis of intimate citizenship.

THE RIGHTS OF EVERYDAY LIFE

For most of the period since World War II, rights have been central to the progressive agenda: the rights of individuals to certain freedoms, and increasingly from the 1960s the rights of minorities to access to public goods. Now there is a developing reaction against what has pejoratively and dismissively been called 'rightism' (as a *locus classicus* of this developing position see Selbourne 1994). The clamant demands of militant minorities, including sexual minorities, it is argued, do not resolve conflict of value or different ethical claims; they merely institutionalize them, with victory going to the loudest, not the most just (if we could only decide who had the most just case). Increasingly, critics argue for responsibilities to balance rights, and the sonorous word 'obligation' has reemerged to offer a master discourse in which rights can be subordinated to what Selbourne (1994) calls the 'principle of duty'.

I have argued, however, that the inadequacy of rights-based arguments lies not in the claim to right in itself, but in the absence of a wider social context in which the notion of rights becomes meaningful (Weeks 1993b). A claim to individual right which abrogates our concern for, and involvement with, others is clearly an appeal to individual good over social responsibility and collective involvement. As such it fails to match the need for that sense of mutuality and 'lightness of care' which has to be the hallmark of a radically pluralist culture. But there are areas of private life, where interference is illegitimate because it denies the possibility of human interactions which add to the general good even while they ostensibly concern only the intimate sphere. This is especially the case when those interactions express minority, even unpopular, lifestyle choices. The kind of 'regulated privacy' (Brill 1990, p. 190), which is encoded in law and custom and which currently organizes intimate life, is based on the assumption that everyday rights are dependent on an ability to force a case on to the public agenda, or on the fortunate coincidence that you happen to share the tastes of the contingently reigning majority. A clarification of intimate rights as the guarantee of intimate citizenship is especially necessary not when we all want to live the same way but when we want to explore our differences, without undermining that wider sense of belonging on which the unfolding of diversity depends.

The need for equal freedom and equal life chances for all is in the end dependent on our willingness to recognize an 'equality of vulnerability' (Brill 1990, p. 190): our equal fallibility in negotiating the conditions of our intimate life; our equal propensity to failure and disappointment as well as happiness and personal transcendence; the equal likelihood that one day we will fall ill, and the certainty that eventually we will all die. Our equality as human beings requires an awareness of the validity of other people's often painful choices as well as the importance of our own in the contingent circumstances in which we live.

It is in this light that it is important, indeed indispensable, to clarify the rights of everyday life, not so much to encode them in statute, but rather to embed them in the practices of daily life. Three rights, I suggest, are crucial: the right to difference, the right to space, and the twin rights of exit and voice.

The right to difference

The right to equality, Melucci (1989, p. 178) has suggested, under whose banner all modern revolutions have been fought, is being replaced by the right to difference. This does not mean that equality has been won, for in many parts of the world the emancipatory project embodied in the claim to equality has barely begun. The right to difference goes beyond this in a critical way, however: it seeks to establish that equality of access to goods is a precondition for, but not the defining element of, an equality of care and concern for individual variety and choice. The recognition of diversity and a respect for individual differences opens the way for new definitions of autonomy and authenticity, and for the development of notions of community, toleration and human solidarity that offer new possibilities for mutual involvement. The freedom to have is, Melucci (1989, p. 177) suggests, being replaced by the freedom to be; a freedom from needs is being replaced by a freedom of needs, in a situation where our dependence on each other as fellow citizens of a vulnerable spaceship earth is becoming apparent to us.

In practical terms the right to difference endorses the value of sexual choices and experimentations which enhance individual growth and sexual exploration, while not offending the equal claims and autonomy of involved and consenting others. It is perfectly conceivable that these explorations will offend countless people, but in an intensely plural society there appears to be no grounds for imposing one's own personal tastes on others if their actions can have no effect on you. The central idea of the endorsement of a right to difference is a respect for different ways of being human, and a recognition of the various ways that potentially exist for achieving your self-defined ends. That respect, however, is dependent on, conditioned by, a respect for people's equal freedom, life chances, and vulnerability as fellow human beings. It depends, in other words, on the relationships in which agency occurs. If values are irredeemably plural and contextual, and the social relations that govern them are necessarily contingent, then all we have by which to judge an act is the context and meaning of that act, the set of human relations within which it takes place.

A relational perspective necessarily involves an awareness of context: of the power relations that shape individual action, of the subtle coercion of daily life which limit autonomy, as well of the greater pressures of social life that provide the limits as well as the opportunities for social action and individual agency (see Weeks 1986). But a right to diversity also involves a recognition of the variety of relationship patterns that provide the space for individual growth and the dense ties of intimate life. If, as Agnes Heller (1987) argues, in late modernity these ties have become 'emaciated', then what Jean Bethke Elshtain calls the 'redemption of everyday life' (1981, p. 335) requires their invigoration and reaffirmation.

The danger is, however, that the redemption will be simply a reassertion of a narrowly familial model of intimate life at the expense of denying the reality of other patterns of intimacy. Elshtain (1981, p. 322) herself strongly affirms that 'familial ties and modes of child-rearing are essential to establish the minimal foundations of human, social existence', and by this very statement apparently invalidates different forms of intimate life. In this, though a liberal feminist, she is clearly at one with the conservative reassertion of family values that appeals to many on the left as well as the right of the political spectrum. Yet many of the obligations of family life she lauds are also present in the alternative focuses of daily life. A sense of moral involvement with others, of common belonging sustained over time, without expectation of direct or immediate reward, except that of mutual support, is characteristic of what Ann Ferguson (1989) has called 'chosen families', whether of lesbians and gays or others who choose to live outside conventional domestic arrangements (see also Weston 1991). It is also a marked feature of the support systems built up as a response to the AIDS crisis, where gay men especially have evolved an ethic of care that embodies many of the values traditionally associated with the ideal of family life (Adam 1992).

Relationships built on a sense of equal vulnerability and mutual care are, as Giddens (1992) has indicated, inherently democratic in their dynamics. In terms of sexual relationships, democratic values would judge acts by the way people deal with each other, the absence of coercion, the degree of pleasure and need they can satisfy. But as Giddens (1992) also points out, there is a need in democratized relationships for authority to be based on commitments. Heterosexual marriage remains the key signifier of commitment, but there are other focuses of personal life where 'self-assumed obligation' (Pateman 1988, p. 178) and overt commitment have begun to redefine the balance between sexual intimacy and friendship.

This is most obvious in the case of the bonding that takes place in the highly politicized contexts of the social movements. Raymond (1986) has spoken of the 'passion for friends' that characterizes relations between women, and Orbach and Eichenbaum have argued that changes in the position of women over the past generation, not least the impact of the women's movement, have given women the chance to evolve friendships that go beyond merged attachments: 'We have the opportunity to acknowledge our need for other women as well as our need for recognition and acceptance of our autonomous selves' (quoted in Limb, 1989, p. 45).

In lesbian and gay communities, as Nardi (1992) observes, friendships take on many of the roles of families. Finch (1994; see also Finch and Mason 1993) has noted the growing rather than diminishing importance of the extended support offered by families of origins in the wake of the social developments of the 1990s (weakening welfare provision, the growth of divorce, changing opportunities of inheritance). For many lesbian and gay people, faced equally by rapid social change as well as the perpetuation of stigma, this sort of support is provided through friendship networks:

> For gay men and lesbians, social approval of intimate relations is typically absent or limited by legal, religious, and cultural norms. For some, their families of origin (parents, siblings, and other close relatives) may not acknowledge or legitimize gay people's friendships and relationships. In the context of these social constraints and the need to sustain a sense of self, friendship takes on the role provided by heterosexual families (Nardi 1992, pp. 109–10).

In both heterosexual and homosexual cases, however, a similar social tendency is evident. The weakening of would-be lifelong sexual unions in the case of heterosexual life, in favour of patterns of serial monogamy, and the less institutionalized nature of sexual partnerships among lesbians and gay men, where emotional loyalty is frequently combined with casual sexual encounters (see Davies et al. 1993), means that it becomes problematic to place all one's emotional trust for a lifetime in one other person, whatever the incentives and desire to do so. Sexual involvement and emotional support may become detached from one another. Friends, especially in the case of lesbians and gays, thus assume an essential emotional support in intimate life:

> In addition to providing opportunities for expressions of intimacy and identity, friendships for gay men and lesbians serve as sources for various kinds of social support (ranging from the monetary to health care) and provide them with a network of people with whom they can share celebrations, holidays, and other transitional rituals (Nardi 1992, p. 112).

The psychoanalyst Heinz Kohut (quoted in Little 1989, p. 149) has argued that friendships flourish when overarching identities are fragmented in periods of rapid social change, or at turning-points in people's lives, and he relates it to lives lived at odds with social norms. Friendships are portable, they can be sustained at a distance, yet they can allow the individual who is uprooted to feel constantly confirmed through changing social experiences. Such developments offer the possibility of developing new patterns of intimacy which may be, but are not necessarily, sexualized.

Commitments, then, can take many, diverse forms, ranging from intense sexual-emotional bonding to intimate though often desexualized friendships. They are also widespread, even though many have yet to achieve social recognition, and therefore tend to be absent from the development of social policies or public validation. How, asked Wendy Mulford (1993), in an obituary notice of her friend Carol Kendrick:

> do we meet the loss of someone who has been an integral part of our inner lives and development, and yet to whom we have, in our society, no recognized familial bond? For whom there can be no public space of recognition of our loss? . . . In our funeral service we tried to celebrate her in our own way, and yet I still feel we did not quite do justice to the passionate commitment she had to maintaining an open network of intimate loving friendships, reciprocally founded on mutual respect and care, in place of the traditional nuclear family.

However much they lack public affirmation, developments such as these in the 'subterranean social order' provide the space for other changes in sexual-social patterns, many of which have become lightning conductors of social anxiety, especially in relation to parenting. The flurries of uncertainty around lesbian and gay parenting, for example, underline the fear that changes in the apparently 'natural order' of intimate life evokes. It is noticeable that moves towards the recognition of legal partnership arrangements ('partnership rights') among lesbians and gay men specifically exclude rights to adoption (Bech 1992a), while conception through donor insemination among lesbians has provoked acute political concern (Mason 1994; Saffron 1994).

At the same time, the fact of these developments is producing a grudging recognition of the need to adjust social responses in the interests of the offspring. A lesbian couple made legal history in June 1994 in Britain by being granted joint parental responsibility. Making the order, the judge said the 'child's welfare was

paramount. The evidence pointed overwhelmingly in its favour'
(*The Guardian*, 30 June 1994). The right to diversity, in sexual
behaviour and in domestic arrangements, is, it appears, being
tacitly accepted in many areas of social life, even though formal
recognition is often tardy and reluctant. The truth is that many
of the changes that are taking place in intimate arrangements
are unstoppable, despite the best endeavours of politicians and
social moralists. The challenge is to provide the social opportunities where they can be fully legitimized, and this brings us to the
second right of everyday life, the right to space.

The right to space

The idea of a space for personal life is a useful metaphor for the
freedom of individuals to determine the needs and conditions
of their lives, on the assumption that this freedom does not
involve the use of another person as a mere means. But the
notion of 'life spaces' (Bech 1992b) transcends the private/
public divide, for what we are talking about is the development
of the possibilities of private life through the growth of public
opportunities. The idea of the city offers a microcosm of the
challenge and the dangers.

It was the growth of the city, with its physical density and moral
anonymity, which provided the possibilities for lives lived at odds
with the norms and values of the culture, both private in that
they expressed personal needs and desires, and often had to be
protected from the threat of exposure and possible social dis-
grace, and public in that new social spaces offered the chance
for different ways of life. Both are made possible by the city,
distant physically and mentally from the normalizing values and
idiocies of traditional life, a peopled world of enforced proximity
where nevertheless space can be carved out for sexual exchange.
As Iris Young (1990) notes, the city instantiates difference as the
erotic, offering the chance to be drawn out of one's routines, to
encounter difference, novelty, the strange and exciting.

The opportunities remain different for men and women, but
for those trapped in rigid roles, male or female, the possibilities

are potentially great. The city, it has been argued, with its mixture of terror and opportunity has provided the space for women to become autonomous beings:

> The city offers women freedom. After all, the city normalises the carnivalesque aspects of life . . . Perhaps the 'disorder' of urban life does not so much disturb women. If this is so, it may be because they have not internalised as rigidly as men a need for over-rationalistic control and authoritarian order. The socialisation of women renders them less dependent on duality and opposition; instead of setting nature against the city, they find nature *in* the city. For them, that invisible city, the 'second city', the underworld or secret labyrinth, instead of being sinister or diseased . . . is an Aladdin's cave of riches. Yet at the same time, it is a place of danger for women (Wilson 1991, pp. 8–9).

It has also provided the possibilities of the anonymous bars, clubs, cruising grounds, 'communities of the night', where first homosexual men, and later lesbians and other erotic outsiders could make sexual and emotional contacts, and develop sexualized identities (see the essays in Duberman, Vicinus and Chauncey 1989). The city has been a breeding ground for sexual diversity, 'a space of pleasure, ecstasy and desire. The city as endless possibility. A confusion of happenings which one can never quite see, understand, order, because they occur simultaneously' (Squires 1994, pp. 80–1), in the public places where private pleasure may be pursued.

Electronic means of communication have compounded both the opportunities and the dangers, anonymizing and distancing in a new way while offering the possibilities of a form of mediated intimacy. Telephone sex lines offer unlimited scope for fantasy and the elaboration of new codes of sexual behaviour, safe from the danger of the promiscuous interchange of bodily fluids. Interactive videos and computer sex offer a virtual reality where bodies become cyborgs. Space ceases to be merely geographical, and becomes infinitely expansive into the realms of the mind and fantasy.

New forms of spatial relations also, however, produce demands for new forms of regulation. The computer has not only produced a new sexualized space, it also encourages new forms of sexual aggression and harassment. Telephone sex promotes safe sex over a distance, but also gives new opportunities for access to sexualization for the young and the vulnerable. Pleasure and danger meet again, in the life spaces on the ground, in the air and in the mind.

These spaces are therefore contested spaces. Intimate interactions in the bedroom, over the telephone, in the streets, on the computer, can be dragged into public view and broadcast to millions. The sucked toe of a duchess in a private garden is on the front page of scandal sheets within hours; fantasies on the phone of a Prince of Wales are transcribed in our morning newspapers, and available to listen to on special toll-free lines. Intimate interactions, yes, but an intimacy devoured by millions, because the electronic and print media, with their own specific agenda, moral and political as well as commercial, have new powers to invade the private. Similarly, geographical spaces are often fought over, sometimes violently. A public sex environment used by gay men may be subjected both to police harassment and waves of 'queer-bashing' as the wheels of different sexual mores grind together. The fear of rape limits the freedom of women, and sometimes men, to walk the streets of the city.

The right to space, then, can never be an absolute right. Like all rights it has to be based on certain common terms, a 'grammar of conduct', the rules of the space (Squires 1994, p. 98). The endorsement of diversity requires a minimum of solidarity, and therefore agreement over what constitutes a legitimate space for private interactions and for public display.

Take the question of dress, with its heavily coded sexual referents. Ordinary common sense might dictate that matters of taste in appearance must be regarded as purely private matters, yet this is easier asserted than worked out in practice. Long hair and hippy clothes in the 1960s generated untold moral fury. Even in the more secluded world of the erotic minorities, matters of dress have driven the righteous to high levels of apoplectic energy. The London Lesbian and Gay Centre almost fell apart in the mid-1980s over the arcane issue of whether members should be allowed to enter wearing leather jackets and what could be construed as Nazi-type insignia (Ardill and O'Sullivan 1987). What you wear or how you look may seem of entirely individual concern, but we know that to many people it matters. Clothes can be a political statement, and can evoke a political response.

A recent example illustrates the complex issues at play. In both France and Britain almost simultaneously at the end of 1989 controversies erupted concerning the wearing of headscarves by young Muslim girls in schools. The issue took on a slightly different flavour in each country. In France many, especially on the secular left, saw the girls' claim as impinging on the hard-won attempt to free the education system of religious influence (Marnham 1989). Wearing the scarf, in compliance with fundamentalist demands, was seen as a threat to secular and republican values. A compromise was reached initially which did in fact allow the use of headscarves, but in 1994 the French education minister issued new instructions to headteachers discouraging their use, though appealing to his respondents 'to convince rather than force' (*The Independent*, 15 September 1994).

In Britain, a very similar incident, in the wake of the controversies raised by the Salman Rushdie affair, brought to the fore the question of the limits and possibility of multicultural education, and the gendered response that Islamic traditions concerning female modesty appeared to require. Two young Muslim girls who had worn white scarves to a local school in Greater Manchester were barred thirteen times from attending until they conformed to school rules of dress. But as the father of one of the girls said: 'education is secondary; faith comes first' (*The Guardian*, 24 January 1990). A compromise was eventually reached which allowed the girls to wear scarves, on written request from their parents, as long as they were in the school colours (*The Independent*, 24 January 1990).

In both cases, what seemed on one level matters of individual taste became charged public issues because of their links with the larger battles in society concerning different cultural traditions and faiths, but also different versions of the female body and moral values. Bhatt notes, for instance, how:

absolutist interventions into these spaces [of gender and sexual

experimentation] can have contingent, highly contradictory out-
comes. Asian feminists have pointed out how the demand for
separate schools for Muslim girls ... the wearing of headscarfs
and modest clothing and the regulation and control of women's
private and public spaces betrays a fundamental concern with the
body. In the need to regulate the voyage of the body, the need to
shield, contain, conceal and repress it, attention is paradoxically
focused on it, and new resistive bodies are produced (1994,
p. 159).

Clearly, what a young Muslim girl wears is not freely chosen,
given that certain standards of discretion and modesty are written
into long traditions. On the other hand, it is difficult to see why
the clothes one wears should concern anyone else as long as they
are not imposed by force or become a danger to others (in fact
in the British case, the school had argued that headscarves were
potentially dangerous in the gymnasium and the laboratories,
though they got round this eventually by insisting that they be
tight-fitting). In the end, the question of what you wear, whether
in a gay club or a school, whatever the wider issues, must be
regarded as matters of cultural taste, however offensive that might
be to some people. It becomes of public concern, however, when
appearance becomes a weapon in, say, the advocacy of violence
(as with a fascist uniform adopted for political purposes), or as
a mark of a fundamentalism which threatens to impinge on the
space of others.

The dilemma lies in the extent to which moral pluralism can
accommodate ('tolerate') a faith which is itself intolerant and
has absolutist and hegemonic claims. Heller comments that:

If people are imprisoned, tortured, killed, humiliated, even discriminated against within particular cultures it is then, and only
then, that the sense of justice enjoins us to apply exactly the same
standards to all of them. Whether women wear veils or mini-skirts
is a matter of particular (unique) cultural taste. However, should
they be *forced* to wear veils, it ceases to be a matter of "cultural
uniqueness" and becomes a matter of coercion or force (1987,
p. 44).

Moral pluralism, and radical tolerance, can work only if individuals and groups are prepared to accept that a condition of freedom for their way of life is a tolerance of others. Protection of minorities must be a condition of a plural society. But within the minorities themselves there is the further requirement, the guarantee of the freedom of individuals. Social pluralism and the proliferation of associations do not necessarily guarantee variety or autonomy for all its members. The intertwined rights to enter, to leave and to speak thus become the critical guarantee of the right to space.

The rights of exit and of voice

I have already cited the warning of Rosenblum (1987) that in pluralist societies membership can be as ascriptive and stifling as in traditionalist societies. Individuals must be free to enter and to leave. Bauman (1988), following a similar line of argument, after A. O. Hirschman (1970), has elaborated an important distinction between the freedom of exit, which he describes as a private freedom, and freedom of voice, which is a public freedom (Bauman 1988, p. 98). Both, he argues, are critical in offering means by which citizens can attempt to exercise control over those who would seek to dominate them.

Freedom of exit in itself suggests a double-sided right: to belong to collectivities of one's choice, and to have the freedom to withdraw from such collectivities when their norms inhibit your freedom to be what you want to be. Such tensions have often come to focus on the position of young women and gays in the family values of minority ethnic community families, as Bhatt (1994, 1995) observes, but it is a wider issue.

Embeddedness, Rosenblum (1987) comments, means you can get stuck. Yet resistance may involve the painful exit from communities of support at a time of great vulnerability, at 'fateful moments' (Giddens 1991) of identity development. Protection of the individual's freedom involves support for a freedom to leave, but it also requires the freedom to speak out with and through others. Support of the private right of exit involves a recognition of a more public right, to have your voice heard. This public freedom of voice is in fact the guarantee of all the freedoms and rights of everyday life. Morality, as Michael Walzer has put it, is 'something we have to argue about' (1987, p. 32). There is no final end, no final proof of what is right or wrong – only the possibility of continuing debate about it.

The idea that the condition for a good life is continuous dialogue provides a yardstick by which we can measure the degree of tolerance of a culture (or a way of life within the culture). It directs our attention to the forces that inhibit free communication. It is also a device by which we can pragmatically align ourselves within debates, and with others in communities of identity. Communication, dialogue, is a condition of the good life not only because it refuses to close debate. It is also the necessary condition for changing the terms of the debate, for effecting change in individual and intimate as well as public life.

In his essay 'On Liberty' Mill endorsed 'experiments in living' on the grounds that:

> There is always need of persons not only to discover new truths, and point out when what were once truths are true no longer, but also to commence new practices (1859/1975, p. 79).

Freedom, autonomy, as Foucault (1988a) observed, does not exist before its practice. Hence the three principles of his morals:

> (1) the refusal to accept as self-evident the things that are proposed to us; (2) the need to analyse and to know, since we can understand nothing without reflection and understanding – thus the principle of curiosity; and (3) the principle of innovation: to seek out in our reflection those things that have never been thought or imagined. Thus: refusal, curiosity, innovation (Foucault 1988a, p. 1).

It is only through a radical toleration of experimentations that these can be tried out and measured against experience, and it is only through continuous dialogue that these can be properly tested. The condition for this, in turn, is the recognition that the best means of continuing the dialogue is the endorsement of the values both of belonging and difference. Practices of freedom require no less.

5

Caught between Worlds and Ways of Being

————————————

Hate is not a family value.

Choose love/Choose life/Kiss the future.
Slogans on tee-shirts, early 1990s

Gently they go, the beautiful, the tender, the kind;
Quietly they go, the intelligent, the witty, the brave.
I know. But I do not approve. And I am not resigned.
Edna St. Vincent Millay, 'Dirge without Music'

PROLOGUE

... to utter the name is a sign of health.
Susan Sontag, The Way We Live Now

Two images. Two worlds?

The first image is by the American pop artist Robert Indiana: his famous series of paintings, sculptures and prints of the 1960s that spell out the word LOVE in a strong graphic formation. The letters are blocked, the L and an (italicized) O placed above the V and the E, in a powerful design that stands as a symbol of the 'decade of love and peace', and of violence and war, in which it was produced. It offers an iconic challenge to the depradations of hate from the reparations of hope. In the years that followed the image circulated round the world: in the form of sculptures, posters, the New York Museum of Modern Art's most popular postcard, wallpaper design, and, according to the artist, '333 million *Love* stamps'. It was also, says Indiana, 'the most ripped-off piece of art the world has ever seen', its originator having failed to copyright the design (Petrow 1992, p. 74).

Here we have a powerful image which presumably spoke to the easy aspirations of millions ('all you need is love . . .'). It also became, as Indiana's rueful comment suggests, a vibrant element in the commercialization of its referent. LOVE sells, and was sold in millions, circulating like any other commodity around the global economy: 'love is all you need . . .'.

The second image is less easy. In the summer of 1993 the San Francisco Museum of Modern Art hosted an exhibition, one stop on an international tour, called *Fin de siècle*, consisting of a number of installations by the Canadian artists' group General Idea (1992). Outside the museum was a sculptural form, in lacquered metal, promiscuously covered in graffiti and stickers, echoing Indiana's design, but this time the word was 'AIDS'. In the exhibition itself the blocked letters provided the dominating, multi-coloured motif. LOVE obliterated by AIDS?

The General Idea design is powerfully ambivalent, evoking and ironically mocking the ambiguities aroused by *its* referent. Like the original this graphic has already circulated widely, from posters to mass-transit decoration to a lighting display in Times Square, New York. 'We see the logo', one of the members of General Idea is quoted as saying, 'as a virus travelling through media and channels of communication', and through widespread dissemination becoming as ubiquitous a part of today's symbolic language as LOVE was in the 1960s (*At the Modern*, San Francisco Museum of Modern Art, July-August 1993, p. 2).

AIDS, it seems, has become in the late twentieth century a mediatory term between love and death. Nineteenth-century Romanticism purported to see a necessary association between the two: only in death, with all obstacles finally obliterated, was true erotic fulfilment truly possible. Now, acts of sexual love, painfully, may set us on the path towards disease and death. The central installation of the *Fin de siècle* exhibition, which also gave the name for the whole event, nods a homage to Caspar David Friedrich's early nineteenth-century masterpiece *The Death of the Hope*, which shows a ship helplessly trapped by mountainous icebergs. That painting's sense of desolation and entrapment is also suggested in General Idea's installation, a pile of white, frostily illuminated polystyrene slabs representing ice floes. Enthroned in glacial isolation on top are three stuffed baby seals, representing perhaps the signature of the three members of General Idea, but also a wider sense of the isolation, imprisonment and hopelessness that an epidemic might evoke.

But naming the danger is also an act of hope, the General Idea's image appears to be suggesting. For the circulation of the imagery of AIDS, pursuing the global circulation of the virus, is a process of giving voice, placing and challenge, and therefore of recuperation. In the same exhibition was another installation: 12,000 little putti (ordinarily defined as representations of children as cherubs, nude or in swaddling bands). These were made of soap, again in the shape of seals, placed in an increasingly amorphous shape in the middle of the floor of a gallery. Visitors were invited to pick up one of these symbols of a sort of knowing innocence, and in so doing contribute $10 to support HIV and AIDS organizations in San Francisco. In choosing these little soap objects the participants were shaping the constantly changing appearance of the installation, just as our individual and collective actions shape the pattern of the epidemic. In taking off the little putti to our own destinations we were replicating the circulation of the virus. But in participating in the event, sharing in the experience, we were also invited to express a solidarity with people with HIV and AIDS, and through that solidarity affirm that this was not solely (though it is very much that) an individual tragedy but a collective, a human experience that touches us all. Just as Robert Indiana's image became a symbol of a culture heavily sold on the hope of love, the General Idea's may be seen as a struggle against the hopelessness produced by a fear of death, expressing a less easy but even more necessary form of love. In line with this, the AIDS image has become a logo for many organizations fighting against HIV and AIDS, and for safer sex: for acts of care, responsibility, respect, knowledge and hope.

Love and death have come to be linked as the twentieth century fades by the powerful shadow of AIDS. What does the epidemic of signification, the continent of meaning built around these three experiences tell us about values in this age of uncertainty?

When my close friend Angus Suttie died of AIDS-related illnesses in 1993 I received a note of condolence from another friend which contained the comment that we are 'caught between worlds and ways of being . . .'. It stirred my imagination because it put into words my strong sense of a culture in uncertain and uneven transition between old traditions that are manifestly crumbling, and new forms of living and loving, and perhaps of dying, that are with us but still lacking full acceptance and validation. And a period of transition, as many commentators since the nineteenth century at least have pointed out, gives rise to many strange anxieties, fears, paranoias – and hopes and opportunities. In such a culture the various forms of love are the site of fierce controversies, even as the general concept is valorized. And death, which appeared neatly tidied away by the scientific, medical and even cultural progress of the twentieth century, has come again to haunt our consciousness.

In the first volume of *The History of Sexuality*, Michel Foucault (1979) argues that it was the fading of epidemics in the eighteenth century (or at least their confinement to the nether regions of the 'uncivilized world') which made possible a governmental regime built round the protection and fostering of life. This in turn provided the conditions of possibility for the construction of the regime of sexuality, with its production of the norm of the reproductive couple and the pathologization of sexual difference. Yet in the late twentieth century a devastating epidemic has returned, not just in the Third but at the heart of the First World, an epidemic moreover that links sexuality and death (and ironically carried off Foucault himself), and which in Western countries has engulfed the population that battled most strongly to escape the 'perverse implantation', and to affirm the values of sexual diversity.

There are countless life-destroying diseases, many of which cause many more deaths than HIV and AIDS have yet latched up. It is the link between sexual activity (both factually and figuratively the embodiment of the drive for life) and potentially fatal illnesses, initially rampant in a highly sexualized, and stigmatized, group, which has given AIDS much of its symbolic power in an epoch that thought it had liberated Eros and uncovered the keys of health and longevity. Now it seemed the dangers of the erotic had returned with a vengeance, the healthy had succumbed to epidemic disease, and the young were dying. Not surprisingly, the most powerful cultural responses have come from the male gay communities of Western nations, as they confront the ambiguous and uneven impact of sexual and moral change and the fear of individual and collective loss. As the American writer Robert Gluck has put it:

> AIDS creates such magnitude of *loss* that now death is where gay men experience life most keenly as a group. It's where we learn about love, where we discover new values and qualities in ourselves. Death joins if not replaces sex as the community sublime (1988, p. 45).

But HIV and AIDS are not simply gay phenomena, nor is premature death a particularist experience. The HIV/AIDS epidemic has had a powerful impact, I have argued, not only because of the devastating human losses it has caused but also as a symbolic crystallization of wider cultural shifts. Through the pain and the grief (and the prejudice and discrimination, fear and anxiety) to which the epidemic has given rise, we can see the working-through of broad tendencies which were already transforming global attitudes and individual lives. AIDS provides a reflector through which we can witness the uncertainties of our attitudes to life, love and death – but also the possibilities which are giving them new meanings.

MATTERS OF LIFE AND DEATH

That isolation and death are certain and universal clarifies
our responsibility.

James Baldwin, *Evidence of Things not Seen*

We can judge a culture by the ways in which it confronts the fact
of death, and the needs of the dying.

Life may be contingent, at the mercy of hazard, chance, the
play of historical forces and the diversity of human needs. The
circumstances of dying may also be contingent – but death itself
is the one certainty of our lives. This harsh fact is the supreme
human tragedy. Individual biographies must always be shadowed
by the inevitability of loss and grief, anguish and pain, the final
extinction of those we love and who love us, and of ourselves.
We can live our lives without a daily sense of that tragedy, but all
too often at the expense of constant denial, repressed fear and
anger.

Yet the tragedy of death, and the ephemerality of life, however
masked by easy truisms and various escape attempts, is also the
precondition of creative human life. Bereavement, illness, war or
epidemics remind us of our transitoriness. But because we will
die we try to live as if we are immortal, as if we had an eternity
to fulfil our lives' tasks – until death, our own or that of loved
ones, finally confronts us.

All cultures have to confront the certainty and universality of
death, and the loss that entails. 'Death is paired with loneliness,'
Michael Ignatieff reminds us, 'even in societies rich in rituals for
its sharing' (1984, p. 101). A peculiarity of our own society, however, is the poverty of the cultural responses to death, marking
the fear of extinction that haunts our lives. Instead of finding
ways of coming to terms with the inexorability of our final end
we live under its shadow. Death, it often seems, is our dirty or
guilty secret (Bauman 1992b, p. 134), and the victims are those
who are dying, often in isolation and terror.

The privatization, or separation of death from life, is, it is now
commonly argued, a product of modernity (see essays in Clark
1993a). Like sexuality, death has been sequestered into a zone

of the purely personal. With the biographical continuity of the self increasingly linked with the body, and with the shrinking of the sacred in everyday life, we have become more sensitized to death even as we shrink from it. Inevitably, the repressed constantly returns with a vengeance, its lurking presence constantly lowering over its public absence. Cultures concerned with death avoidance, Bauman (1992b, p. 9) reminds us, are dominated by an acute fear of death-making agents, and an obsessive concern with health. Since the nineteenth-century sexuality has never ceased to proliferate into discourse, despite (or because of) the forms of regulation which seek to delimit what can be said or not said, done or not done, leading to a rich language of desire and love. Unlike the language of sexuality the language of loss remains impoverished, as a result of what Bauman (1992b, p. 136) has called a 'collective de-skilling' in public responses to death. Death has been hidden away, and become a technical matter (Giddens 1991, p. 161), the private end of a private thing called life.

Death gives rise to feelings of shame; our response is embarrassment and the obfuscations of fear. Because modern life is shaped so much by the exclusion of thoughts of its end, we find it painful and difficult to live with the inevitability of death. Sexuality is crawling out of the closet, but we still hold the door shut on our finitude (Bronski 1988).

Death has always been surrounded by fear and anxiety, and there is no reason to believe that there has never been, or could be, a golden age of easy acceptance (see Hockey 1990). As Elias (1985, p. 13) notes, challenging the rosier picture of Ariès (1977/ 1983), people did not die more serenely in the Middle Ages than they do now: life was nasty, brutal and short (see Gittings 1988; Whaley 1981). Death was often spoken of in terms of terror, especially in times of plague. But death was spoken of more openly and frequently in premodern times because it was a more public, or at least less privatized experience; it was a collective experience precisely because whole populations were threatened by mass extinction, and because death was a frequent visitor in pre-scientific times. By the mid-twentieth century, however, the decline of the infant mortality rate, longer life expectancy, growing prosperity, improved medical care – the fruits of 'civilization' – meant that in most Western countries, where wars largely remained cold, and famine and plague seemed abolished for ever, death had become 'unfamiliar' (Kubler-Ross 1979) to most people for most of their lives. But there was no new language to deal with this unprecedented situation, rather the silence and fear that Kubler-Ross encountered when she began her researches on the needs of the dying in the 1960s.

The 'collective wishful fantasies' (Elias 1985, p. 15) of earlier times may have been coloured by fear of hell-fire and damnation, and the hope of redemption, but there was also a language of communal transcendence and salvation, which if it did not give hope may have given solace. John Donne's well-known sonnet 'Death be not Proud' expresses anguished loss, but also a defiance rooted in a sense of an afterlife:

> One short sleepe past, wee wake eternally,
> And death shall be no more; death thou shalt die.

Today as a culture we lack the certainty, or even hope, of a life after death. It is our contingency not our eternal spirit that shapes our consciousness. Whatever our individual faiths and beliefs, the reality of our lives revolves around our individual sense of self and the frailty of our bodies. As the collective is downgraded so it is in our bodies and our individuality that we are expected to find salvation. And individuals die . . .

Death has always been a frightening final horizon, argue Heller and Fehér, but it has never been such an *idée fixe* as it is now: 'We are afraid of seeing a person die or of looking at the sight of death. Since our common fate has become contingent, we are afraid of looking it in its face' (1988, p. 18).

Taylor (1992, p. 10) has identified what he describes as 'three malaises about modernity': a loss of meaning, and the fading of moral horizons; an eclipse of ends in face of rampant instrumental reason; and a loss of freedom. All three, complexly interacting, can be seen operating in modern attitudes to sexuality and death.

The 'desacralization' of contemporary culture has created a void, a sense of the meaninglessness of life. We can face this with despair, with stoicism, with frenetic activity in work or sex, or with calm resignation, but face it somehow we must. The secular religions that sought to fill that emptiness, from Enlightenment humanism to Marxism, and a host of other imperialistic philosophies, have been variously tried, tested, failed and now rigorously deconstructed until little is left. The new foundationalisms and fundamentalisms that abhor and race to fill the vacuum may hold the blind allegiance of millions but (mercifully, to me at least) have little hope of imposing their meanings on all, simply because they express the faiths of particular groups and traditions rather than a true universal aspiration for humankind. What we have in their place are the diverse ends of countless atomized individuals, some giving their allegiance to collective belief systems, most seeking their individual ends. And what could the ultimate end be but the cultivation and preservation of individual lives?

We have lost confidence in the cure of souls, so we have sought meaning in the cure of individual bodies. As Walzer puts it, 'as eternity receded in the popular consciousness, longevity moved to the fore' (1983, p. 87). It is now our bodies that give a sense of location for our sense of ourselves, an anchor for our individual identities; and so our bodies, despite the fact that they must decay, become the locus for our avoidance of death.

But bodies, as we know, are no longer the simple givens of existence, the natural ground on which all else is built. They themselves are shaped and reshaped in the reflexive organization of contemporary life. Death like birth is increasingly bound up in the technological management of life (Giddens 1991). Even the definition of death (like that of life) is now a matter of scientific judgement: not when the soul departs, or the vital functions collapse, or when the patient is past recovery and in an endless slumber, but when the machine is turned off. Medical triumphalism, Sontag (1989, p. 34) has argued, has ensured that death now occurs because of a failure of medicine.

This technological reorganization of life does, however, have a curious effect. For while it socializes the management of the body, it also individualizes diseases, and our responsibility for them. Before the nineteenth century, Coward (1989) argues, disease was seen as part of the corruption of mortal life. The greatest symbol of Christian love was to reach out to the perfectible human soul, however encased in illness or death. Contemporary beliefs, however, insist that we do not have to accept disease. No disease seemed beyond our control: 'The corporeal body is no longer something which holds us back on our quest for perfectibility. Instead it has become the place where this perfectibility can be found' (Coward 1989, p. 43).

Within the framework of medical organization, the body can now be constantly renewed: new limbs, new (or at least recycled) organs, new hope of longer and longer life – if individuals take responsibility for their health and hence also for warding off death. The desire to explain sickness and death in terms of acts of will – action done or not done – may, as Rosenberg (1988, p. 27) suggests, be a powerful and ancient one, but in the late twentieth century it has taken a new, more positive form, in the search for ever more rigorous regimens of diet, physical fitness and general healthy living. Increasingly, it has been widely argued, health is displacing sex as the focus for personal identity (see Coward 1989); and by extension for thinking of right and wrong: a healthy mind in a healthy body may be a time-honoured aspiration but in contemporary culture it has become a ruling morality.

It follows, however, that it also becomes possible to think of disease (dis-ease, lack of ease with the body) as the effect of an individual's failure to act responsibly – to exercise, give up overeating, drinking and smoking, or to fight sexual addiction and sexual excess. If death can be indefinitely postponed by constant battle against a series of discrete attacks on the perfectible body, a battle led by the medical profession with the bodily disciplined rank and file of the healthy, then disease and death can be blamed on individuals who fail to live by the new norms. Death becomes a curable disease.

The paradox is that the stress on individual autonomy and responsibility, which aims to speak for an increasing individual freedom, is overlaid with, and in part vitiated by, an extension of social intervention into questions of health, including sexual health, through the power of definition of what is appropriate behaviour. The pathologization of certain types of behaviour in the name of individual health actually creates new categories of outsiders, and ends up limiting individual freedom. The delineation of new types of risk behaviour constructs risk groups, who can then be subjected to administrative decisions about who should be treated or not. In the name of individual responsibility for health, whole categories of people are in danger of being excluded from advanced medical care.

In saying this I am not attacking medicine as such, nor am I pushing a desire to return to, or invent, more 'natural' medicines. On the contrary, the denial of real scientific breakthroughs, and the search for alternative therapies is often a symptom of the same cultural tendencies: a search for individual solutions in a fertile pot of fantasies that if only we could escape the tyranny of science we could somehow find more natural ways to live. Nor am I denying the importance of individual responsibility for avoiding forms of behaviour which can put at risk oneself and others. The problem lies not in medicine or science in themselves but in a culture which asserts the rights and responsibilities of individuals, but denies them the appropriate context for making informed choices, for becoming truly autonomous. A culture which asserts the responsibility of individuals while denuding them of meaningful communal belongings accentuates the fear of illness and the isolation of death – and increases the power of those who have the right in our culture to decide who should live or die. The hospitals alone, Auden wrote, 'remind us of the equality of man' (quoted in Walzer 1983, p. 181). They also remind us of our vulnerability, and that some people are more equal than others.

Yet the culture also constantly shows the need for something more. When members of the public pile flowers and toys at the site of a murder, natural disaster, catastrophic accident or terrorist assault, or when the families, loved ones and friends of people who have died of AIDS make quilts or memorial plaques, they are offering a communal response which says that no one should die in this way, unexpectedly or alone or stigmatized; that death like this is a tragedy that affects us all. Throughout the era when death has been hygienically hidden away, countless millions have expressed their sense of loss in personal and family rituals of remembrance. Communal traditions, Christian, Jewish, Hindu, Muslim or secular, have survived or been created to celebrate a life and commemorate a death. The circumstances of terminal illness and death have been humanized. The hospice and palliative care movements, and increasing numbers of hospitals, have sought to support the sick and their carers in choosing the circumstances of death, so that the ill can die in dignity, and the living can work through their grief (Clark 1993b).

Increasingly, too, people decide to die at home with their loved ones with them, taking some control of the circumstances of their own deaths (Duda 1987). We strive to listen to the needs of the dying, or of the survivors. The problem lies not in the human response, but in a cultural configuration which celebrates individual life not because of but in terror of the fact of death. In a world without apparent meaning, death itself is in danger of becoming meaningless.

As the journalist Polly Toynbee wrote, in response to hearing of the fatal illness of her friend Jill Tweedie:

> Through all this suffering we learn . . . What? With the wound comes the bow . . . Does it hell? In the midst of death there is life . . . Where? No, only rage, rage against the dying of the light (*The Guardian*, 14 September 1993, 2, p. 4).

If this is the response to an illness (motor neurone disease in this case) which is not stigmatized, of a person who is not marginalized but on the contrary much admired (Jill Tweedie, a prominent feminist journalist), how much truer is it of an epidemic which affects vulnerable communities and individuals? As Froman argues:

> Death by any cause is never easy to face. The sadness and grief connected with death are as inevitable as they are painful. An AIDS death adds more elements to the grieving process . . . We must also deal with the politics of AIDS: the fear, the ignorance, the bigotry, the guilt, the outrage, and the mushrooming numbers of those who are dying (1992, p. 2).

Here we have the threat of death, hidden away from life, suddenly reappearing as a universal threat, confronting people with the question of not only how they should die but also how they should live. When it was first named in the early 1980s, it was an epidemic which appeared to defy the triumph of science in obliterating epidemics, and where medicine seemed at first helpless. The sick were segregated from the healthy (and the professionals from the patients) by barrier nursing, special isolation wards, rituals of decontamination, and fear. AIDS was a syndrome that was seen as particularly affecting individuals who lacked a sense of personal responsibility, either because they indulged in risky sexual activities, or abused their bodies by drugs. The 'victims' of AIDS were neatly categorized into high or low risk groups, with prescriptions about how to separate the guilty from the innocent, the responsible from the irresponsible. Some people with AIDS sought to restore the body's immunities by rigorous diets, exercises, healthy living. Some took refuge in denial (of, for instance, the role of the virus in leading to AIDS), or in the search for a 'magic bullet' cure. Instead of love and compassion, the most vulnerable were often subjected to acute isolation in sickness and at the moment of death. And grief, on a massive scale in the community most affected, was accompanied by prejudice and rejection:

> One of my clients was locked out of his own home by his partner's angry family, who immediately flew his partner's body back to the Midwest. He was not allowed to see the body or attend the funeral (Froman 1992, p. 20).

This experience is echoed in that of many others, 'wise before their time' (Richardson and Bolle 1992).

AIDS, Sontag has written, has become 'the generic rebuke to life and to hope' (1989, p. 24). Of course, much has changed since the early days of the epidemic in the early 1980s. Science has made many breakthroughs; medicine has shown compassion; new standards of care have evolved; people with HIV and AIDS have participated to an unprecedented degree in the definition of, and response to, their illnesses, and to the management of their own deaths. Hope *has* developed from disaster. But what I want to underline through the experience of AIDS is the ways in which it revealed the ambivalences of our attitudes to death, and to different patterns of life, especially sexual life. The return of epidemic in the metropolitan areas of the West in some ways involved a return for many people to premodern experiences of life and death in marginalized communities. In its global spread, but local patterning, it can be seen as the first postmodern plague. But the language and values that existed to deal with it were resolutely those of modernity, with its sequestration of death from everyday life – and clearly inadequate to the challenge.

A major reason for this, as I have already suggested, has been the association of death with sexuality. Twins in the modern sequestration of experience, they have waltzed a macabre *dance à deux* in the era of postmodernity, though the connection of sex and death is an ancient one. St Augustine, as the first philosopher of subjectivity in the early Christian era, bound it into desire, transgression, original sin and an intense preoccupation with death (Dollimore 1991, p. 132). Postlapsarian man is riven with death and desire, the former having entered the world through the latter. This has been a recurrent theme in Western literature and art, but what is particularly important with regard to the impact of AIDS is the association of homosexuality with death. As, during the course of the past century, the homosexual has become the personification of perverse desires, so the shadow of death has hovered around this new historical personage. It has become a cliché that the twentieth-century literature of homosexuality has usually ended in the despair or death of the homosexual hero or heroine. After the emergence of a new gay activism from the late 1960s, and the resulting new sexual openness and vibrancy in the gay community, a new inflection was given to this ancient tradition: no longer homosexuality leading to death, but sexual pleasure as a challenge to death: 'The sweatshirt slogan "so many men, so little time" was our contemporary *carpe diem*: seize the day; eat, drink, and be merry, for tomorrow you die' (Woods 1992, p. 158). But in the popular discourse that attributed AIDS to homosexuality, a new impetus was given to the original dying fall.

In October 1990 the *New York Times* published an essay on the conductor and composer Leonard Bernstein, who had recently died of lung cancer, and who was widely known to have been at the very least bisexual. Although there is no explicit reference to AIDS, his death is clearly linked to his homosexuality. His death is portrayed as a logical result of a life where 'death was always standing in the wings':

> ... his compulsive smoking and other personal excesses certainly could be interpreted in classic death-wish terms. In the Romantically committed mind, for every plus there must be a minus, for every blessing of love, a compensating curse.

As Judith Butler observes, here death is understood as a necessary compensation for homosexual desire, 'as the *telos* of male homosexuality, its genesis and its demise, the principle of its intelligibility' (1992, p. 359).

For many, AIDS has served to confirm this link, and in Western discourse the response to the epidemic has inevitably been shaped by ambivalence towards homosexuality. But of course the link between sex, AIDS and death is more complicated than that. If sex and the health, fitness and well-being of the body are principal elements of personal identity in the modern world, and if modern identity is in part at least based on an avoidance of death, then inevitably an epidemic which associates sexual activity (heterosexual as well as homosexual) with death is likely to have a profound existential impact. Sexual passion, the expression of Eros, of life, is perilously embraced by Thanatos, the drive to death:

> My thoughts are crowded with death
> and it draws so oddly on the sexual
> that I am confused
> confused to be attracted
> by, in effect, my own annihilation.

The lines belong to Thom Gunn's poem 'In Time of Plague' (1992, p. 59), which is elegizing his friends who have died of AIDS. The experience is that of the North American gay community. But the resonance is surely much more universal. In the spread of the heterosexual epidemic in the West, and in the pandemic nature of AIDS in the non-Western world, it is the reproductive sexual chain that is mostly deeply threatened. The transient extinction of individuality in sexual ecstasy appears as the harbinger of that more final extinction which faces us all.

That, however, is not all that can, or has been said.

People do not live with AIDS, said the British film maker Derek Jarman bitterly, as he faced his own death; they die of it. Yet the most powerful cultural response from people living with HIV and AIDS has been a celebration of life and a resistance to death. 'We are not victims, but survivors'; 'Militancy not mourning' (Crimp 1989). Such slogans are more than desperate denials from the threatened. They speak of a reassessment of the meaning of life in face of the universal fact of death. For Michael Callen, who lived with AIDS for over ten years:

> AIDS has taught me the preciousness of life and the healing power of love . . . I've tried to see AIDS as a challenge to begin living, instead of a sign to begin dying. AIDS forced me to take responsibility for my own life – for the choices I had made and the choices I could still make (1990, p. 10).

The fact of looming death – or perhaps we should say, *because of* the reality of death – life becomes meaningful. Instead of being astonished at the spiritual emptiness, the meaningless of our times, we should be amazed, with Michael Ignatieff, that individuals somehow manage, 'in both the silence and the babble, to find sufficient meaning and purpose' (1984, p. 79). We care for life, and for individual lives, because we are going to die. That is the human paradox, and the sublime human achievement: death 'makes permanence into a task, into an urgent task, into a paramount task' (Bauman 1992b, p. 4), even though we know that nothing can be permanent, that evanescence is our collective lot.

That makes the way we should live the key question, both cultural and political. For the radical humanist, aware of the contingencies of existence but alert to the meanings of life, the key to meaningfulness must lie in our ties to others. As modernity and individualization have emphasized freedom from restraints, have denied the value of bonds that are not freely chosen or contractual, so the individual has been left naked in the face of death: Elias's loneliness of the dying. But there are other traditions. For the Romans the verb 'to live' was synonymous with 'to be among men', and 'to die' with 'to cease to be among men' (Arendt 1958, p. 7). We no longer live or die like Romans, but a crisis like that unleashed by AIDS forces us to remember that our life can have meaning only because of the human bond, our links with others.

For those facing death, sooner than expected, life may seem out of control, like a feeble raft borne haphazardly but relentlessly through the rapids. But with and because of our involvements with others we can still learn to control the raft, even if we cannot avoid the final fall. The contingency of life, and the imminence of death, forces us to take responsibility for our lives and for the lives of others. With others we have the possibility of 'suspending the pressure of time', as Heller (1988, p. 178) says. We can act as if life's promise were still eternal, even though we know it is not. Through others we can learn to live with loss and grief. Grieving well, writes Froman, 'means telling the truth, and nothing but the truth, in an attitude of gentle respect and love' (1992, p. 78): the truth of our vulnerability and finitude, of our need for others, of the inevitability of death and the possibilities of life lived with others. *Not* victims, driven hither and thither by forces beyond control, but survivors, because we need not be, should not be, isolated individuals, passive before fate. The responses to AIDS 'remind us, despite the simplest impulse to withdraw from each other, how bound we are each to the other. And . . . that we are to seize not the day, but rather each other' (Dewey, 1992, p. 38). Or, in Froman's words, in a book about coping with grief from the death of people with AIDS: 'Before, during, and after you say goodbye, be willing to love. Be willing to be loved. Be willing to live today well' (1992, p. 265).

A LOVE ETHIC

When love comes so strong
There is no right or wrong
Your love is your life.

Leonard Bernstein/Stephen Sondheim, *West Side Story*

Love in the modern world, as the popularity of Robert Indiana's pop-art icon suggests, all too often has become a panacea or 'escape attempt': a vehicle for individual meaning in a world without meaning. As Otto Rank (quoted in Bauman 1992b, p. 28) argues, the modern person's dependency on the love partner is the result of the loss of spiritual ideologies, and on the need for something, somebody to provide an escape from spiritual isolation and meaninglessness. Partners are desolated by loss in part because the fragile meanings that love gave to their life has gone beyond recall. Love may be a necessary antidote to the terror of death, yet it proves a frail and crumbling barrier. But love need not be, in practice often is not, so narrowly confined. Love gives meaning not because it provides an escape from death but because it illuminates life shadowed by death, because in its broadest sense it is precisely about being willing to live life today well.

The literature of AIDS, largely a product of the suffering and grief and resilience of the gay community, has seen a resurgence of the literature of love in the face of death. In his novel about AIDS, *Second Son*, Robert Ferro (1988) counterposes the dysfunctional families, fear of the other and marginalization of people with AIDS of a culture beset by fear with the fragile, hesitant but committed relationship of two men living with AIDS, Mark and Bill. Until they meet, Mark has been surrounded by occasionally well-meaning but inadequate members of the family, isolated by the fact of his illness and his sexuality. With Bill he found a new hope: 'For it seemed that what they would do together ... was a kind of trip, a voyage home' (Ferro 1988, p. 215). Against the possibility of isolation, and retreat into the self that a harsh and uncompassionate culture might promote, the novel counsels a courageous commitment to emotion, 'the fragile, private, man-made constructions of passion and compassion, that can serve as the heroic counterforce to the sort of poisonous webbing suggested by the insidious spread of the disease' (Dewey 1992, p. 31). Love is seen as a counterpart and challenge to the fear and isolation caused by the virus and its associated prejudices.

That does not wipe out, or hide, the likelihood of an end. The characters are not free of fantasies of escape, of a fragile hope that a 'magic bullet' would release them from their fate. But love becomes meaningful for them not as an escape from death but because of its inevitability:

> As Mark and Bill prepare, as AIDS patients must, for inevitable closure, they wait with each other. That commitment offers them a healing of a sort, a summer that is in its brevity the very mother of beauty. The disease itself creates the occasion of their passion, for only the knowledge of their mutual infection creates the courage to love . . . Mark and Bill define a fragile community, an achievement of man-made magic as artificial, as momentous, as incandescent as the string of lights along an autumnal shoreline (Dewey 1992, p. 33).

The example is particular, the circumstances dictated by a painful and unresolved history. Yet the message is wider. Death makes love necessary: the reassurance that you will not go into that dark night alone.

Love takes many forms, is given many meanings, endures many clichés, and yet apparently remains a fundamental of individual lives. But what do we mean by love? It is difficult to 'love' humankind, except as a metaphysical flight. W. H. Auden famously removed the line 'We must love one another or die' from the poem 'September 1, 1939' in later versions published in his collected works on the grounds that this was a pious sentimentality which did more harm than good (Hecht 1993, pp. 167–70). Or as Jessica Benjamin argues, the injunction to love our neighbour is less a testimony to our abiding concern for others than a reflection of the opposite: our constant propensity for aggression against our fellow humans (1990, p. 4). Apart from those expressing the grosser abuses of nationalist or racist fervour, we tend to love not our communal attachments but our individual partners and nearest and dearest. Even on this level there are various forms of love. We may not wish to emulate the Native Americans who are reported to have had some six hundred categories of love experience (Douglas and Atwell 1988, p. 35), yet even the Western experience has been dominated by at least four major types: *filial* (the love of parents for children); *philia* (the love embodied in friendship); *agape* (the love of God); and the *erotic* (the urge to union, which embraces passionate sexual love). It is the last of these, however, that has come to symbolize the real power of love, becoming, perhaps 'the primary vehicle for self-realization, transformation, and transcendence' in our time (Person 1989, p. 354).

In the discourse of romantic love, the classical form which passionate love has taken in modern societies, it is the individual and the pair, not the large social unit that we celebrate. Love is transcendent because it bridges the yawning gap between autonomous and atomized individuals. Romantic love, by its nature, is exclusive, the property of the couple involved. It provides meaning in a meaningless world, the vehicle by which the inner experiences and needs of subjects is mutually recognized and validated, and through which, potentially, both individuals are transformed. And sex has become the vehicle for the expression of that love.

But just as romantic love has been a product of a complex history, so *its* history is being transformed under the impact of the changes that are shaking the world of relationships. Simone de Beauvoir (1962) distinguished between long-term loving relationships, 'essential love' (which she enjoyed, if that is the correct word, with Sartre), and what for her were more short-term passionate sexual involvements, what she called 'contingent love' (see also Evans 1985, pp. 43–6). It is at least arguable, however, that in the Western world, contingent love is not very far removed from becoming the norm. The stress now, I have argued, is not so much on the qualities that make for a lifetime's sexual partnership but on the pleasures and satisfactions that can be obtained from the particular relationship – so long as it lasts. Meaning resides less in the 'ties that bind' than in the passions that unite, until they fade; then we start all over again. In this the sexual bonds are critical: through the cultivation of the *ars erotica* we can help find meaning, however ephemeral, and certainly find pleasure. Yet what Giddens (1992) calls confluent love, an openness to the other in the exploration and satisfaction of sexual love, has to be worked at, negotiated, constructed and reconstructed. It does not just happen, and it does not always last. Erotic love may be transcendent, but it also appears transient.

Auden's poem 'Lullaby', also known by its first line (Auden 1937/1979) beautifully captures the two moments of transcendence and transience, as various writers have observed (Person 1989, p. 323, Giddens 1992, p. 197):

> Lay your sleeping head, my love,
> Human on my faithless arm . . .

Individual beauty fades, vision like the body dies, certainty and fidelity may pass on the stroke of midnight 'like vibrations of a bell', but in the haven of the night, there is only the other:

> Mortal, guilty, but to me
> The entirely beautiful.

Love to be immortal need not be eternal. It is, on the contrary, an act of faith, a Pascalian wager: it is better to act as if love will last a lifetime, even if you know it might not.

But again, there is more to be said. Person comments in her book on love, *Dreams of Love and Fateful Encounters* (1989), that passionate love between two people has been ignored in recent literature. But it is difficult not to escape the conclusion that it is this form of love that uniquely dominates the literature, at the expense of other forms of love, equally intense. The problem of love lies less in its transcendence or transience than in its supposed exclusivity: the assumption that passionate love between two people is not only qualitatively different from love of friends but on another and superior plain. It must by its nature close out others.

The language of love is highly conventionalized. Yet in the psychoanalytic literature, Eros is more than sexual desire. It may take the form of intense commitment to the Other, but the urge to communion with others is not limited to this. Modern transformations in the meanings of intimacy, with their inherently democratizing tendencies, indicate that love in the broadest sense is coming to mean more than the passionate links that bind the dyad against the world. It is also about the possibilities of intimate ('loving') communication with others, in a variety of forms that go beyond the model of conventional coupledom. This has been especially important as HIV and AIDS have swept through the gay male community, offering narratives of tenderness and care in confronting the indifference and fear of a hostile world, but it has a wider resonance. Love is not a thing in itself. Its possibility may be a constant of our psychological make-up, but the forms in which it is expressed are necessarily social and historical. It offers a language, a series of narratives, codes of behaviour, and a multiplicity of possibilities for making sense of our need for each other, embracing, but not being limited to, the passionate sexual and emotional involvements that conventionally define love.

I am reminded that Auden's love poem and lullaby, despite its careful gender neutrality, was written by a homosexual man to another man, expressing in the most intimate and tender language the depth of feeling that even a casual and ephemeral sexual relationship might release. But transience is not simply a characteristic of casual sex, nor is contingency the fate merely of contemporary relationships. Both are markers of the uncertainty of postmodern lives. Love by its nature must be ephemeral because as a human phenomenon it is bounded by our transience. As Hecht comments: 'What Auden does is to equate fidelity and life itself, since both are of necessity brief' (1993, p. 107). But brevity makes the human connection more not less important, and reminds us that intimacy and tenderness, 'love' in its broadest sense, are not confined to the sexual bond: they potentially reach out to all those we recognize as our 'significant others' (plural, not singular).

To illustrate this I want now to go back to the four principles, or virtues, that I briefly outlined earlier: 'care', 'responsibility', 'respect' and 'knowledge'. In his vastly popular essay *The Art of*

Loving (1957/1971), a book which greatly influenced me a decade or so after its publication, Erich Fromm described these as basic elements which were common to all forms of love. Rereading it after many years, I am struck now by how much a product of its time and its dominant assumptions the book is. 'Mature' heterosexual love is seen as the finest human achievement, while homosexual relations are denigrated, in the liberal language of the time, as a sad and unfortunate deviation. But while challenging that, I am still impressed by the ways in which the elements he defined are central to any revaluation of loving relations in this era of uncertainty – precisely because they ask us to reflect on the possibilities of seeing certain common features across different forms of relationship. It is not the terms themselves which are problematic, but the limited meanings they have been given. I want now to offer a rereading of these terms which point the way to an alternative ethics of love.

Care

Love as care involves an active concern for the life, hopes, needs and potentialities of the person, or people we love: parents or carers for children or dependants, partner for partner, carer for those who are ill or dying. The term 'carer' itself has become an almost universal signifier for the combinations of involvement and trust that such relationships require, though in Western cultures it is still seen as overwhelmingly a female responsibility.

Yet we also know that 'caring' is an ambiguous activity. There are many forms of destructive care: the smothering love of the overpossessive parent or lover, or the love that crushes the hope and life out of those we claim to love, or the symbiotic love where the pair give up everything for each other. The structured inequalities that still shape our lives, of age, or race, or gender and sexuality, make genuine caring relationships an often perilous achievement, enforcing dependencies that make love a duty, a punishment, or a trap. Women particularly, as Coward argues, are victims of their 'treacherous hearts':

Not only do they contort themselves to accommodate all the contradictory expectations of the prevailing ideal, but they try to fend off social problems with individual solutions. Viewed from one side, such gyrations are heroic. But viewed from another, they show a failure of will, an acceptance of the status quo, and a collusion with men's expectations of women (1992, p. 199).

Women's continuing identification with the caring role traps them within the privacy of their own guilt and contradictory desires, and individualizes problems, and therefore solutions. The resolute belief of our individualistic culture that we are sufficient unto ourselves, that we do not need anyone else, is a major manifestation of male hegemony today and:

far more pervasive than overly authoritarian forms of male domination. Indeed, this one-sided ideal of individuality has not been diminished by the undermining of paternal authority and superego. It may even have been strengthened: the lack of manifest authority intensifies the pressure to perform independently, to live up to the ideal without leaning on a concrete person who embodies it (Benjamin 1990, p. 172).

Yet even when we ostensibly escape the egoism of the self-sufficient individual, we are as likely to re-create what Fromm (1957/ 1971, p. 65) calls an 'egoism *à deux*', love as a haven from aloneness, the couple against the world, which is as much a pathology as the individuality which refuses love at all. 'Care' here becomes an escape from wider involvement, and a perpetuation, despite decades of 'rethinking masculinity', of female responsibility.

This is the reality that lurks behind such fashionable panaceas in social policy as 'care in the community'. The assumption here is that care for the vulnerable is what women are expected to do, and do do, as part of their family obligations (Finch and Groves 1983; Dalley 1988; Graham 1991, 1994). But this privatizing of care produces its own distortions. There is the care we do out of a sense of weary obligation and duty to the helpless, while all the time we resent the intrusion into our own sense of self of an enforced altruism (Finch 1989). There is also the private care that covers for a wider lack of communal care for the marginal and ill. Cindy Patton (1990) has vividly described the 'new altruism' that has arisen in the response to HIV and AIDS: the 'immune' (often well-meaning middle-class women in a passable revival of nineteenth-century philanthropic intention) have sometimes taken responsibility for caring for the 'vulnerable' as part of a prolonged process of state avoidance of, or disengagement from, caring for people with a feared disease; 'self-help' has become a motto for privatizing concern.

There is, no doubt, 'love' in all these activities, but it is a love where an active concern for the lives of others impedes care for the self, and in certain situations threatens to obliterate the autonomy of others, to crush their sense of self and self-worth, and to deny the possibility of, and need for, more complex involvements.

A truly loving care can be built only on a recognition of the autonomy of the other, the equality of carer and the person cared for, the reciprocal needs thus addressed, and ultimately on the recognition that the autonomy of oneself is dependent on the autonomy of others. Love as care, in other words, implies an act of imagination, an ability to enter sympathetically into the life of others. But that in turn requires that we love responsibly.

Responsibility

Responsibility as a term carries with it a drear echo of prescription, of enforced duty. As I write, it also appears to be well on the way to becoming a code word for returning to 'traditional values'. If only, the ideologues of conservative values argue, we could build in our youth a sense of responsibility to authority, if only parents could be more responsible, that is more disciplining, of their offspring, if only we could return to the tranquillity and decency of that golden age somewhere in our past of self-control and decency and discipline, then the pathologies of our age would gently dissipate: the young would cease to take drugs and steal cars, the teenager would not become pregnant to scrounge on the welfare state, adults would not neglect their children, adultery and divorce would diminish, families would grow in strength and become again the building blocks of our society. If only . . .

conclusion ?

And yet, the concept circulates as a political cliché because it resonates with a sense that a selfish commitment to self does destroy, not only the individual and his or her relationships, but also the wider culture. A culture of individualism, of personal freedom, puts responsibility firmly on the agenda. Individual freedom implies that people are made more self-responsible, and that means responsibility for sinking lower, or climbing higher. The difficulty, therefore, does not reside in the idea of responsibility but in the various meanings caught up in it.

Responsibility as duty, as a must, is bound up with sanctions, with enforcing the laws of behaviour laid down by others, or by traditions, which often means the same thing. There is, however, a more valuable sense to the term: responsibility as a voluntary act, expressing our response to the needs, expressed or unexpressed, of others; and receiving in return the responsible behaviour of others. Love, as Person puts it, 'determines one's sense of obligations and time, or transforms them' (1989, p. 23). A responsible love is one based on mutual obligation, and on the recognition that what I do has consequences for the other.

I earlier referred to the work of Carol Gilligan. In her influential book *In a Different Voice* (1982), she underlined the conflicts between an ethics of justice and rights, reliant on a strong sense of individual separation and an ethic of responsibility, which assumes the mutual dependency between individuals. She argues that the first concept of morality essentially reflects the masculine experience of psychological growth, while the second reflects the feminine. Her researches on how the moral psychology of individuals develops suggest that while men might indeed find it necessary to subordinate relational responsibilities to the needs of autonomy and achievement, women are more likely to espouse values associated with sharing, caring and obligation. In a male-dominated world, it is the masculinist ethic of rights which dominates the culture, confining ideas of mutual responsibility to the private, 'feminine' sphere.

There is no reason to assume, however, that these qualities are exclusively 'male' or 'female', whatever the historical associations may be. Both, as Anne Phillips (1991, pp. 155–6) suggests, are necessary for a good society, balancing the qualities of justice and compassion. Nor is there any reason to suppose that these cannot at the same time be both private and public qualities, with a fuller sense of private responsibility to others being the real building-block of a more humane and just public culture. The discourse of 'safer sex' in the context of the HIV/AIDS epidemic vividly again provides a useful illustration of this.

The notion of safer sex is, of course, not new. Sex workers have long been aware of the risks of unprotected sex, and have sought means to protect themselves against sexual disease. Male punters throughout the centuries have similarly used a variety of primitive protectives, from rags to sheep bladders. State authorities have sought, in a variety of ways, to minimize risk, from the punitive state control of prostitutes pioneered in the nineteenth century to the armies floating on a sea of condoms in the twentieth – though such measures were usually adopted in war-time, to protect the health and morale of the armed forces. But it was among the gay male communities of American cities such as San Francisco and New York in the early 1980s, as AIDS began to stalk their experience, that a public discourse of safer sex as mutual responsibility first emerged. It was pioneered by gay men to protect themselves and their loved ones, and to learn 'how to have sex in an epidemic' (Callen and Berkowitz 1983). As national agencies began to intervene to limit the spread of HIV in the mid-1980s, the idea of safer sex took on a different echo: basically how the wider (by implication, mainly heterosexual) population could be protected from the risk groups (King 1993; Watney 1994). But in the communities most at risk the term retained and strengthened the earlier tone. Safer sex became a means of negotiating sex and love, of building a respect for self and others, in a climate of risk and fear. From this point of view, safer sex was a way of recovering the erotic, not a defensive reaction to it, based on the minimization, if not complete elimination, of risk, in relationships of mutual trust and responsibility.

I take this as a powerful example of the ways in which a responsibility for the self requires a responsibility to others, in a web of reciprocity that takes for granted that a small concession

of absolute freedom to do as you desire guarantees a wider
freedom. Safer sex, despite the well-known hazards, difficulties
and 'backslidings' that make it often problematic, can be taken
as symbolic of a wider need for a sense of caring responsibility
that extends from sexual behaviour to all aspects of social life.
Love as responsibility means accepting that we are not isolated
monads, sufficient unto ourselves. Our humanity is dependent
on our caring and responsible involvements with others. This in
turn means respecting the other.

Respect

People are worthy of respect when they strive to achieve their
life-plans in ways that do not harm others, that express care for
and responsibility to others in the pursuit of individual goals.
Our culture, however, denies worth and respect, even full citizenship, to many categories of people: because of their colour and
ethnicity, their gender or age, their physical or mental capacities,
their class or status, and because of their sexuality. Respect for
individuals, in their individuality and their diversity, already therefore implies a cultural and political programme which seeks to
eliminate institutionalized discrimination and domination.
'Exclusion from power', Brittan observes: 'is in reality a denial
of dignity to the excluded. It is a way of saying that the excluded
group has no "respect-worthiness" ' (1989, p. 163).

Respect involves taking seriously the dignity of the other: both
their autonomy as a person, and their needs for you and for
others. Dignity is lost when the possibilities of autonomy and of
mutual respect, of achieving an appropriate balance between
full subjectivity and reliance on the other, are thwarted by false
polarities and hierarchical relations. In the sphere of love the
balance is difficult to sustain and hold. Domination, as Jessica
Benjamin (1990, p. 5) reminds us, is a two-way process, involving
the participation of those who submit to power as well as those
who exercise it. Desire plays around the poles and hierarchies of
erotic attraction. Fantasies of domination and submission are
inextricably linked with mutual attraction, and are unlikely ever

to be eliminated. The problems lie not in the fantasies, or even enactment of sexual play around such fantasies, but in the ways in which domination and subordination become locked into social assumptions and cultural norms and traditions: when the polarities and hierarchies of our sexualized desires become located in gendered and other polarities, and with the social hierarchies associated with them. In such situations the work of love becomes less a mutual recognition of need and more a way of sustaining the power relations themselves.

Respect for the dignity of the other is impossible when men and women 'do' emotional work differently. Duncombe and Marsden (1993) speak of 'gender assymetry in emotional behaviour'. Women's responsibility for caring and responsiveness are balanced against male fear of intimacy and male non-disclosure in the context of family responsibilities where emotional work is solidified into poles of gender. The challenge is to recognize the paradox while avoiding the polarity. That, ultimately, requires much more than an act of will, but rather a working through of the transformations of personal relationships that have already fundamentally undermined the basis of gender relations. Respecting the dignity of others, the paradoxical tension between sense of self and recognition of the other, is a necessary first step.

Knowledge

The capacity to do the above implies knowledge, an openness to understanding both of your own needs, and the needs of others. The democratization of love that is implicit in the broad developments of our culture assumes that human relationships should be based on what Heller (1987) describes as 'symmetric reciprocity', or what Benjamin (1990, p. 16) calls 'mutual recognition'. This in turn suggests that knowledge of the other has to be based on an awareness of the complexities of human subjectivity and social belonging. As Benjamin argues:

> The vision of recognition between equal subjects gives rise to a
> new logic – the logic of paradox, of sustaining the tension between

contradictory forces. Perhaps the most fateful paradox is the one posed by our simultaneous need for recognition and independence: that the other subject is outside our control and yet we need him [sic]. To embrace this paradox is the first step towards unravelling the bonds of love. This means not to undo our ties to others but rather to disentangle them; to make them not shackles but circuits of recognition (1990, p. 221).

Reciprocity and recognition suggest an attention to the lives of others which Foucault and others have termed 'curiosity' (see White 1991, p. 92): not a heavy wish for total knowledge of others, which is a denial of the privacy of the other, but a delicacy of concern which is sensitive to the needs of our partners, creating a space for understanding where difference can flourish while solidarity grows.

Love in its broadest sense, based on care, responsibility, respect and knowledge, is not an escape from a life without meaning, but a recognition that we make our individual lives meaningful through our involvements with (our love for) others. We cannot retreat from the contingency and arbitrariness of the world, but we can make life meaningful if we face it with love based on our recognition of our mutual need for one another. Those who strive for a meaningful life may recognize the inherent limitations of life's strivings, while all the time seeking to make sense of them, to develop their capacities to live with and love others. The individual who is attempting to live a meaningful life, Heller argues, 'is not a closed substance but a developing one who shrinks from no new challenges. . . . It is a process to which death alone sets a term' (1984, p. 267). Self-development in these terms is not simply about cultivation of the self; it is concerned with developing one's abilities, to transform one's contingency into destiny (Heller and Feher 1988, p. 27). Or to change the language, it is to transform the language of authenticity from one of individual need into a recognition of meaningfulness with and for others.

The language of self-fulfilment, self-determination, autonomy and authenticity, the 'motivating ideals' (Taylor 1992) of our culture, contains within it some concept of our being-with-others.

But the introduction of a word like 'ideal' presupposes that what we have are goals to be achieved, values that we can struggle to realize, rather than the current givens of everyday life. This discussion of the elements of love, care, responsibility, respect and knowledge has already suggested the ambiguities of their meanings, and the barriers to their realization. A love ethic starts with these individual experiences, and their hazards, but ends with a sense of the indissoluble link between the individual and the social, and, in the hallowed phrase, the personal and the political. For what is clear is that the limits to the achievement of authenticity do not lie in the individual alone, but in the culture which valorizes individual gain above social solidarity. The ability to love others depends, as Fromm (1957/1971) argued, on one's ability to love oneself; but one's ability to love oneself in turn depends on one's recognition by others. A hierarchical culture, based on relations of domination, might leave space for the aesthetic life; it does not create opportunities for a fully self-determining, meaningful and authentic life. There may well be an inherently democratizing imaginary in the motivating ideals of the culture. The challenge still remains of realizing it.

EPILOGUE: BEING ALIVE

> Unless there's love, the world's an empty place
> And every town's a lonely town.
> Leonard Bernstein, *On the Town*

The ethics of love is about finding ways of loving and living, of conduct, relationships and solidarities, that make life meaningful in the aching void of meaninglessness. White (1991) speaks of the 'grieving delight' that is a characteristic tone of the postmodern mood. There is grief at the death of illusions, of the hope for delivery, of the aspiration towards transcendence, at the fragility and transitory nature of all that we value and want to affirm. But there is delight in the love and care, the effort and will, the resilience and affirmations that carry us frail humans forward whatever the obstacles and disappointments; and delight above all in the 'continuing presence of difference, of the other' (White 1991, p. 110).

There is a constant ambiguity and paradox in the world we inhabit but do not fully possess. That is a source of the sense of uncertainty that dogs our lives. It leads, too readily, to what Raymond Williams (1983, p. 4) called the 'settled pessimism' of so much of the culture of the late twentieth century: an absolute loss of the future, of any real belief that anything can be both different and better. We do not know how to find a settled home in an era of spiritual homelessness.

But in the tragedies of our time we do find the resources for hope. There are many examples I could offer, but I will confine myself to the one I have used many times in this book, because it sums up for me the pain and the passion, the anger and love, of contemporary life: the AIDS crisis. In the acts of love so characteristic of the epidemic we find elements of the wider solidarities that the construction of a radical humanism requires. I can end this book in no better way than by describing one aspect of that response: the NAMES Project based in San Francisco, but now world-wide, and its Quilt which commemorates those who have died of AIDS.

The Quilt stands, as Cleve Jones who founded the NAMES Project has said, 'as a statement of hope and remembrance' (quoted in Elsley 1992, p. 188) and therefore for the possibilities of life in the shadow of death.

The Quilt is made up of thousands of embroidered panels commemorating individuals who have died from the epidemic: black and white, gay and straight, male and female, young and old, citizens not only of the USA but of the world, who have died prematurely of diseases associated with HIV and AIDS. The panels have been sewn by the bereaved: mothers and fathers, brothers and sisters, friends and lovers, working individually or collectively, marking deep loss, celebrating love, underlining the democracy of the dead, and the solidarities of the living.

When it was displayed on the Ellipse, south of the White House in October 1988, it contained 9000 panels, covered 375,000 square feet, and had completed a 12,000 mile national tour. Now it is too large ever again to be assembled in one place, as the dead accumulate at a relentless pace, and still people go on embroidering.

Making the Quilt is both deeply symbolic, reminding us, as Woods suggests, that 'it was beneath our bed covers that we loved those who have died' (1992, p. 163); and severely practical, giving 'cathartic relief, enabling relief, comfort and community and emotion' (Dawidoff 1988, p. 157). But whether symbolically potent or practical, in both spheres it lovingly mourns, affirms and celebrates the lives of those who have died, and attests to the continuities of life, the hard-won community of those who are living in the shadow of our frailties and the knowledge of loss and death:

> the AIDS quilt shifts the consciousness of a whole society from a single, fearful view of AIDS to multivocal diversity, and by doing so enables us to begin to face our fears (Elsley 1992, p. 193).

The Quilt stands for many things. For rootedness, evoking not only the traditions of the American communities of women who embroidered for weddings and family occasions, individually and collectively, but now also the newly invented, but no less powerful, traditions of people dying of AIDS or living with HIV in their diverse imagined communities. For participation, in the changing rituals of life, and death, where the equality of loss forces us to rethink and challenge the inequalities of life and where the connections between self and others are affirmed and reaffirmed. And for the future: the construction of the Quilt reminds us that life goes on. Just as the Quilt is constantly changing as new panels are added, so the pattern of death, and the impact of AIDS on life, changes.

Earlier in this book I quoted Sontag (1989) and her rejection of AIDS as a metaphor. AIDS is too real to be a metaphor for anything. But in the Quilt as an imaginative response to the AIDS epidemic we *can* see a metaphor: for the possibilities of ways of being which respect the diversity of life, which empathize with the pains and suffering of others because they are also our pains and sufferings, and which, against and because of the tragedies of agonizing death, affirm the possibilities of life. Here, caught in the rapids of change, in a world of giddy uncertainty, we find an invented morality that confirms an ethic of love and the possibilities of the human bond.

Bibliography

Adam, B. D. 1992, 'Sex and caring among men: impacts of AIDS on gay people', in Plummer 1992.

Aggleton, P., Davies, P. and Hart, G. (eds) 1989, *AIDS: Social Representations, Social Practices*, London, New York and Philadelphia, The Falmer Press.

Aggleton, P., Davies, P. and Hart, G. (eds) 1991, *AIDS: Individual, Cultural and Policy Dimensions*, London, New York and Philadelphia, The Falmer Press.

Alibhai-Brown, Y. and Montague, A. 1992, *The Colour of Love: Mixed Race Relationships*, London, Virago.

Altman, D. 1986, *AIDS and the New Puritanism*, London and Sydney, Pluto Press; as *AIDS in the Mind of America*, New York, Doubleday.

Altman, D. 1971/1993, *Homosexual Oppression and Liberation*, New York, New York University Press.

Andrews, G. (ed.) 1991, *Citizenship*, London, Lawrence and Wishart.

Ardill, S. and O'Sullivan, S. 1987, 'Upsetting an applecart: difference, desire and lesbian sado-masochism', in Feminist Review (ed.), *Sexuality: A Reader*, London, Virago.

Arendt, H. 1958, *The Human Condition*, Chicago, University of Chicago Press.

Ariès, P. 1977/1983, *The Hour of our Death*, London, Peregrine.

Arroyo, J. 1993, 'Death, desire and identity: the political unconscious of "new queer cinema" ', in Bristow and Wilson 1993.

Auden, W. H. 1937/1979, *Selected Poems*, London, Faber and Faber.

Bakhtin, M. 1984, *Rabelais and his World*, Bloomington, Indiana University Press [written 1930s; Russian edn 1965].

Baldwin, J. 1956/1963, *Giovanni's Room*, London, Corgi.

Baldwin, J. 1986, *Evidence of Things not Seen*, London, Michael Joseph.

Bartlett, N. 1988, *Who Was that Man? A Present for Mr Oscar Wilde*, London, Serpent's Tail.

Bauman, Z. 1988, *Freedom*, Milton Keynes, Open University Press.

Bauman, Z. 1989, *Legislators and Interpreters: On Modernity, Post-modernity and Intellectuals*, Cambridge, Polity Press.

Bauman, Z. 1990, 'From Pillars to Post', *Marxism Today*, February 1990.

Bauman, Z. 1992a, *Intimations of Postmodernity*, London and New York, Routledge.

Bauman, Z. 1992b, *Mortality, Immortality and Other Life Strategies*, Cambridge, Polity Press.

Bauman, Z. 1993, *Postmodern Ethics*, Oxford, Blackwell.

Bayer, R. 1991, 'AIDS and the future of reproductive freedom', in Nelkin et al. 1991.

Beauvoir, S. de. 1960/1962. *The Prime of Life*, London, Andre Deutsch.

Bech, H. 1992a, 'Report from a rotten state: "marriage" and "homosexuality" in "Denmark" ', in Plummer 1992.

Bech, H. 1992b, 'Living together in the (post) modern world', paper given at the European Conference of Sociology, Vienna 1992.

Benhabib, S. 1987, 'The generalized and the concrete other: the Kohlberg-Gilligan controversy and feminist theory' in Benhabib and Cornell 1987.

Benhabib, S. and Cornell, D. (eds) 1987, *Feminism as Critique: Essays on the Politics of Gender in late-Capitalist Societies*, Cambridge, Polity Press.

Benhabib, S. and Dallmayr, F. (eds) 1990, *The Communicative Ethics Controversy*, Cambridge, MA, and London, The MIT Press.

Benjamin, J. 1990, *The Bonds of Love: Psychoanalysis, Feminism and the Problem of Domination*, London, Virago.

Benton, S. 1991, 'Gender, sexuality and citizenship', in Andrews 1991.

Berlin, I. 1984, 'Two concepts of liberty', in Sandel 1984.

Bernauer, J. and Rasmussen, D. (eds) 1988, *The Final Foucault*, Cambridge, MA, The MIT Press.

Berridge, V. and Strong, P. (eds) 1993, *AIDS and Contemporary History*, Cambridge, Cambridge University Press.

Bersani, L. 1987, 'Is the rectum a grave?', *October* 43, Winter 1987.

Bérubé, A. and Escoffier, J. 1991, 'Queer/nation', *Outlook: National Lesbian and Gay Quarterly* 11, Winter 1991.

Bhatt, C. 1994, 'New foundations: contingency, indeterminacy and black translocality', in Weeks 1994.

Bhatt, C. 1995, *Liberation and Purity: Race, New Religious Movements and the Ethics of Postmodernity*, London, UCL Press.

Bland, L. 1996, 'The shock of the *Freewoman* journal: feminists speaking on heterosexuality in early twentieth century England', in Weeks and Holland (forthcoming).

Blum, L. A. 1980, *Friendship, Altruism and Morality*, London, Boston and Henley, Routledge and Kegan Paul.

Bray, A. 1982, *Homosexuality in Renaissance England*, London, GMP.

Brill, A. 1990, *Nobody's Business: The Paradoxes of Privacy*, Reading, MA, Addison-Wesley.

Bristow, J. and Wilson, A. (eds) 1993, *Activating Theory: Lesbian, Gay, Bisexual Politics*, London, Lawrence and Wishart.

Brittan, A. 1989, *Masculinity and Power*, Oxford, Basil Blackwell.

Bronski, M. 1988, 'Death and the erotic imagination', in Preston 1988; also in Carter and Watney 1989.

Bullough, V. L. 1994, *Science in the Bedroom: A History of Sex Research*, New York, Basic Books.

Butler, J. 1990, *Gender Trouble: Feminism and the Subversion of Identity*, New York and London, Routledge.

Butler, J. 1991, 'Imitation and gender insubordination', in Fuss 1991.

Butler, J. 1992, 'Sexual inversions', in Stanton 1992.

Butler, J. 1993, *Bodies that Matter: On the Discursive Limits of Sex*, New York and London, Routledge.

Callen, M. 1990, *Surviving AIDS*, New York, HarperCollins.

Callen, M. and Berkowitz, R. 1983, *How to Have Sex in an Epidemic: One Approach*, New York, privately circulated pamphlet.

Campbell, B. 1988, *Unofficial Secrets: Child Sexual Abuse. The Cleveland Case*, London, Virago.

Canovan, M. 1988, 'Friendship, truth and politics: Hannah Arendt and toleration', in Mendus 1988.

Carol, A. 1993, 'Porn, perversion and sexual ethics', in Harwood et al. 1993.

Carter, E. and Watney, S. (eds) 1989, *Taking Liberties: AIDS and Cultural Politics*, London, Serpent's Tail.

Chapman, R. and Rutherford, J. (eds) 1988, *Male Order: Unwrapping Masculinity*, London, Lawrence and Wishart.

Chauncey, G. 1994, *Gay New York: Gender, Urban Culture, and the Making of the Gay Male World 1890–1940*, New York, Basic Books.

Clark, D. (ed.) 1993a, *The Sociology of Death*, Oxford, Blackwell Publishers/The Sociological Review.

Clark, D. (ed.) 1993b, *The Future of Palliative Care: Issues of Policy and Practice*, Buckingham and Philadelphia, Open University Press.

Clark, D. (ed.) 1994, *The Jackie Burgoyne Memorial Lectures, Volume 1, 1989–1993*, Sheffield, Pavic Publications, Sheffield Hallam University.

Clark, D. and Haldane, D. 1990, *Wedlocked? Intervention and Research in Marriage*, Cambridge, Polity Press.

Cohen, A. P. 1985, *The Symbolic Construction of Community*, Chichester and London, Ellis Horwood/Tavistock.

Cohen, A. P. 1992, 'The personal right to identity: a polemic on the self in the enterprise culture', in Heelas and Morris 1992.

Cohen, A. P. 1994, *Self Consciousness: An Alternative Anthropology of Identity*, London and New York, Routledge.

Connell, R. 1987, *Gender and Power*, Cambridge, Polity Press.

Cooper, D. 1993, 'The citizen's charter and radical democracy: empowerment and exclusion within citizenship discourse', *Social and Legal Studies* 2, 1993.

Coward, R. 1983, *Patriarchal Precedents: Sexuality and Social Relations*, London, Boston, Melbourne and Henley, Routledge and Kegan Paul.

Coward, R. 1989, *The Whole Truth: The Myth of Alternative Health*, London and Boston, Faber and Faber.

Coward, R. 1992, *Our Treacherous Hearts: Why Women let Men get their Way*, London and Boston, Faber and Faber.

Crimp, D. 1987, 'AIDS: cultural analysis/cultural activism', *October* 43, Winter 1987.

Crimp, D. 1989, 'Mourning and militancy', *October* 51, Winter 1989.

Crimp, D. 1993, 'Right on, girlfriend!', in Warner 1993.

Dalley, G. 1988, *Ideologies of Caring: Rethinking Community and Collectivism*, London, Macmillan.

Davies, P. M., Hickson, F. C. I., Weatherburn, P. and Hunt, A. J. 1993, *Sex, Gay Men and AIDS*, London, New York and Philadelphia, The Falmer Press.

Davis, M. S. 1983, *Smut: Erotic Reality/Obscene Ideology*, Chicago and London, University of Chicago Press.

Dawidoff, R. 1988, 'The NAMES project', in Preston 1988.

Devlin, P. 1959, *The Enforcement of Morals: Maccabean Lecture in Jurisprudence*, London and Oxford, Oxford University Press.

Dewey, J. 1992, 'Music for a closing: responses to AIDS in three American novels', in Nelson 1992.

Dollimore, J. 1991, *Sexual Dissidence: Augustine to Wilde, Freud to Foucault*, Oxford, Clarendon Press.

Douglas, J. D. and Atwell, F. C., with Hillebrand, J. 1988, *Love, Intimacy and Sex*, Newbury Park, Beverley Hills, London and New Delhi, Sage.

Duberman, M. B., Vicinus, M. and Chauncey, G. (eds) 1989, *Hidden from History: Reclaiming the Lesbian and Gay Past*, New York, New American Library.

Duda, D. 1987, *Coming Home: A Guide to Dying at Home with Dignity*, New York, Aurora Press.

Duncombe, J. and Marsden, D. 1993, 'Love and intimacy: the gender division of emotion and "emotion work": a neglected aspect of sociological discussion of heterosexual relationships', *Sociology* 27, 2, May 1993.

Durham, M. 1991, *Sex and Politics: The Family and Morality in the Thatcher Years*, Basingstoke and London, Macmillan.

Ehrenreich, B. 1983, *The Hearts of Men: American Dreams and the Flight from Commitment*, London, Pluto Press.

Elias, N. 1985, *The Loneliness of the Dying*, Oxford, Basil Blackwell.

Eliot, G. 1871/1966, *Middlemarch*, Harmondsworth, Penguin.

Elshtain, J. B. 1981, *Public Man, Private Woman: Woman in Social and Political Thought*, Oxford, Martin Robertson.

Elsley, J. 1992, 'The rhetoric of the NAMES project quilt: reading the text(ile)', in Nelson 1992.

Epstein, S. 1990, 'Gay politics, ethnic identity: the limits of social constructionism', in Stein 1990.

Epstein, J. and Straub, K. (eds) 1991, *BodyGuards: The Cultural Politics of Gender Ambiguity*, London and New York, Routledge.

Etzioni, A. 1993, *The Spirit of Community: Rights, Responsibilities, and the Communitarian Agenda*, New York, Crown.

Evans, D. T. 1993, *Sexual Citizenship: The Material Construction of Sexualities*, London and New York, Routledge.

Evans, M. 1985, *Simone de Beauvoir: A Feminist Mandarin*, London, Tavistock.

Faderman, L. 1981, *Surpassing the Love of Men*, London, Junction Books.

Fee, E. and Fox, D. M. (eds) 1988, *AIDS: The Burdens of History*, Berkeley, Los Angeles and London, University of California Press.

Fee, E. and Fox, D. M. (eds) 1992, *AIDS: The Making of a Chronic Disease*, Berkeley, Los Angeles and Oxford, University of California Press.

Fekete, J. (ed.) 1988, *Life after Postmodernism: Essays on Value and Culture*, Basingstoke, Macmillan.

Feminist Studies 1992, 18, 3, Fall 1992.

Ferguson, A. 1989, *Blood at the Root: Motherhood, Sexuality and Male Dominance*, London, Pandora.

Ferro, R. 1988, *Second Son*, London, Arrow.

Feyerabend, P. 1987, *Farewell to Reason*, London and New York, Verso.

Finch, J. 1989, *Family Obligations and Social Change*, Cambridge, Polity Press.

Finch, J. 1994, 'Kith and kin in the 1990s', in Clark 1994.

Finch, J. and Groves, D. 1983, *A Labour of Love: Women, Work and Caring*, London, Boston and Henley, Routledge and Kegan Paul.

Finch, J. and Mason, J. 1993, *Negotiating Family Responsibilities*, London, Routledge.

Fitzgerald, F. 1987, *Cities on a Hill: A Journey through Contemporary American Cultures*, London, Picador.

Foucault, M. 1963/1977, 'A Preface to Transgression', in D. F. Bouchard (ed.), *Language, Counter Memory, Practice: Selected Essays and Interviews by Michel Foucault*, Ithaca, NY, Cornell University Press.

Foucault, M. 1976/1979, *The History of Sexuality, Volume 1, An Introduction*, London, Allen Lane.

Foucault, M. 1982, 'Sexual choice, sexual acts', *Salmagundi* 58–9, Fall 1982.

Foucault, M. 1984a, 'Sex, power, and the politics of identity: an interview', interview with Bob Gallagher and Alexander Wilson, *The Advocate* 400, 7 August 1984.

Foucault, M. 1984b, *The Foucault Reader*, ed. P. Rabinow, New York, Pantheon.

Foucault, M. 1984/1985, *The History of Sexuality, Volume 2: The Use of Pleasure*, London, Viking.

Foucault, M. 1984/1986, *The History of Sexuality, Volume 3: The Care of the Self*, London, Viking.

Foucault, M. 1988a, 'Power, moral values, and the intellectual: an interview with Michel Foucault', *History of the Present* 4, University of California, Berkeley, Spring 1988.

Foucault, M. 1988b, 'The ethic of care for the self as a practice of freedom', in Bernauer and Rasmussen 1988.

Foucault, M. 1989, *Foucault Live (Interviews, 1966–84)*, ed. Sylvere Lotringer, New York, Semiotext(e) Foreign Agents Series.

Franc, H. M. 1992, *An Invitation to See: 150 Works from the Museum of Modern Art*, New York, The Museum of Modern Art.

Froman, P. K. 1992, *After you Say Goodbye: When Someone you Love Dies of AIDS*, San Francisco, Chronicle Books.

Fromm, E. 1957/1971, *The Art of Loving*, London, Allen and Unwin.

Fuss, D. (ed.) 1991, *Inside/Out: Lesbian Theories, Gay Theories*, New York and London, Routledge.

Gagnon, J. H. and Simon, W. 1973, *Sexual Conduct: The Social Sources of Human Sexuality*, London, Hutchinson.

Garber, M. 1992, *Vested Interests: Cross-Dressing and Cultural Anxiety*, London and New York, Routledge.

Gates, H. L. Jr. 1993, 'The black man's burden', in Warner 1993.

Geertz, C. 1984, 'Anti anti-relativism', *American Anthropologist* 86, 2, June 1984.

General Idea 1992, *Fin de siècle*, Stuttgart, Wurttembergischer Kunstverein.

Gerard, K. and Hekma, G. (eds) 1988, *The Pursuit of Sodomy: Male Homosexuality in Renaissance and Enlightenment Europe*, New York, Haworth Press.

Gever, M., Greyson, J. and Parmar, P. (eds) 1993, *Queer Looks: Perspectives on Lesbian and Gay Film and Video*, New York and London, Routledge.

Giddens, A. 1990, *The Consequences of Modernity*, Cambridge, Polity Press.

Giddens, A. 1991, *Modernity and Self-Identity: Self and Society in the Late Modern Age*, Cambridge, Polity Press.

Giddens, A. 1992, *The Transformation of Intimacy*, Cambridge, Polity Press.

Gilligan, C. 1982, *In a Different Voice: Psychological Theory and Women's Development*, Cambridge, MA, and London, Harvard University Press.

Gilroy, P. 1987, *There ain't No Black in the Union Jack: The Cultural Politics of Race and Nation*, London, Hutchinson.

Gittings, C. 1988, *Death, Burial and the Individual in Early Modern England*, London, Routledge.

Gluck, R. 1988, 'HIV 1986–88', *City Light Review* 2, San Francisco.

Goldstein, R. 1991, 'The implicated and the immune: responses to AIDS in the arts and popular culture', in Nelkin, et al. 1991.

Graham, H. 1991, 'The concept of caring in feminist research: the case of domestic service', *Sociology* 25, 1, 1991.

Graham, H. 1994, 'The woman who cares', in Clark 1994.

Grant, L. 1993, *Sexing the Millennium: A Political History of the Sexual Revolution*, London, HarperCollins.

Grimshaw, J. 1993, 'Practices of freedom', in Ramazanoglu 1993.

Gross, L. 1993, *Contested Closets: The Politics and Ethics of Outing*, Minneapolis and London, University of Minnesota Press.

Gunn, T. 1992, *The Man with Night Sweats*, London, Faber and Faber.

Hall, C. 1992, *White, Male and Middle Class: Explorations in Feminism and History*, Cambridge, Polity Press.

Halley, J. E. 1991, 'Misreading sodomy: a critique of the classification of "homosexuals" in Federal Equal Protection Law', in Epstein and Straub 1991.

Halley, J. E. 1993, 'The construction of heterosexuality', in Warner 1993.

Hamer, D. et al. 1993, 'A Linkage between DNA markers on the X chromosome and male sexual orientation', *Science* 261, 1993.

Haraway, D. 1991, *Simians, Cyborgs, and Women: The Reinvention of Nature*, London, Free Association Books.

Hart, H. L. A. 1963, *Law, Liberty and Morality*, London and Oxford, Oxford University Press.

Hart, G., Boulton, M., Fitzpatrick, R., McLean, J. and Dawson, J. 1992, ' "Relapse" to unsafe sexual behaviour amongst gay men: a critique of recent behavioural HIV/AIDS research', *Sociology of Health and Illness* 14, 2, June 1992.

Harvey, D. 1989, *The Condition of Postmodernity: An Enquiry into the Origins of Cultural Change*, Oxford, Basil Blackwell.

Harwood, V., Oswell, D., Parkinson, K. and Ward, A. (eds) 1993, *Pleasure Principles: Politics, Sexuality and Ethics*, London, Lawrence and Wishart.

Healey, E. and Mason, A. (eds) 1994, *Stonewall 25: The Making of the Lesbian and Gay Community in Britain*, London, Virago.

Hecht, A. 1993, *The Hidden Law: The Poetry of W. H. Auden*, Cambridge, MA, and London, Harvard University Press.

Heelas, P. and Morris, P. (eds) 1992, *The Values of the Enterprise Culture: The Moral Debate*, London and New York, Routledge.

Held, D. 1987, *Models of Democracy*, Cambridge, Polity Press.

Held, D. 1991, 'Between state and civil society: citizenship', in Andrews 1991.

Heller, A. 1984, *Everyday Life*, London, Routledge and Kegan Paul.

Heller, A. 1987, *Beyond Justice*, Oxford, Basil Blackwell.

Heller, A. 1988, *General Ethics*, Oxford, Basil Blackwell.

Heller, A. and Fehér, F. 1988, *The Postmodern Political Condition*, Cambridge, Polity Press.

Herbert, S. 1993, 'Consent no defence in acts of violent degradation: law report', *The Guardian* 12 March 1993.

Herdt, G. (ed.) 1992, *Gay Culture in America: Essays from the Field*, Boston, Beacon Press.

Herdt, G. (ed.) 1994, *Third Sex, Third Gender: Beyond Sexual Dimorphism in Culture and History*, New York and Paris, Zone Books.

Herman, D. 1994, *Rights of Passage: Struggles for Lesbian and Gay Legal Equality*, Toronto, Buffalo and London, University of Toronto Press.

Himmelweit, S. 1988, 'More than a "woman's right to choose"?', *Feminist Review* 29, Spring 1988.

Hirschman, A. O. 1970, *Exit, Voice and Loyalty*, Cambridge, MA, Harvard University Press.

Hockey, J. 1990, *Experiences of Death: An Anthropological Account*, Edinburgh, Edinburgh University Press.

Holland, J., Ramazanoglu, C., Sharpe, S. and Thomson, R. 1994, 'Power and desire: the embodiment of female sexuality', *Feminist Review* 46, Spring 1994.

Hollis, M. and Lukes, S. (eds) 1982, *Rationality and Relativism*, Oxford, Basil Blackwell.

Hunter, J. D. 1991, *Culture Wars: The Struggle to Define America*, New York, Basic Books.

Hutcheon, L. 1989, *The Politics of Postmodernism*, London, Routledge.

Ignatieff, M. 1984, *The Needs of Strangers*, London, Chatto and Windus/ The Hogarth Press.

Interrante, J. 1987, 'To have without holding: memories of a life with a person with AIDS', *Radical America* 20, 6, 1987.

Jackson, M. 1994, *Fucking with Miners: The Story of Lesbians and Gays Support the Miners*, London, privately circulated.

Jeffery-Poulter, S. 1991, *Peers, Queers and Commons: The Struggle for Gay Law Reform from 1950 to the Present*, London and New York, Routledge.

Jeffreys, S. 1990, *Anti-climax: A Feminist Perspective on the Sexual Revolution*, London, The Women's Press.

Jowers, P. 1994, 'Towards a politics of a "lesser evil": Jean-François Lyotard's reworking of the Kantian sublime', in Weeks 1994.

Julien, I. and Savage, J. (eds) 1994, *Critical Quarterly: Critically Queer* 36, 1, Spring 1994.

Katz, J. N. 1995, *The Invention of Heterosexuality*, New York, NAL/Dutton.

Kay, J. 1991, *The Adoption Papers*, Newcastle upon Tyne, Bloodaxe Books.

Keane, J. 1989, *Democracy and Civil Society*, London and New York, Verso.

Kermode, F. 1967, *The Sense of an Ending: Studies in the Theory of Fiction*, London, Oxford and New York, Oxford University Press.

Kern, S. 1992, *The Culture of Love: Victorians to Moderns*, Cambridge, MA, and London, Harvard University Press.

Kershaw, A. 1992, 'Love hurts', *Guardian Weekend*, 28 November 1992.

King, E. 1993, *Safety in Numbers: Safer Sex and Gay Men*, London, Cassell.

Kinsey, A., Pomeroy, W. B. and Martin, C. 1948, *Sexual Behavior in the Human Male*, Philadelphia, W. B. Saunders Company.

Kippax, S., Connell, R. W., Dowsett, G. W. and Crawford, J. 1993,

Sustaining Safer Sex: Gay Communities Respond to AIDS, London and Washington DC, The Falmer Press.

Kooten Niekerk, A. van and Meer, T. van der 1989, *Homosexuality? Which Homosexuality?*, Amsterdam, An Dekker/Schorer, London, GMP.

Kroker, A. and Kroker, M. 1988, *Body Invaders: Sexuality and the Postmodern Condition*, London, Macmillan.

Kubler-Ross, E. 1979, *On Death and Dying*, London, Tavistock Publications.

Laclau, E. 1990, *New Reflections on the Revolution of our Time*, London and New York, Verso.

Laclau, E. and Mouffe, C. 1985, *Hegemony and Socialist Strategy: Towards a Radical Democratic Politics*, London and New York, Verso.

Larrabee, M. J. (ed.) 1993, *An Ethic of Care: Feminist and Interdisciplinary Perspectives*, London and New York, Routledge.

Lasch, C. 1980, *The Culture of Narcissism*, London, Abacus.

Lasch, C. 1985, *The Minimal Self: Psychic Survival in Troubled Times*, London, Pan Books.

Lash, S. and Urry, J. 1987, *The End of Organized Capitalism*, Cambridge, Polity Press.

Laumann, E. O., Michael, R. T., Gagnon, J. H. and Michaels, S. 1994, *The Social Organization of Sexuality: Sexual Practices in the United States*, Chicago, University of Chicago Press.

Lauretis, T. de. 1991. 'Queer theory: lesbian and gay sexualities: an introduction', *Differences: A Journal of Feminist Cultural Studies*, 3, 2, 1991.

LeVay, S. 1991, 'A difference in hypothalmic structure between heterosexual and homosexual men', *Science* 253, 1991.

Limb, S. 1989, 'Female friendship', in Porter and Tomaselli 1989.

Little, G. 1989, 'Freud, friendship and politics', in Porter and Tomaselli 1989.

Luhmann, N. 1986, *Love as Passion*, Cambridge, Polity Press.

Lynch, M. 1989, *These Waves of Dying Friends*, New York, Contact II Publications.

Lyotard, J. 1979/1984, *The Postmodern Condition*, Manchester, Manchester University Press.

MacCannell, D. and MacCannell, J. F. 1993, 'Violence, power and pleasure: a revisionist reading of Foucault from the victim perspective', in Ramazanoglu 1993.

McIntosh, M. 1993, 'Queer theory and the war of the sexes', in Bristow and Wilson 1993.

MacIntyre, A. 1985, *After Virtue: A Study in Moral Theory*, London, Duckworth.

MacIntyre, A. 1988, *Whose Justice? Which Rationality?*, Notre Dame, Indiana, University of Notre Dame Press.

Mackie, J. L. 1977, *Ethics: Inventing Right and Wrong*, Harmondsworth, Penguin.

McNay, L. 1992, *Foucault and Feminism*, Cambridge, Polity Press.

McNay, L. 1994, *Foucault: A Critical Introduction*, Cambridge, Polity Press.

Madonna 1992, *Sex*, New York and London, Calloway Publications/ Martin Secker and Warburg.

Maffesoli, M. 1988, *Le temps des tribus: le declin de l'individualisme dans les sociétés de Masse*, Paris, Meridiens Klincksieck.

Marnham, P. 1989, 'Muslim girls unveil a French crisis of culture', *The Independent* 25 October 1989.

Marquand, D. 1990, 'A language of community', in Pimlott et al. 1990.

Marshall, T. H. 1963, *Sociology at the Crossroads*, London, Heinemann.

Mason, A. 1994, 'The scientific baby and the social family: the possibilities of lesbian and gay parenting', in Healey and Mason 1994.

Melucci, A. 1989, *Nomads of the Present: Social Movements and Individual Needs in Contemporary Society*, London, Radius.

Mendus, S. (ed.) 1988, *Justifying Toleration: Conceptual and Historical Perspectives*, Cambridge, Cambridge University Press.

Mendus, S. and Edwards, D. (eds) 1987, *On Toleration*, Oxford, Clarendon Press.

Mercer, K. 1990, 'Welcome to the jungle: identity and diversity in post-modern politics', in Rutherford 1990.

Mercer, K. and Julien, I. 1988, 'Race, sexual politics and black sexuality: a dossier', in Chapman and Rutherford 1988.

Mill, J. S. 1859/1975, 'On Liberty', in *Three Essays: On Liberty, Representative Government, The Subjection of Women*, Oxford, Oxford University Press.

Milne, A. J. M. 1986, *Human Rights and Human Diversity: An Essay in the Philosophy of Human Rights*, London, Macmillan.

Moore, B. 1984, *Privacy: Studies in Social and Cultural History*, London and Armonk, NY, M. E. Sharpe Inc.

Morgan, D. 1985, *The Family, Politics and Social Theory*, London, Routledge and Kegan Paul.

Mort, F. 1987, *Dangerous Sexualities: Medico-moral Politics in England since 1830*, London and New York, Routledge and Kegan Paul.

Mort, F. 1994, 'Essentialism revisited? Identity politics and late twentieth century discourses of homosexuality', in Weeks 1994.

Mouffe, C. 1991, 'Pluralism and modern democracy: around Carl Schmitt', *New Formations: On Democracy* 14, Summer 1991.

Mouffe, C. 1993, 'Liberal socialism and pluralism: which citizenship?', in Squires 1993.

Mount, F. 1982, *The Subversive Family*, London, Cape.

Mulford, W. 1993, 'Appreciation: Carol Kendrick: uniting the two sides of the good doctor', *The Guardian* 14 August 1993.

Murray, C. 1994, *Underclass: The Crisis Deepens*, Choice in Welfare No. 20, London, Institute of Economic Affairs.

Nardi, P. 1992, 'That's what friends are for: friends as family in the gay and lesbian community', in Plummer 1992.

National Deviancy Conference (ed.) 1980, *Permissiveness and Control: The Fate of Sixties Legislation*, London, Macmillan.

Nelkin, D., Willis, D. P. and Parris, S. V. (eds) 1991, *A Disease of Society: Cultural and Institutional Responses to AIDS*, Cambridge, Cambridge University Press.

Nelson, E. S. (ed.) 1992, *AIDS: The Literary Response*, New York, Twayne Publishers/Macmillan Publishing Company.

Newburn, T. 1992, *Permission and Regulation: Law and Morals in Post-War Britain*, London and New York, Routledge.

O'Brien, C. C. 1994, 'A great defeat for the Vatican', *The Independent*, 16 September 1994.

Osborne, P. (ed.) 1991, *Socialism and the Limits of Liberalism*, London, Verso.

Page, B. 1993, 'Two skins to mask hypocrisy', *The Guardian* 13 March 1993.

Panos 1994, *Private Decisions, Public Debate: Women, Reproduction and Population*, London, Panos Books.

Parekh, P. 1991, 'British citizenship and cultural difference', in Andrews 1991.

Parker, A., Russo, M., Sommer, D. and Yaeger, P. (eds) 1992, *Nationalisms and Sexualities*, London and New York, Routledge.

Pateman, C. 1985, *The Problem of Political Obligation: A Critique of Liberal Theory*, Cambridge, Polity Press.

Pateman, C. 1988, *The Sexual Contract*, Cambridge, Polity Press.

Patton, C. 1990, *Inventing AIDS*, London and New York, Routledge.

Peiss, K. and Simmons, C., with Padgug, R. 1989, *Passion and Power: Sexuality in History*, Philadelphia, Temple University Press.

Person, E. S. 1989, *Dreams of Love and Fateful Encounters: The Power of Romantic Passion*, London, Penguin.

Petrow, S. 1992, 'Robert Indiana's love story', *The Advocate* 598, 10 March 1992.

Phillips, A. 1984, 'Fraternity', in Pimlott 1984.

Phillips, A. 1991, ' "So what's wrong with the individual?" Socialist and feminist debates on equality', in Osborne 1991.

Phillips, A. 1994, 'Pluralism, solidarity and change', in Weeks 1994.

Pimlott, B. 1984, *Fabian Essays in Socialist Thought*, London, Heinemann.

Pimlott, B., Wright, A. and Flower, T. (eds) 1990, *The Alternative: Politics for a Change*, London, W. H. Allen.

Plummer, K. (ed.) 1992, *Modern Homosexualities: Fragments of Lesbian and Gay Experience*, London and New York, Routledge.

Plummer, K. 1995, *Telling Sexual Stories*, London and New York, Routledge.

Porter, R. and Tomaselli, S. (eds) 1989, *The Dialectics of Friendship*, London and New York, Routledge.

Preston, J. (ed.) 1988, *Personal Dispatches: Writers Confronting AIDS*, New York, St Martin's Press.

Radical America 1993, 'Becoming a spectacle: lesbian and gay politics and culture in the nineties', *Radical America* 24: 4, September–December 1990, published April 1993.

Rajchman, J. 1991, *Truth and Eros: Foucault, Lacan and the Question of Ethics*, London and New York, Routledge.

Ramazanoglu, C. (ed.) 1993, *Up against Foucault: Explorations of Some Tensions between Foucault and Feminism*, London and New York, Routledge.

Ramazanoglu, C. and Holland, J. 1993, 'Women's sexuality and men's appropriation of desire', in Ramazanoglu 1993.

Raymond, J. 1986, *A Passion for Friends: Towards a Philosophy of Female Affection*, London, The Women's Press.

Reed, R. 1993, 'The religious right reaches out', *New York Times*, 22 August 1993.

Richardson, A. and Bolle, D. (eds) 1992, *Wise before their Time: People with AIDS and HIV talk about their Lives*, London, Fount/HarperCollins.

Riley, D. 1988, *'Am I that Name?' Feminism and the Category of 'Women' in History*, London, Macmillan.

Robertson, R, 1990, 'After nostalgia? Wilful nostalgia and the phases of globalisation', in Turner 1990.

Romans, P. 1992, 'Daring to pretend? Motherhood and lesbianism', in Plummer 1992.

Rorty, R. 1989, *Contingency, Irony and Solidarity*, Cambridge, Cambridge University Press.

Rose, J. 1988, 'Margaret Thatcher and Ruth Ellis', *New Formations* 6, 1988.

Rosenberg, C. 1988, 'Disease and order in America: perceptions and expectations', in Fee and Fox 1988.

Rosenblum, N. 1987, *Another Liberalism: Romanticism and the Reconstruction of Liberal Thought*, Cambridge, MA, Harvard University Press.

Rubin, G. 1984, 'Thinking sex: notes for a radical theory of the politics of sexuality', in Vance 1984.

Rutherford, J. (ed.) 1990, *Identity: Community, Culture, Difference*, London, Lawrence and Wishart.

Saffron, L. 1994, *Challenging Conceptions: Pregnancy and Parenting beyond the Traditional Family*, London, Cassell.

Sandel, M. J. 1982, *Liberalism and the Limits of Justice*, Cambridge, Cambridge University Press.

Sandel, M. (ed.) 1984, *Liberalism and its Critics*, Oxford, Basil Blackwell.

San Francisco Museum of Modern Art. 1993, *At the Modern*, San Francisco, July/August 1993.

Scarman, L. 1987, 'Toleration and the law', in Mendus and Edwards 1987.

Scruton, R. 1986, *Sexual Desire: A Philosophical Investigation*, London, Weidenfeld and Nicolson.

Sedgwick, E. K. 1985, *Between Men: English Literature and Male Homosocial Desire*, New York, Columbia University Press.

Sedgwick, E. K. 1990, *Epistemology of the Closet*, Berkeley and Los Angeles, University of California Press.

Segal, L. 1994, *Straight Sex: The Politics of Pleasure*, London, Virago.

Segal, L. and McIntosh, M. (eds) 1992, *Sex Exposed: Sexuality and the Pornography Debate*, London, Virago.

Seidman, S. 1992, *Embattled Eros: Sexual Politics and Ethics in Contemporary America*, London and New York, Routledge.

Selbourne, D. 1994, *The Principle of Duty: An Essay on the Foundations of the Civic Order*, London, Sinclair-Stevenson.

Shilts, R. 1993, *Conduct Unbecoming*, London, Penguin.

Shklar, J. 1984, *Ordinary Vices*, Cambridge, MA, The Belknap Press of Harvard University Press.

Showalter, E. 1991, *Sexual Anarchy: Gender and Culture at the Fin de Siècle*, London, Bloomsbury.

Shusterman, R. 1988, 'Postmodernist aestheticism: a new moral philosophy', *Theory, Culture and Society* 5, 2–3, June 1988.

Signorile, M. 1994, *Queer in America: Sex, the Media and the Closets of Power*, London, Abacus.

Sinfield, A. 1994, *The Wilde Century: Effeminacy, Oscar Wilde and the Queer Moment*, London, Cassell, and New York, Columbia University Press.

Singer, L. 1993, *Erotic Welfare: Sexual Theory and Politics in the Age of Epidemic*, London and New York, Routledge.

Smith, A-M. 1990, 'A symptomology of an authoritarian discourse: the parliamentary debates on the prohibition of the promotion of homosexuality', *New Formations: A Journal of Culture/Theory/Politics* 10, Spring 1990.

Smith, A-M. 1992, 'Resisting the erasure of lesbian sexuality: a challenge for queer activism', in Plummer 1992.

Smith, A-M. 1993, 'Outlaws as legislators: feminist anti-censorship politics and queer activism', in Harwood et al. 1993.

Smith, A-M. 1994, 'Hegemony trouble: the political theories of Judith Butler, Ernesto Laclau and Chantal Mouffe', in Weeks 1994.

Smith-Rosenberg, C. 1985, 'The female world of love and ritual', in *Disorderly Conduct: Visions of Gender in Victorian America*, New York and Oxford, Oxford University Press.

Smyth, C. 1992, *Lesbians Talk Queer Notions*, London, Scarlet Press.

Sontag, S. 1989, *AIDS and its Metaphors*, London, Allen Lane.

Soper, K. 1993, 'Productive contradictions', in Ramazanoglu 1993.

Spivak, G. C. 1991, 'Remembering the limits: difference, identity and practice: a transcript', in Osborne 1991.

Squires, J. (ed.) 1993, *Principled Positions: Postmodernism and the Rediscovery of Value*, London, Lawrence and Wishart.

Squires, J. 1994, 'Ordering the city: public spaces and political participation', in Weeks 1994.

Stanton, D. M. (ed.) 1992, *Discourses of Sexuality: From Aristotle to AIDS*, Ann Arbor, University of Michigan Press.

Stein, E. (ed.) 1990, *Forms of Desire: Sexual Orientation and the Social Constructionist Controversy*, New York and London, Garland Publishing.

Stoddard, T. B. and Rieman, W. 1991, 'AIDS and the rights of the individual: towards a more sophisticated understanding of discrimination', in Nelkin et al. 1991.

Taylor, C. 1992, *The Ethics of Authenticity*, Cambridge, MA, and London, Harvard University Press.

Thompson, B. 1994a, *Soft Core: Moral Crusades against Pornography in Britain and America*, London, Cassell.

Thompson, B. 1994b, *Sadomasochism: Painful Perversion or Pleasurable Play?*, London, Cassell.

Turner, B. S. (ed.) 1990, *Theories of Modernity and Postmodernity*, London, Newbury Park and New Delhi, Sage.

Turner, B. S. (ed.) 1993, *Citizenship and Social Theory*, London, Newbury Park and New Delhi, Sage.

Vance, C. S. (ed.) 1984, *Pleasure and Danger: Exploring Female Sexuality*, London and Boston, Routledge and Kegan Paul.

Vance, C. S. 1989, 'Social constructionist theory: problems in the history of sexuality', in Kooten Niekerk and Meer 1989.

Walkowitz, J. R. 1993, *City of Dreadful Night: Narratives of Sexual Danger in Late-Victorian London*, London, Virago.

Walzer, M. 1983, *Spheres of Justice*, Oxford, Blackwell.

Walzer, M. 1987, *Interpretation and Social Criticism*, Cambridge, MA, and London, Harvard University Press.

Walzer, M. 1988, *The Company of Critics: Social Criticism and Political Commitment in the Twentieth Century*, New York, Basic Books.

Warner, M. (ed.) 1993, *Fear of a Queer Planet: Queer Politics and Social Theory*, Minneapolis and London, University of Minnesota Press.

Warnock, M. 1987, 'The limits of toleration', in Mendus and Edwards 1987.

Watney, S. 1989, 'The subject of AIDS', in Aggleton, Davies and Hart 1989.

Watney, S. 1991, 'Safer sex as community practice', in Aggleton, Davies and Hart 1991.

Watney, S. 1994, *Practices of Freedom: Selected Writings on HIV/AIDS*, London, Rivers Oram Press.

Weeks, J. 1977/1990, *Coming Out: Homosexual Politics in Britain from the Nineteenth Century to the Present*, London, Quartet.

Weeks, J. 1981/1989, *Sex, Politics and Society: The Regulation of Sexuality since 1800*, Harlow, Longman.

Weeks, J. 1985, *Sexuality and its Discontents: Meanings, Myths and Modern Sexualities*, London and Boston, Routledge and Kegan Paul.

Weeks, J. 1986, *Sexuality*, Chichester and London, Ellis Horwood and Tavistock.

Weeks, J. 1991, *Against Nature: Essays on History, Sexuality and Identity*, London, Rivers Oram Press.

Weeks, J. 1993a, 'Rediscovering values', in Squires 1993.

Weeks, J. 1993b, 'An unfinished revolution: sexuality in the twentieth century', in Harwood et al. 1993.

Weeks, J. 1993c, 'AIDS and the regulation of sexuality', in Berridge and Strong 1993.

Weeks, J. (ed.) 1994, *The Lesser Evil and the Greater Good: The Theory and Politics of Social Diversity*, London, Rivers Oram Press.

Weeks, J. and Holland, J. (eds) 1996, *Sexual Cultures: Communities, Values and Intimacy*, London and Basingstoke, Macmillan.

Wellings, K., Field, J., Johnson, A. M. and Wadsworth, J. 1994, *Sexual Behaviour in Britain: The National Survey of Sexual Attitudes and Lifestyles*, London, Penguin.

West, C. 1993, *Race Matters*, Boston, Beacon Press.

Weston, K. 1991, *Families we Choose: Lesbians, Gays, Kinship*, New York, Columbia University Press.

Whaley, J. (ed.) 1981, *Mirrors of Mortality*, London, Europa Publications.

White, S. K. 1991, *Political Theory and Postmodernism*, Cambridge, Cambridge University Press.

Williams, R. 1983, *Towards 2000*, London, Chatto and Windus/The Hogarth Press.

Williams, R. 1989, *Resources of Hope*, London, Verso.

Wilson, E. 1985, *Adorned in Dreams: Fashion and Modernity*, London, Virago.

Wilson, E. 1991, *The Sphinx in the City: Urban Life, the Control of Disorder and Women*, London, Virago.

Wilson, E. 1993, 'Is transgression transgressive?', in Bristow and Wilson 1993.

Wolfenden, J. 1957, *Report of the Committee on Homosexual Offences and Prostitution*, Cmnd 247, London, HMSO.

Woods, G. 1992, 'AIDS to remembrance: the uses of elegy', in Nelson 1992.

Young, I. M. 1987, 'Impartiality and the civic public: some implications of feminist critiques of moral and political theory', in Benhabib and Cornell 1987.

Young, I. M. 1990, *Justice and the Politics of Difference*, Princeton, NJ, and Chichester, Princeton University Press.

Young, I. M. 1993, 'Together in difference: transforming the logic of group political conflict', in Squires 1993.

Index